SOCIAL ENTERPRISE as PEACEBUILDING

To learn more about the Tessendorf Consulting Group, visit www.tessendorfconsulting.com

First Edition August 2021 in ebook & paperback

Project by New Voices Publishing Services

guiding authors to self-publish

www.newvoices.co.za

Edited by Brenda Burgess *www.brendaburgesseditor.com*
Cover designed by Barbara Mueller
Cover art work from depositphotos.com
Graphic design by Christopher Lee Jones

Printed by Booklogix, Atlanta GA, USA

ISBN: 978-0-620-95208-8

SOCIAL ENTERPRISE as PEACEBUILDING

Megan-Lee Meredith & Harold Tessendorf

CONTENTS

ACKNOWLEDGEMENTS

Harold - I wish to acknowledge the support and encouragement that I received from the following people.

Dr. Tammy Crutchfield and the Stetson-Hatcher School of Business at Mercer University for inviting me to create and teach a Social Business course.

The students who brought their energy and passion to the BUS MGMT 477 class on Social Business. Their questions and comments helped to challenge my assumptions, and their zeal for creating a more inclusive and just world through social enterprise continues to inspire me.

Dr. Walter "Buddy" Shurden, the founding Executive Director of the Center for Baptist Studies at Mercer University and one of my Sunday School teachers, for providing me with the necessary encouragement and advice on how to write a book with the specific purpose of helping those who are in the field.

My numerous work colleagues in the United States of America, South Africa, Haiti, Sierra Leone, and Mozambique who lovingly taught and corrected me whilst I worked alongside them. Something of each of you is reflected in this book.

My family, in particular Karen, Claire, and Matthew, for your loving support and encouragement, and for reviewing sections of this book.

My co-author, Megan, for partnering with me on this book and for subjecting my ideas and work to rigorous review. Thank you for that and for the boundless energy, experiences and ideas that are reflected in this book.

Megan – This book is the product of a continuing life journey in search of better ways to implement leadership and development for the good of all humanity. A collective thank-you to those colleagues, mentors, lecturers, partners, companies, and non-profits who have assisted me with developing my thoughts and practice of leadership and social development over time, for providing me with a learning environment that facilitated this insight and understanding, and for helping me to fully engage with the subject of social development. Within the book itself, many wonderful people have directly and indirectly contributed to the examples of improving the way of doing leadership and social enterprise development, with special mention to trailblazers, Sihle Tshabalala and the Nation Builder team. The wonder, creativity, innovation, and tenacity of all these people and social enterprises never ceases to amaze and inspire me.

A special thanks to my mum and dad who encouraged me from an early age to not waste what you have within and around you but instead to continuously seek out and make the most of every opportunity, and to Harold, my co-author, for inviting and challenging me to come along on this book-writing journey.

Lastly, we both wish to thank Barbara Mueller and her team at New Voices Publishing for their guidance, support, and excellent service; to Brenda Burgess of Brenda Burgess, Editor for her tireless editing services and patience with us which allowed us to meet our deadlines; and to Christopher Lee Jones for the graphic design work. It is always a pleasure to work with such a professional team.

INTRODUCTION

"The greatest danger in times of turbulence is not the turbulence; it is to act with yesterday's logic." – Peter Drucker

It is our belief that the social enterprise is an example of business operating with today's logic. Correctly established and well-managed social enterprises will play an increasingly crucial role in addressing the escalating challenges of the 21st Century. In the pages that follow, we will share our definition of the "social enterprise" and expand on our statement by exploring the context in which social enterprises find themselves, as well as the logical concepts which we believe make them such crucial actors.

History has taught us that turbulence and change remain constants throughout the ages and all around the globe. The words most often used to describe turbulence include *"turmoil, unrest, instability, upheaval, pandemonium or a state of confusion, movement or agitation"* (Collins Dictionary, 2018). Modern day global turbulence manifests in the form of frustration, anger and, at times, violence. This turbulence comes in response to ever-increasing levels of unemployment, poverty, crime, inadequate access to housing, health and sanitation, and socio-economic difficulties, as more and more people compete for what seem to be 'smaller slices of the proverbial resource pie'. The gap between the 'haves' and 'have nots', if anything, is becoming wider. In 2019, Oxfam International reported that the wealth gap between billionaires and the poorest half of the world's population grew by 12% in 2018 alone, fueling perceptions of unfairness and growing public anger (Holland, 2019). The quickening pace of climate change with its increasingly unpredictable and extreme weather patterns and related national disasters; the financial crises that lead to the global erosion of social capital, household income and wealth; and the rise of populism, nationalism, extremism, and political polarization have amplified this turbulence. Added to this is the growing unease fueled by the social, economic, and political shocks unleashed by a pandemic such as COVID-19. If anything, the COVID-19 pandemic seems to have highlighted the growing distrust that individuals, communities, and nations have in their institutions, be they governmental, business, and even those in civil society.

When these institutions prove themselves incapable of addressing the challenges brought about by the turbulence, the resulting inter- and intra-group competition and mistrust often flares into violence. Institutional inertia results from a combination of factors: these include institutions that lack the necessary resources to address the source of turbulence, the absence of political will on the part of their elected leaders (whose actions serve to protect special interest groups rather than address the causes of this turbulence), and a lack of mechanisms to effectively manage crises and conflict at all levels of society. By way of example, 2020 saw an increase in xenophobia-motivated violence in South Africa. The year also saw largely non-violent demonstrations across the United States in response to systemic racism, election outcomes, and the COVID-19 pandemic (Human Rights Watch, 2020; ACLED, 2020). The post-Cold War consensus around the benefits of market economies continues to unravel as many ask whether they will ever get a seat on the "gravy train".

Turbulence, however, is not always a bad thing. For one, it creates pressure to change unacceptable behavior or create solutions to a pressing social issue or problem. In other words, it brings about change to the status quo. The rise of the social enterprise is an example of a positive response to the aforementioned turbulence. Outdated business models, overburdened welfare systems, and failing government structures have led a younger generation of students and entrepreneurs to question what types of institutions can better address these local and global social problems. This group is creating new institutions to do just that because they are motivated to improve the lot of those who continue to find themselves marginalized and exploited, those for whom inaction is not an option and whose daily survival requires bold action. Then there is the post-Cold War generation of activists who reflect on the experiences they gained while leading and managing institutions, and who are now looking to add value to the efforts of this younger generation.

Social enterprise is not a new idea. However, this concept has been growing in scale and popularity over the past few decades. Social enterprises are a viable vehicle to address the very real social, economic, and environmental issues in the 21st Century. We ascribe to the definition of social enterprises as

> *disciplined institutions, purposefully established to address specific social issues by harnessing social, community and market forces to profitably deliver a product (goods or services). Social issues arise from an imbalance between social, community and market forces. Social enterprises seek to address that imbalance.*

Another way of stating this is that social enterprises are disciplined, democratic, human-scaled institutions which use competition to accomplish their social mission.

We were motivated to write this book to share the best practices, insights, and hard lessons learnt from serving and leading social enterprises over the past three decades. *Social Enterprises as Peacebuilding* is the product of a trans-Atlantic partnership that seeks to ensure that social enterprises are built better and outlast their founders. The framework and stories stem from three decades of working with communities and institutions in South Africa, the United States of America, Sierra Leone, Haiti, and Mozambique. Today, we continue to draw from our wider experiences of these institutions' eco-systems in our roles as funders, university instructors, consultants, and executive coaches. We will therefore include the best practices and theories from the fields of social science and business studies and will also include some case studies from our respective experiences.

We have strong roots in South Africa, and consequently, our worldviews are informed by the interaction between Western and African theory and thought. These worldviews have been tempered by the realities of applying these principles to social enterprises in five countries across the globe. The multi-decade work undertaken by the King Committee on Corporate Governance, including King IV (2016), has helped to shape our arguments in favor of a more inclusive, stakeholder-based model of capitalism that promotes sustainable local economic development. We have found that this process and end-goal inspires all the enterprises, leaders, and students with whom we continue to engage.

We have also drawn on our extensive experience in conflict management and peacebuilding. Social enterprises are charged to be instruments of peace as they provide productive channels to engage those community members across the world whose human needs are frustrated by continued socio-economic marginalization. The violent circumstances within which these people find themselves pose a significant threat to both individual and community safety and peace. Social enterprises which are put into action and result in meaningful change therefore serve as vehicles of local economic development; they provide a "parallel narrative" to polarization and hate. We argue that sustainable social enterprises are a crucial (and often overlooked) component in efforts to build lasting peace in their communities and beyond. By intentionally incorporating conflict management practices into their structure and operations, and through their practice of enlightened local and global citizenship, social enterprises use conflict productively to create and deliver their products and services. As such, we are influenced by the guiding principles and elements found in the Peace Continuum model and its manifestation in South Africa's National Peace Accord (NPA) of 1991.

Scholar-practitioners of conflict management and resolution have introduced the Peace Continuum to explain the ideal progression of communities and societies as they transition from the absence of violence (keeping the peace) to addressing the underlying causes of social conflict (peacebuilding). This continuum can be represented as follows.

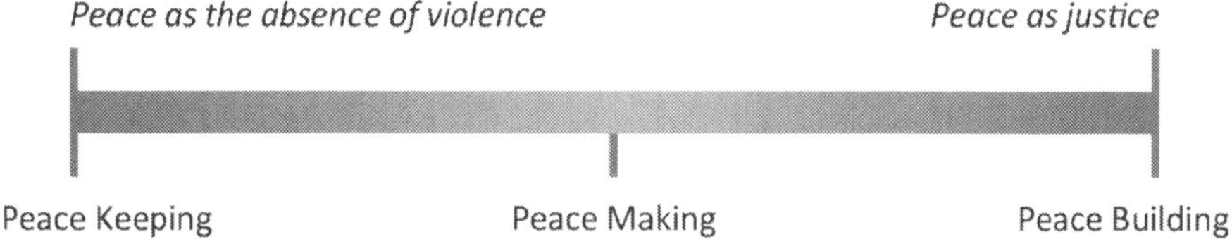

Fig.1: Diagram of Peace Continuum

Social enterprises belong in the peacebuilding space. They employ market forces and business disciplines to deliver a product or service in a sustainable manner, whilst simultaneously meeting a pressing social need or issue. Through their legal structure, governance and management structures, operational practices and stakeholder mindset, social enterprises can model an alternative form of business that is economically, socially, and environmentally sustainable. The absence of violence, along with a strong adherence to the rule of law, is a precondition for sustainable social enterprises. Social entrepreneurs and businesses operate in and serve communities beset by inequality and social turmoil; however, they can only operate effectively if their staff can work in safety and the legal system allows for corporate law which upholds and enforces property and contractual rights. While it is preferable that the legal system be formal and regulated, informal systems may also suffice if government authority and services are weak or disrupted.

In the early 1990s, the National Peace Accord (NPA) created South Africa's first institutionalized peacekeeping and peacemaking instrument and, as the values and principles underlying this accord focused on compliance, they can be applied to the building of sustainable social enterprises. There were specified codes of conduct for the different stakeholders, and detailed standards and operating procedures to ensure compliance and which promoted the democratic principles of good governance, mutual responsibility, and accountability. The NPA also established a conflict management structure that promotes negotiation, mediation, and participatory socio-economic development to manage and address the causes of South Africa's deep-rooted social conflict.

This book relies on a systems approach to enterprises. We understand social enterprises as having interrelated components and that these enterprises exist within a larger social system. In doing so, we draw on the philosophical insights of Ubuntu and Holism, both of which have strong roots in South African history and society.

We believe this is applicable to social enterprises, in both Northern and Southern Hemispheres, which seek, irrespective of the way the enterprise is legally incorporated, to address a given social problem in a disciplined way.

It is written specifically for students and practitioners (managers, executive leaders, and board members) alike, to provide the reader with:

- An understanding of the theory and practice of sustainable social enterprise.
- A practical framework within which to locate their social enterprise.
- Proven practices to govern the way their social enterprise operates and result in a superior product.
- A road map to create an enduring institution that increases the size and shape of the 'pie', leading to healthier outcomes for stakeholders, with an impact and growth that surpasses the vision of the institution's founders.

OVERVIEW

The inter-connected components of a social enterprise system remain constant throughout the enterprise's growth journey. However, the specific areas they address will depend on the challenges and opportunities they face along that journey. The chapters which follow will look at each of these components in greater detail.

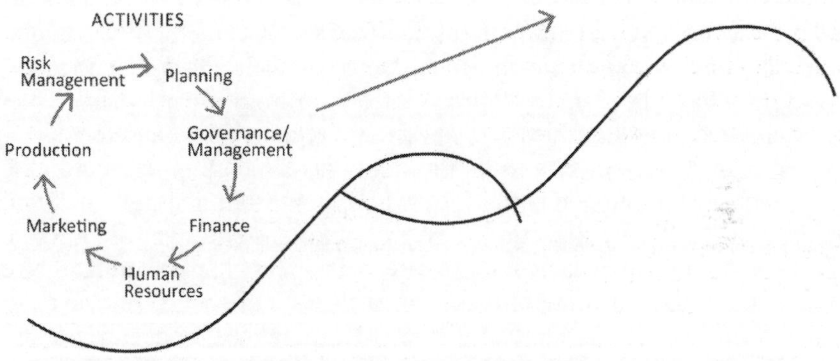

Fig.2: Chronology of the Social Enterprise

Influences that shape social enterprises

The performance and sustainability of any social enterprise is measured against how well they meet their triple bottom line (TBL) while applying the Six sources of Capital. These include natural, human, financial, manufacturing, social and relationship, and intellectual capital. By their very nature, social enterprises originate on or near the margins of their local communities. As institutions, they play an important part in building local resilience through community economic development. Chapter 1 introduces readers to the intellectual influences that shape the world of social enterprises by locating each of these in one of four holons. These include the philosophical, legal, economic, and spiritual holons. The insights gained from this chapter will provide the reader with a framework of intellectual insights and wisdom for the ensuing practical chapters.

Planning for social enterprises

The need for regular planning and continuous, structured evaluation forms the basis of Chapter 2. In addition to delving into the components of a sustainable social enterprise, we also apply these principles over the life of the enterprise by drawing on the theory and practice of the Sigmoid Curve (S-Curve) to show how it applies to any social enterprise, from start-up through to its second generation or "finding its second wind". Important tools and insights that help the leaders of a social enterprise to plan and evaluate their programs and impact include the Theory of Change and Systems Thinking. Another important tool is the Business Plan, used not only at the inception of the social enterprise, but also when it decides whether to take advantage of growth opportunities.

Structuring social enterprises

Chapter 3 introduces readers to a framework that allows them to better understand the various legal or corporate formats that a social enterprise can adopt. It considers how this strategic choice is shaped by their purpose and values, the way in which the social enterprise intends to meet a particular market and social need, how it proposes to attract and retain capital, and the extent to which it feels accountable to its different stakeholders. These corporate forms generally fall into either the for-profit or non-profit/non-governmental organization (NGO) framework. There are variations and hybrid corporate forms to be found within each of these categories. This chapter will therefore introduce the reader to some of these forms that are of special relevance to social enterprises such as joint ventures, B-Corporations, cooperatives and worker-owned business, and employee stock ownership programs (ESOPs). The chapter concludes with a look at emerging trends in the structure and operationalization of corporate governance for social enterprises.

Financing social enterprises

Chapter 4 introduces the formal and community sources of funding available to social enterprises during the start-up phase and again when they plan for additional growth and expansion. Since the legal form adopted by the social enterprise will influence which sources of capital it can readily access, these sources will be examined through the lens of those legal forms. In addition to attracting financing, the staff, managers, and Boards of Directors of social enterprises also need to understand their financial operations. This includes the financial ratios they include on their financial dashboards and financial statements, such as their balance sheets and income and expense statements.

Financial statements are a key component of the plans that social enterprises create when they start up and grow. The chapter concludes with an introduction to the principles and some practices of Open Book Management. This practice empowers the employees and teams of a social enterprise to better understand how their institution operates, assess its financial health, and measure how their daily efforts impact the social enterprises' success or failure.

Social enterprises and their human capital

Chapter 5 discusses the use of the well-structured and executed Human Resource Management (HRM) system in the deployment of human capital in social enterprises. We explore the creation, operation and evaluation of this system before looking at the emerging HR practices of Open Hiring and Business Vocations in social enterprises.

Marketing social enterprises

The marketing of both mission and product is a key part of every social enterprise. Chapter 6 introduces the reader to the marketing framework and language. It looks at the ethics that every social enterprise must adhere to when marketing their product so that they remain true to their mission. We share the concept of a cross-functional marketing team and show the components of a virtuous marketing plan. The chapter also speaks to the challenges and opportunities presented by cause marketing; it provides insights for managing cause marketing partnerships and provides an overview of the proven marketing tactics and platforms that social enterprises can adapt to their unique circumstances. The concepts and practices of Stakeholder and Impact Reporting and how these are becoming part of the marketing done by a social enterprise are also covered.

Risk management

Chapter 7 explores how social enterprises manage risk when they employ their Six Capitals in the sustainable pursuit of their social mission. The principles and practices behind Risk Management, and how a social enterprise can institutionalize these through its planning and operations, are mentioned. Historically the field of Risk Management has focused specifically on the individual institution's internal financial risks and compliance with government regulations. It has long been associated with auditors, tax entities, and human resources managers. However, the growing awareness of environmental and political risks, along with the growing interest in economic and social reporting, has expanded the focus of Risk Management to include non-financial risks that are peculiar to each social enterprise. This expanded view of Risk Management is increasingly associated with the practice of integrated reporting.

Managing operations at social enterprises

The practicalities of creating and managing lean and efficient social enterprise operations are covered in Chapter 8. Continuous improvement of market place delivery of products and services is key if social enterprises are to remain sustainable. The chapter outlines how Systems Theory and the S-Curve have influenced the field of operations management and how this has translated into the contemporary focus on Lean Production, as well as operational techniques such as Value-Mapping and 5S. Social enterprises need to be nimble learners and their senior managers are required to create and support teams. The chapter ends by acknowledging that there is a season for all products and processes and that these seasons do come to an end. This reality means that social enterprises should create an abandonment protocol which allows them to swiftly transition to new products.

Wise growth to ensure sustainability and impact

Chapter 9 focuses on some of the challenges facing the maturing social enterprise. Once the enterprise has progressed past its initial start-up and growth phase and its systems and personnel are comfortably in place, it faces the dilemma of how to scale up its operations, either by adding additional business lines or by growing its core business. The chapter takes a critical yet hopeful look at how social enterprises can grow responsibly to deliver greater social impact in their chosen area whilst continuing to nurture their core identity and purpose. Beginning with the philosophical dilemmas and questions which underpin the debate around "scaling up", it then considers the structure of a growth plan and the process which is followed to arrive there. The chapter ends with a look at the operational structure of business federalism, and whether a social enterprise can adopt this to facilitate expansion.

Leadership and Management

Chapter 10 looks at what social enterprise leaders can expect when they introduce change, and it provides a guideline of how to manage the associated transitions. The S-Curve not only applies to social enterprises, but also to their leadership and staff. Social enterprises rely a great deal on their founders' "sweat equity", but this often results in burnout and an existential threat to the institution's sustainability. While necessary changes in staff, products, and services can be planned for and managed, leaders also need to manage the protracted psychological transitions. The chapter concludes with vital information on how leaders and managers can keep themselves healthy and resilient for the long haul.

Towards a definition of social enterprise

A social enterprise is a disciplined institution, purposefully established to address specific social issues by harnessing social, community and market forces to profitably deliver a product or service. Social issues arise from an imbalance between social, community and market forces. Social enterprises seek to address that imbalance.

Social Enterprise

Social enterprises can be legally incorporated as for-profit businesses, non-profits or NGOs, or may be a hybrid blend of both. They may also be incorporated as cooperatives. These enterprises span the gap between traditional business activity and traditional charity work. Social enterprises fund their operations from a diverse assortment of revenue streams. These revenues allow them to meet their social purpose and mission.

Institutions

It is incorrect to assume that institutions refer only to buildings and their occupants. Scholars from across the academic disciplines agree that the term refers to something much more enduring. Hodgson (2006) defines institutions as "integrated systems of rules that govern social interactions."

We argue that the term "institution" is appropriate when describing a social enterprise. Social problems are large in scale and complexity, and it takes time to address them. Sustainable institutions are committed to addressing these problems over the long haul. Sustainable social enterprises have a well-developed strategy, have created the necessary rules and processes to mobilize the Six Capitals to deliver a product or service, and are held accountable for reporting on their positive social impact to their stakeholders.

Social Problems

Social problems refer to conditions in a community or society that negatively affect groups of people, either directly or indirectly. To qualify as a social problem, a condition or practice must be recognized as such by a large section of the public because its persistent existence goes against their accepted values. Furthermore, they recognize that the solution to the problem can only come from collaboration and by sharing community resources. Examples of social issues include, but are not limited to, racism, poverty, unemployment, inadequate housing and education, substance abuse, corruption, food insecurity and poor health outcomes. Addressing a social problem is one of the two reasons for the existence of any social enterprise. The social enterprise captures this aspiration in its mission statement and marketing strategy and serves to motivate its internal and external stakeholders.

Sources of Capital

The rise of integrated reporting to help corporations, social enterprises and non-profits/NGOS measure their impact has coincided with the emerging consensus that these institutions employ the Six sources of Capital. These include natural, human, financial, manufacturing (production), social and relationship, and intellectual assets.

Sustainable

Sustainability is tied to the concepts of longevity and to the stewardship of resources. The idea of sustainable resource management was first introduced through the environmental movement, but the term has migrated into other disciplines and is recognized as being equally applicable across the Six Capitals referenced above. In the context of social enterprise, sustainability also refers to the enterprise itself, to its commitment to respond to market forces, and to the sense that it is structured and managed in such a way that the enterprise will outlast its founders.

Discipline

Discipline refers to the application of rigorous business practices to all aspects of a social enterprise's operations. In this way, their product or service meets an identified market need, responds to market forces, and generates a profit or surplus which is re-invested to further the enterprise's ongoing operations and mission.

Product or service to meet a given market need

Social enterprises do not depend on charity. They exist because they create a tangible product or intangible service which is valued by the wider community and society, and which *they are willing to pay for*. Social enterprises understand that their survival depends on their ability to respond to these changing market needs.

A word on social entrepreneurship

Lynch and Walls (2009) reference a study by the Schwab Foundation when they describe the traits that are commonly associated with social entrepreneurs. By implication, the traits also apply to social enterprises, and can be summarized as follows:

- Believing that everyone can make meaningful contributions.
- Creating opportunities for people to make their meaningful contributions.
- Having a practical, innovative stance towards addressing social problems and using the discipline of market forces and practices to measure the success of the enterprise.

- Continuously monitoring impact by using qualitative and quantitative data.
- Having a healthy impatience with bureaucracy.

A word about Peacebuilding

Peacebuilding interventions are aligned with the "peace with justice" at the end of the peace continuum introduced earlier. "Peace with justice" was popularized by non-violent civil rights leaders such as Mahatma Gandhi and Martin Luther King Jr. This understanding of peace considers that lasting peace is only possible when the underlying causes of the conflict are addressed. Since these causes are tied to social and economic inequalities, lasting peace will thus only be realized when meaningful steps are taken to address these long-standing injustices and inequalities.

Designing peacebuilding interventions that address these inequalities gives rise to long-term community and economic development plans along with new or re-invigorated institutions. Common peacebuilding mechanisms include participatory forums and institutions which focus on addressing the underlying social, economic, and political causes of violence and conflict. If these conflicts are taking place within an existing democratic system, then an appropriate peacebuilding intervention is to identify delays in the democratic decision-making process. The next step is to eliminate those delays so that the necessary resources can address the underlying causes of the conflict. Although it is tempting to place all the responsibility for peacebuilding on political institutions, it is important to acknowledge that business and civil society institutions can, and must, address socio-economic inequality. The decisions made by these institutions when allocating their resources should also be examined to see how they can speed up peacebuilding initiatives. Conflict management practitioners encourage peace builders to institutionalize conflict management systems within their peacebuilding initiatives and to become powerful advocates of this practice in the official and unofficial arenas where they operate. This is a worthy cause that all social enterprises must embrace.

Having introduced the reader to our definition of social enterprises and the conceptual milieu within which they function, we will continue to build on this definition and framework by examining the inter-related components that make up a social enterprise in the following chapters. Our intention is that the chapters will serve as a roadmap for all those who lead social enterprises and aspire to address the pressing challenges that face our communities, nations, and planet.

Chapter 1

INFLUENCES THAT SHAPE SOCIAL ENTERPRISES

The context of social enterprises is shaped by several key intellectual influences. We will provide the reader with a brief introduction to those intellectual schools that have influenced and shaped our approach to working with, and leading, social enterprises.

HOLONS

We have placed each of these influences in holons. The word "holon" comes from the Greek and means "whole" and we will draw on Koestler's view that holons refer to the whole system as well as to its components. These components are simultaneously autonomous and interdependent. In this chapter we will use the image of intellectual or thought holons.

The first holon is the philosophical one. We introduce readers to two South African philosophical traditions that continue to influence businesses and civil society organizations in South Africa and around the world. These are the traditions of *holism* and *ubuntu.* A third insight in this holon will be provided by the phenomenon known as *paradox.*

The second holon is the legal holon with particular attention being paid to how insights into business and corporate law have shaped the way in which we approach our work with social enterprises. Through our exposure to the King Code on Corporate Governance, we share more about the concepts of the Triple Bottom line and Six Capitals that this Code has popularized. We explore these insights against the backdrop of the ongoing intellectual and political debate between proponents of a shareholder-centric model of governance and those who favor a more inclusive stakeholder-centric model.

These two ideas of the Triple Bottom line and Six Capitals are finding favor with international business leaders, multi-nationals, political and environmental leaders. We have found that more companies have begun to incorporate some or all of them into their operations because of the benefits that accrue to their financial position, reputation, and ability to attract and retain employees when they do so. However, we have found that these concepts are less familiar amongst smaller social enterprises. We believe that social enterprises can greatly improve their operations and reputation by adopting these concepts and practices. One of the goals of this book is to advocate that more social enterprises do so, since we believe that social enterprises can help to address the turbulence which we referred to in the introduction.

The third holon is the economic holon. If the leaders of social enterprises and community groups feel that Triple Bottom line and Six Capitals are lofty ideas that do not apply to their circumstances, or if they feel that these ideas are compromised because they have found favor with elites, or if they are concerned that these ideas may be too costly to implement, then this next idea may be easier for them to embrace. This is the idea of local or community economic development which argues that communities need to own, participate in, and benefit from the economic activities taking place in the area that they call home.

The fourth holon is the faith holon which speaks to the sacredness of individual needs being met through harmonious social interaction. We can testify from both our personal and professional experiences that faith is an important force behind the social enterprises we are involved with.

We will now explore each of these holons in greater detail.

The Philosophical Holon

Holism

The South African political leader and international statesman, Jan Christian Smuts, introduced the world to the term "holism" when he published his book *Holism and Evolution* in 1926. As already mentioned, the term *holism* owes its origin to the Greek word "*holos*" which can be translated to mean *whole.* Wholeness is at the heart of every human and natural system or being. Smuts understood Holism to be more than just the sum of its constituent parts. It also includes the energy that arises from the interaction between these parts or subsystems. When this concept is applied to social enterprise, the valued product or service, along with the maturation that results within its people and operational processes that comprise the enterprise, contribute towards the larger whole.

After studying the works of Charles Darwin, Smuts arrived at a more harmonious and less deterministic interpretation of evolution. He stated that there are two components and forces at play in each system. The inner factor refers to those characteristics that are unique to each system and which allow them to exercise control. It is here that all systems, however small they may be, make choices. It is here that they incorporate lessons learnt from their external environment to improve and create something better. Smuts considered these deliberate alterations to be evolution. He also reminded his readers that prior knowledge serves as the building blocks for the new. These insights into the inner factor provide us with a better understanding of the origin and nature of reinforcing feedback loops, a topic that we will consider in more detail when we study the systems approach to organizations. Another insight that is of particular significance to enterprises is that their subsystems can change them. Enterprises co-create a more perfect community and society when they incorporate influences and effects from their environment and stakeholders into their ongoing actions.

The outer factor is the second component of each system. It consists of the other subsystems which exist outside each system; systems theorists refer to this as the "external environment". Smuts argued that holism refers to the external environment which lies outside the boundary of each individual system. But holism is more than a static condition. It is also a dynamic force that produces balancing feedback loops that order and restrain each individual system. These feedback loops help smaller units to adapt and survive.

Smuts viewed individual freedom as the highest order priority in human systems. However, he embraced neither libertarianism nor totalitarianism which he saw as antithetical responses to the larger debate between proponents of Free Will and Determinism (Beukes, 1989). He understood freedom as involving self-discipline which emerges when individuals exercise their choices, and that self-discipline is shaped, in part, by the feedback that the individual system gets from its external environment. Human personality is shaped by the interplay between individual choices, self-discipline, and the ability to co-create something new while engaging with their external environment. Based on this insight, the leaders and managers of social enterprises need to create conditions for, and appeal to, the individual's desire for beauty and freedom.

As a child of Africa, Smuts' philosophy of holism emerged from the interplay between the core teachings of his Christian faith; his intellectual and political opposition to the determinism which informed Social Darwinism and which led to the rise of totalitarianism in the early to mid-20th Century; and the lessons he drew by observing the natural world where he lived, fought, and farmed in South Africa. Unfortunately, Smuts failed to extend his enlightened views of human freedom and holism to most of his fellow South Africans. His racist views and actions towards the early African National Congress and the non-violent civil rights efforts organized by Mohandas Gandhi has therefore overshadowed his contribution as an original thinker and as an international statesman. These views blinded Smuts to a parallel philosophy held by Black South Africans, namely that of Ubuntu, which we will consider next. Despite this oversight, holism has helped to inform numerous sub-fields of social, biological, and physical sciences, all of which weigh in on how sustainable social enterprises are structured and operated. Other insights from holism show that the role and actions of every individual and department in the enterprise have an effect on the whole. Furthermore, enterprises need to be sensitive and responsive to their external environments and stakeholders.

Ubuntu

Ubuntu can be described as a moral philosophy that addresses the relationship between individuals and the groups to which they belong. Ubuntu traces its origins to pre-colonial African traditions and philosophy. It continues to be used to affirm the intrinsic dignity and value of Black South Africans, something denied to them by the ideologies of colonialism and apartheid. The fusion of Ubuntu philosophy and Christian values is present in the teachings and writings of Archbishop Desmond Tutu.

Writers such as Khoza (2012) remind us that the essence of Ubuntu is contained in the Nguni phrase "*Umuntu Ngumuntu Ngabantu*" which is translated to read that "A person is a person through others". Ubuntu and Holism reinforce each other. The inner factor – the unique soul and personality of a person – is shaped and influenced by the outer factor, which is the social group in which they find themselves, work, and are nurtured. Ubuntu views people as being both rational and relational. Morality emerges from the interaction between these two parts of every person.

Ubuntu views the inner and outer factors which we read about previously in the section on holism as being in a non-hierarchical and complementary relationship. Ubuntu views people as being essentially social in nature. The individual person is as crucial to the social group as that community is to its individual member. This lateral relationship is captured in the related phrase "I am because they are, and they are because I am." This phrase not only points to the intrinsic value of each unique person, it also points to the fact that the individual's welfare can only be sustainably satisfied when people collaborate in pursuit of the common good. While individuals are nurtured and sustained by their community, Ubuntu also views individuals as having unique qualities and being equal in their community.

Attempts to dismiss Ubuntu as a philosophy that only applies to Africa disregards its universal message. It speaks to workplace identity (where most economically active adults spend the bulk of their workday) by reminding us that all people have meaningful contributions to make and that they are to be accorded dignity. It supplies us with a lateral concept of leadership, where leaders and managers are accorded legitimacy by the rest of the enterprise to set its direction based on the aspirations of the members of that enterprise. That legitimacy must be earned through regular feedback and competence. When leaders and managers set a new direction for the enterprise, they draw inspiration from the rest of the members. Khoza (2012) writes that the practice of servant leadership, after it is updated to include 21st Century sensitivities, allows for Ubuntu to be experienced at the organizational level.

Paradox

Our experience has demonstrated the persistent value of entertaining and embracing paradox. In the enterprise setting, paradox refers to two opposing viewpoints which appear to contradict each other. Upon investigation and further thought, they are found to be equally valid. It has been our experience that the tension generated by attempting to balance these opposing viewpoints can and must be creatively channeled (by both individuals and social enterprises) to create value. This insight has been confirmed by Lynch and Walls (2009) who define paradox as being "challenge-opportunity sets". By opening our minds to the challenges which face the enterprise and then sharing our different perspectives about their underlying dynamics, we begin to view these discussions as opportunities to create new products and ways of operating.

Authors' Corner: The principle of paradox was demonstrated by a discussion around energy retrofits at one of the small social enterprises where we worked. This discussion revealed that the enterprise was home to two schools of thought: those who were for the retrofit of the enterprise's program services building and those who were against it. The opposition said this would result in serving fewer clients. This faction continued to justify their stance by stating that they were being responsible stewards of limited financial resources and that they were honoring the commitments the enterprise had made to clients and donors.

Proponents of the energy-retrofit argued that the upgrades would pay for themselves over the long haul by lowering the enterprise's energy bill. They pointed out that these upgrades would allow the enterprise to market itself as a wise financial and environmental steward. They agreed with their opponents that the retrofit would reduce the financial resources that the enterprise had available to provide program services in the short-term. However, they pointed out that over the long-term these savings would allow the enterprise to develop new products. The proponents of the energy retrofit also offered to raise additional funds to help cover the costs associated with the energy retrofits so that the enterprise could remain focused on delivering their core service and product. By employing paradox, this enterprise was able to increase its operational efficiency by creatively engaging its people to solve a problem and deliver an improved service.

The practice of paradox introduces us to the need to always think "Both... and...". We have subsequently employed this approach while working in conflict management and within social enterprises. Paradox stands in contrast to either/or thinking.

Paradox also highlights the reality that social enterprises cannot easily resolve the big questions and challenges they face. Nor do any solutions they arrive at endure forever. These solutions will generate their own unintended consequences which, in turn, will give rise to a new generation of paradoxes for successive leaders and enterprises to address.

The Legal Holon

This holon is of particular importance when social enterprises attempt to answer two questions. The first concerns which legal structure will be most appropriate for it to adopt. The second concerns the proper working relationship between the enterprises' Board of Directors, staff, and its supporters. We trace the origins of these questions to the ongoing debate between proponents of a shareholder-centric model and those who favor one which is stakeholder-centric in nature. This debate is influenced by contending views of capitalism as they seek to answer the question: "*To whom does the enterprise owe its allegiance?*" This debate reflects an essential paradox that all social enterprises must negotiate, irrespective of whether they are incorporated as a for-profit or non-profit entity.

In the case of the United States, Coy (2020) writes that this paradox was enshrined in business law with a decision made by the Michigan Supreme Court in 1919. In the case of *Dodge vs. Ford Motor Company*, the court ruled that corporate boards were responsible for ensuring that their companies maximized financial returns to their investors. However, the court went on to also issue the business judgment rule, which gave boards of directors the discretion to decide how best to protect a corporation's interests to maximize those returns. Navigating this paradox has been a major responsibility of Boards of Directors and executive teams ever since.

This argument is not limited to large, for-profit corporations. It applies equally to social enterprises as well, especially as they begin to access funding from government agencies, private donors, or investors. It lies at the heart of the ongoing debate between proponents of limiting board responsibility to that of financial oversight and maximizing financial returns to investors and donors, and the investment perspective which argues that enterprises must take environmental, social and governance (ESG) issues into account. While recent governance codes such as the King Code in South Africa, the Malaysian Code on Corporate Governance and the Philippines Code of Corporate Governance for Publicly Listed Companies encourage enterprise leaders to apply the concept of the Six Capitals when making strategic decisions about the enterprise, it is also clear that this paradox will not go away. (The concept of the Six Capitals will be explored later in this chapter). Instead, it will need to be navigated, as it will remain a source of conflict.

In the following sections, we will explore the arguments that have been put forward by proponents of both camps so that we can better understand this paradox.

Shareholder-centric Model

Advocates of the Shareholder-centric model of governance draw on the insights of Milton Friedman when they argue that capital investment is a risk. Since investors put their financial interests at risk by investing in an enterprise, they should be the first to receive a portion of its profits. Furthermore, they argue that there is a close correlation between business success and its financial returns. By using financial returns and profitability as their metrics when measuring success, the management of an enterprise is concerned with maximizing those inputs and factors which lie within their control. Environmental and social variables, on the other hand, are much harder for a given enterprise to manage since it has no control over the actions of other players. When Boards of Directors allow an enterprise to focus on more than one form of return, they inadvertently encourage mediocrity on the part of their managers, who can then conveniently blame their less-than-stellular performance on factors beyond their control. An enterprise's management and leadership can use this argument to protect their own interests rather than those of the groups whom they purport to serve.

Advocates of the shareholder-centric approach to governance also point to the growing concentration of investment power in a few private banks and equity firms. They point out that these actors, as part of an urban elite, can amass and exercise inordinate political power and influence over vast swaths of the economy. These actors include investment firms that offer mutual funds as investment pools for individual and organizational retirement funds. Privately held investment firms are often unaccountable to their investors and to the economy on Main Street since their ESG biases are not subject to regulation.

These advocates also point out that businesses quickly adapt environmentally beneficial technologies and approaches when it is profitable for them to do so. In doing so, they help to reduce the costs of bringing these newer technologies to market, allowing them to be adopted more widely.

While it is tempting to say that this school of shareholder primacy only applies to for-profit organizations, the reality is somewhat different. Many non-profits have a similar approach as they work to attract and retain key donors and foundations. They focus more on meeting the reporting guidelines laid down by the latter, rather than adopting advocacy positions that challenge the social conditions their clients find themselves; yet these same social conditions are caused by the (in)actions of corporations behind those donations and foundations.

Stakeholder-centric model

Advocates for a stakeholder approach to governance argue that enterprises that grant equal weight to their financial, environmental, and social returns and impact are more enduring and generate greater profits over the longer-term. This approach argues that all levels of leadership within an enterprise need to mobilize and be accountable to their internal and external stakeholders for the value that their actions create. The Six Capitals model provides them to do this with a systematic framework.

The stakeholder approach is underpinned by an approach known as the tragedy of the commons. Popularized by Garrett Hardin in 1968, this theory posits that an unintended consequence of individual and enterprise-level focus on a single goal, for example profits, come at the detriment of the wider environment on which they depend and which they share with others. These groups consume the common resources at an unsustainable rate resulting in them becoming depleted. While the actors are behaving rationally by adopting this narrow, short-term focus, their sub-optimizing behavior causes all these groups to suffer economic and social harm.

The stakeholder approach points to the limitations of the shareholder approach. Proponents of this approach argue that businesses and non-profits are created and governed by social rules. These rules are set by officials who are publicly elected or overseen by elected officers. Since government rules make it possible to create these organizations, their rights are offset by their commensurate responsibilities to be good corporate citizens. Enterprises are expected to minimize the harm they cause to their community and environment whilst going about their business.

Advocates of the stakeholder approach agree with the proponents of the shareholder-centric model that organizations and investors must be profitable and seek a return on their investment. But they would add that enterprises need to adopt a wider and longer-term lens. It is perfectly consistent for these investors to be social activists whilst simultaneously protecting their financial interests from being harmed by the actions of others.

Khoza (2012) traces the renewed rise of the shareholder-centric model to the 1970s and 1980s when, in response to mediocre returns and complacent management, investors began to demand that corporate boards focus primarily on generating consistent profits and paying stock dividends. The stakeholder-centric model gained popularity in the 1990s with this trend continuing into the 21st Century. However, the shareholder-centric model is still present. The efforts of the US Labor Department during the Trump Administration to limit the role of the Boards of publicly traded companies to prioritizing financial returns over social and environmental considerations bear witness to this.

In our opinion, invaluable lessons can be drawn from both models. From the shareholder-centric model, social enterprises can learn that measured accountability matters and that financial results are a straightforward way of measuring an enterprises' health and value. Furthermore, the board and management need to be held accountable on a regular basis so that mediocre performance does not seep into an enterprises' behavior and culture.

From the stakeholder-centric model, social enterprises should learn that they are accountable to more than just those who provide them with financial capital (investors, banks, and donors) and those who consume their products. Social enterprises are also accountable to the wider local community and they must ensure that their governance and management structures reflect the diverse make up of that community. Social enterprises need to be transparent and deliberate in understanding how they use and replenish natural capital, and the way in which they value and invest in their human, manufacturing, and social capital.

Both models respond to how executive leaders and managers have implemented the stewardship model of governance. The latter assumes that these leaders will always act in the organization's best interests. Our experience has been that this is not always the case. Executive leaders can, and often do, act in a spirit of enlightened self-interest if two conditions are present. The first is that they are keenly aware of whom they are accountable to. The second is that they surround themselves with people, policies and procedures that institutionalize stewardship as the organization's operating system.

We anticipate that enterprises will continue to navigate this paradox.

Established as a staff investment company in 2007, Thokozani Staff Holdings is an example of a shareholding model of responsible transformation, development, and empowerment. Thokozani, which means "let's celebrate" in Zulu, is the empowerment partner of the Diemersfontein Wine & Country Estate in Wellington, South Africa. Its ownership is comprised of Thokozani Staff Holdings (30%), external investors (30%) and the Diemersfontein Group (40%).

The farmworkers, who are also the shareholders of Thokozani company, are allocated a block of shares in exchange for their commitment to remain with the company for a minimum of five years. They also commit to increase their understanding of, and develop skills in, the principles of small enterprises. These requirements are meant to address the criticism levelled against earlier efforts at South African farmworker equity schemes that failed because of poor governance and the failure to equip farmworkers with the skills that they needed to make a business work.

Thokozani makes sure these skills are learnt firsthand and accompanies this training with credit counseling to ensure the sustainable economic empowerment of all its employees.

A recent groundbreaking development, and a significant event in the history of the South African wine industry, is Thokozani's purchase of fifty-five percent (55%) shareholding in Diemersfontein Wines, the trading company for this wine estate. This trading company includes its wine label, farming, marketing, and infrastructure business. Taking transformation one step further, apart from the allocated block shares, shareholders can now acquire additional shares by a contributing a small part of their salary every month. Thus, instead of buying the land, workers have bought into the brand. This in turn contributes towards sustaining and growing the enterprise and secures the financial future of the shareholders.

The King Code on Corporate Governance

In 1993, South Africa's Institute of Directors approached retired judge, Mervyn King, and tasked him to create a set of voluntary principles and practices that would help shape corporate governance in post-apartheid South Africa. This document become known as the King Code and it has subsequently undergone three revisions. The most recent revision was released in 2016 and is commonly referred to as King IV. This version extends the principles and practices of good governance to include small enterprises, government bodies, state-owned enterprises, non-profits, and NGOs. The King Code influences corporate governance practices internationally. Malaysia, Australia, and the Philippines are three countries which have recently updated their corporate governance regulations to reflect the principles and practices found in King IV. Our research also shows that subsequent iterations of the King Code are interwoven with the practice of integrated reporting which is being adopted in the fields of accounting and auditing.

We argue that the King Code is relevant to social enterprises for the following reasons.

- The Code provides social enterprises with a holistic, systems-focused approach for developing business plans, operationalizing these plans, measuring their outcomes, and reporting these to their stakeholders.
- The Code and these practices reflect insights and practices which some US-based social enterprises have begun to follow, especially those which are organized as B (Benefit) Corporations or which intend to be organized as such. The United States has a long history of member-owned cooperatives for whom this Code will provide invaluable insights as they adapt to meet their stakeholders' expectations in the 21st Century.

- As the principles and practices in this Code are adopted by more countries and businesses around the world, they will become more relevant to social enterprises. Many enterprises engage in international trade, either when they source inputs for the products they create (think Fair Trade Rooibos tea), or when they sell their products. Adopting these principles and practices, or at least aligning themselves with them, adds to the social enterprises' competitive advantage.
- While this is a voluntary code, it will be prescient for social enterprises to adopt and use these principles as more businesses and countries begin to institutionalize its practices.

The King Code on Governance is influenced by the philosophies of holism and ubuntu where it emphasizes stakeholder engagement and its view that all businesses operate within a larger social and environmental system. The success of all enterprises depends on them acknowledging that this comes from adhering to the social and environmental contract which governs how they steward their relationship with their social stakeholders and the natural environment.

King IV lays out sixteen principles and best practices for the governance of social enterprises and locates this holon within a larger canvas that is framed by the concepts of the triple bottom line and the Six Capitals. The fourth version of the King Code refers to how these concepts inform the role, structure, and behavior of the Board of Directors. While it does not address the role of management and how the Board and Management interact, the King Code points to the desired appearance, behavior, and outcomes of enlightened corporate governance. When taken together they allow social enterprises to see how they uniquely combine the Six Capitals and it gets them to think more deeply about their bottom line, how they are reaching it and the depth of their impact.

We will revisit the subject of governance in Chapter 3 when we consider the best ways for social enterprises to structure and operationalize their governance and management through using the sixteen best practices that are found in the King code, as well as the operational model of governance known as Aligned Influence.

The Economic Holon

The Triple Context and the Triple Bottom Line

The origins of the term *triple context* are unclear. The consensus though is that the idea of a triple context began to surface in various intellectual disciplines in the 1970s. Purvis (2018) attributes the first visual diagram of this concept to Barbier, who included it in his article *The Concept of Sustainable Economic Development* which was published in 1987. The 2005

World Summit on Social Development added more legitimacy to this idea. The Summit popularized the concept of the triple context by explaining that social development is located within the three interrelated spheres of society, economy, and natural environment. The implication then is that organizations are responsible for improving social, economic, and environmental conditions and that they are held accountable for doing so. At the very least, they should do no harm. However, given the social and environmental challenges facing communities, nations, and the world, these organizations must do more than just maintain the status quo.

In 1994, John Elkington introduced the world to the idea of the Triple Bottom Line. His goal was to transform capitalism by expanding its focus from just financial returns and profits to a broader one which considers economic, social, and environmental impact and returns. Elkington believed that such a focus would drive innovation by channeling capital away from harmful products and services to ones that are ecologically sound, and which also benefit communities and the environment. This growing pool of capital would also make it possible to scale up innovative products and services.

Elkington revisited his concept in an article that he published in the Harvard Business Review in 2018. He lamented that the concept had become yet another talking point and tool employed by the accounting profession, and managers and executives had been slow to adopt it. Although Elkington wished to recall his concept to fine-tune it, the real issue is not that the concept is impractical, but rather that it needs to be more mainstreamed. Thinking about the Triple Context and Triple Bottom Line forces all organizations, not just traditional business, to move beyond a narrow definition of success and sustainability.

Does this mean that business discipline and success no longer matter? Absolutely not. We know that social enterprises are required to be wise stewards of the Six Capitals and that they need to employ them in ways which are financially, socially, and environmentally sustainable. Leaders of social enterprises need to be conscious that these enterprises operate in, and are accountable to, a local and larger economy, society, and environment. They need to intentionally incorporate these *triple* concepts when designing and operating enterprises to generate valued services and products. Social enterprises have a moral duty to do so. This book shows how students and practitioners of social enterprise can do just that.

The Six Capitals

The concept of Six Capitals was the logical outgrowth of Elkington's (1995) triple context. Jane Gleeson-Smith (2020) writes that use of the concept of Six Capitals continues to grow amongst business leaders, scholars, and professional services such as the accounting field. Accountants and auditors have incorporated it into the national and international standards they use, and this concept continues to inform their integrated system of reporting. Thanks to the governance work of the King Committee in South Africa and the International Integrated Reporting Council (IIRC), more work has been done to define the elements of these capitals and how they might be measured. While most of the characteristics of each capital are unique to them, some others fall into the spaces "in between" one or more of these capitals.

We have found that the International Integrated Reporting Council's image of the Six Capitals as being "stores of value" has resonated with us (IIRC, 2013). When we close our eyes, we envisage six stores. They are different colors, have different floor prints, and they offer different products. While each store is unique, we compare them to a bazaar or farmers market, where a myriad of entrepreneurs buy and sell products. These entrepreneurs know one another, and they collaborate out of a sense of enlightened self-interest. Just as in our bazaar, the contents of these Six Capitals stores that make up the social enterprise are never static. Instead, the social enterprise "buys" or "borrows" capital from each of them to create value. The content increases and decreases on a regular basis as these transactions take place. The returns that it earns are used to replenish those stores, perhaps even bringing back more capital than it withdrew, to ensure that there is enough for future investments and periods when revenue is lower.

The fact that accountants continue to debate the characteristics of each of these capitals and where they should be placed in an enterprise's integrated report, does not invalidate the concept. The real value of the Six Capitals is that they force every social enterprise to have a robust internal discussion about how they employ each capital, determine their unique mix, and how their leaders will be accountable to the enterprises' stakeholders for the way in which they have employed these capitals to create value. It forces the leaders and managers of social enterprises to think strategically about how they engage with each set of stakeholders. It also helps them to shift their decision-making horizon to include both the short- and long-term.

The term "Capital", as opposed to the commonly used "resources and relationships", best describes these stores of value. We favor this term because our Christian faith tradition teaches us to value people as being created in the image of God; that we inhabit God's creation and that we are temporary stewards of the material and non-material resources that have been entrusted to our care. While we understand and accept that assets – especially those reflected in the economic sphere – are defined as resources which are used to create value, we will continue to draw on our experience to argue that these resources originate at levels which we often do not fathom. Capital speaks to something of great value that is entrusted to someone in a position of authority. Those who entrust them with that capital expect a return on their investment. They expect that the capital will grow and be productively used. Look no further than the Parable of the Talents in the Christian New Testament to read about this expectation.

While our current economic model of capitalism has demonstrated both the importance and fragility of financial capital, it has also been our experience that much work still needs to be done to incorporate or "mainstream" the other five concepts into the design and operations of social enterprises. Doing so will also help these enterprises as they market their unique products and services.

We will now begin to explore the Six Capitals.

Natural Capital

We have started with the capital that social enterprises tend to overlook when they think about how they employ the Six Capitals. If each of the subsequent capitals are the trees, then natural capital is the soil that nourishes them and serves as their foundation. It speaks to "the commons" within which a social enterprise co-exists with other organizations and over which it has little control.

The term *natural capital* emerged from the field of ecology. There is wide-spread consensus that the term *natural capital* applies to three inter-related components: natural resources (air, water, minerals, soil, fossil fuels and carbon sinks), the animals and plants that make up living systems, and the interaction, nutrient and energy that flows between these living and non-living components of the ecosystem.

Human beings are dependent on this system remaining healthy. Since social enterprises are composed of humans, it should come as no surprise that the viability of such an enterprise is dependent upon this same natural ecosystem of which it is a part. As this view of natural capital includes the idea that some resources are renewable while others are nonrenewable, social enterprises must be accountable for their use of natural resources in both the present as well as the long-term.

We were first introduced to the concept of *natural capitalism* when we read a book with this title written by Paul Hawken and Hunter and Amory Lovins in 1998. In it, they contrasted what they termed the "conventional economic model" with one that they termed the "natural capital model".

The conventional economic model is the prevailing capitalist one. It argues that the market forces of supply and demand associated with a lightly regulated economy optimally allocates resources to their best and highest use. The efficiencies which are generated by this arrangement generally raises living standards and wealth. These are measured through commensurate increases in national gross domestic product (GDP). Proponents of this economic model argue that any concerns for the environment must be balanced with the need for economic growth to sustain human well-being. When these concerns come into conflict, then they argue that economic growth needs to win out. They also feel environmental problems are likely to be resolved through technological innovations.

Economists and activists who have been concerned about environmental issues have long argued that pollution results from the failure of the conventional economic model to adequately account for its costs. Pollution is an externalized cost that does not appear on the traditional balance sheet. Thus, the natural capital model has emerged as a critique of the conventional economic model promulgated by both the traditional capitalist and socialist camps during the Cold War. It is also proposed as an alternative which employs market forces without being constrained by the narrow self-interest of economic and political elites.

The natural capital model adopts the ecologists' view of the natural environment with its interrelated parts of living and non-living systems which interact with one another. Proponents of this school maintain that future economic development will be limited by the availability of natural capital. They argue that efforts should be made to replenish renewable natural capital and to conserve those elements which are in limited supply. Natural capital is lost through excess consumption, a growing population and poorly designed business systems. Proponents of natural capital are confident that this source of capital can be better utilized when market-based systems of production and distribution utilize the Six Capitals approach, when these systems are more localized, and when they are subject to democratic checks and balances. Champions of natural capital also argue that economic and environmental sustainability depend upon steps being taken to address growing socio-economic inequalities.

Building on Hawken and Lovins' initial work (1998), proponents of this economic model have used one or a combination of the following four strategies to replenish and utilize their natural capital more efficiently:

- Using technology to get more value and use from the natural resources they consume.
- Applying the principle of biomimicry to their production cycles and materials to eliminate waste and the generation of pollutants.
- Moving to a service and flow model where the consumer purchases the service that an instrument produces rather than the instrument itself. The manufacturer continues to own the machine and is responsible for recycling it when it reaches the end of its life.

- Replenishing natural capital and viewing these actions as a long-term investment in new and ongoing local economic development.

These two frameworks form a paradox when discussing how to engage in economic activity which improves human standards of living and the natural environment. There are diverse opinions as to the best ways to accomplish these as they are accompanied by inevitable trade-offs. While the climate crisis continues to grow, we are also encouraged by the efforts of many social enterprises to embrace this paradox. It is clear however, that much more needs to be done to replenish and sustainably manage natural capital and this needs to be done urgently.

Human Capital

This source of capital speaks to the technical, managerial and leadership skills, competence, motivation and learned experiences that an individual employee brings to an enterprise. It refers therefore to the human beings who employ these variables to create a valued product or service. The value of an enterprise's human capital also increases when its employees are permitted to express their values through their work at the social enterprise, and when their values and those espoused by the enterprise are aligned. Our experience reinforces the findings of management research: an enterprises' competitive advantage lies in how well it recruits, motivates, develops, and retains its human capital.

Manufacturing Capital

Manufacturing capital refers to the equipment, buildings (and their related systems) and tools used by a social enterprise to create its product and services. Manufacturing capital is what remains behind once the product or service leaves the place where it was created. As a tangible capital, manufacturing capital also includes the public and community infrastructure that surrounds the social enterprises' physical location. These include the water system, the electrical grid and transportation routes, all of which the social enterprise depends upon to function well.

Social and Relationship Capital

The knowledge and value that is created between a social enterprise and its stakeholders is known as social and relationship capital. It is found in the formal and informal networks where the enterprise engages with other organizations. This space begins with their regular customers, suppliers, and competitors. It then expands to include the local community, that is, the neighborhoods and political units which provide it with further capitals to create valued products and services; the local, regional, and international economic networks; and those governmental entities that are responsible for creating a predictable, safe, and healthy environment in which the social enterprise can operate. Social and relationship capital is where social enterprises meet their legal and regulatory obligations. *Legal* in the sense of their contracts to provide products to customers to ensure their loyalty, their timely and fair treatment of their suppliers and vendors, and the way they negotiate and behave towards their competitors. *Regulatory* in the sense that they understand and comply with all the government and business regulations which pertain to their operations and products.

Financial Capital

Financial capital refers to all sources of funds a social enterprise taps into to start up, operate and grow so that it can deliver valued products over the long-term. These include debt financing such as loans, equity that is issued to community or institutional investors, grants received from the philanthropic sector, and the income the social enterprise earns from the sale of its products and services. Inventory is also considered part of a social enterprises' financial capital since it is a key part of its working capital.

Intellectual Capital

This source of capital refers to the social enterprise's tangible and intangible intellectual property (such as patents, copyrights, and secret recipes), brand and community reputation, organizational culture, and business strategy. We include the processes associated with its governance, management, and operations under intellectual capital, as these are integral to the enterprise's resilience. A helpful way to determine whether something is part of an enterprise's intellectual capital is to ask where ownership of that skill or process resides. If it belongs to the enterprise rather than to an individual, then it should be considered as intellectual capital.

Intellectual capital is valuable and requires protection. With much of an enterprises' communications and commerce now transacted via the internet, there is an increased risk of cyberattacks. Consequently, social enterprises should not only invest in technological platforms but also adopt and enforce policies and protocols that secure their data and their media platforms. We have noted with interest that, increasingly, governance codes such as the King Code include technology in their risk management policies and plans.

Local or Community Economic Development

The philosophy behind Community Economic Development (CED) is based on a proverb that has Chinese, Greek, and Native American origins. This proverb is often stated as follows: "Give a person a fish and they will eat for a day. Teach a person to fish and they will eat for life." CED challenges us to move beyond this focus on education by asking "*Who owns the lake?*" If the person has the equipment that they need to fish but find that they are barred from the shore of the lake, then they will be unable to meet their basic needs.

Our experience is that CED emphasizes the need for widespread local ownership of necessary resources to ensure that local communities enjoy economic vitality and resilience. A vibrant local economy consists of a tapestry of sustainable and connected local organizations which meet the basic needs of their members. These organizations add value to the community's resources and use the circulation of money between them to build individual, household, and community wealth and wellbeing. In practical terms, a local and regional economy which embraces the principles and practices of CED would consist of locally owned farms and businesses, civic and religious organizations, media, arts organizations, and elected local government bodies. These institutions would be responsive to the needs of all the residents in their community. These residents would be healthy, educated and gainfully employed or engaged in other volunteer activities that add value and vibrancy to the community. Residents would feel valued and have some form of ownership in one or more of these local organizations or enterprises.

The Canadian CED Network defines Community Economic Development as "action (taken) by people locally to create economic opportunities and better social conditions, particularly for those who are most disadvantaged." According to them, effective CED occurs when community members lead these initiatives and draw on local community knowledge. These projects recognize and strengthen the connections between individuals, their local communities, and the surrounding regions.

A review of the history of CED shows that it has emerged during periods of tumultuous change and amongst communities such as women, immigrants, and people of color in response to institutionalized discrimination. St. Mary's Bank was established by French-Canadian immigrants in Manchester, New Hampshire, and became the first credit union in the United States. It was created in response to the dominant English-speaking establishment's refusal to extend financial services to these immigrants despite their employment in local industries and businesses. Today, financial cooperatives, better known as credit unions, are important sources of community capital and local economic growth around the world. In 1848 in Rochdale, United Kingdom, 28 textile workers established a cooperatively-owned and -operated shop; this led to the emergence of a worldwide movement which, by 2014, included over 2.6 million cooperatives (https://www.un.org/esa/socdev/documents/2014/coopsegm/grace.pdf.).

The idea of CED experienced a resurgence in the 1980s when it arose in response to the loss of jobs and economic opportunities in rural communities, regions, and historically marginalized communities of color in cities across the world. Many rural communities experienced a decline as the resource extractive industries (such as mining and forestry) on which they depended underwent dramatic changes. Another factor that helped with this resurgence was the rise of the first generation of social entrepreneurs. The idea of micro-credit was popularized by the work of Mohammed Yunus and the Grameen Bank in Bangladesh. Meanwhile, in the USA, Millard and Linda Fuller's work to re-imagine how low-income households, volunteers, and community capital could be woven together to address the problem of substandard housing resulted in the emergence of Habitat for Humanity, an organization that is now active in 70 countries around the world.

Over the past decade we have witnessed how the principles and practices of CED have inspired both business and social enterprises in the areas of sustainable tourism and natural resource management. One of the goals of this book is to provide both new and existing social enterprises with the necessary framework and tools they need to endure and thrive.

The Spiritual Holon

A characteristic of enduring social enterprises is that their founders are motivated not only by the need and suffering that they witness, but also by a spiritual calling which compels them to respond to that suffering. From our experience of creating and sustaining social enterprises, we can testify that doing so requires not only a leap of faith, but also the support of a community or faith tradition which provides inspiration for the inevitable challenges that face the enterprise. Faith traditions have a long history of incubating social enterprises. A major player in the world of cooperatives is the Mondragon Corporation, which traces its origins to a priest named José María Arizmendiarrieta. He drew his inspiration from the social teachings of the Catholic Church.

In addition to the inspiring examples and teachings of Father Arizmendiarrieta, Mohandas Gandhi, Reverend Martin Luther King Jr., we have drawn encouragement from two other sources. One is from the writings of a trained farmer and New Testament scholar Clarence Jordan whose work inspired Habitat for Humanity International. The other is Francois van Niekerk.

In 1942, Jordan co-founded an intentional Christian social enterprise that was established outside Americus, Georgia, in the southern United States. This community is still known today as Koinonia Partners. Jordan viewed Koinonia Farms as a "radical demonstration plot" for local economic development and social justice. He drew his inspiration from Jesus' Sermon on the Mount and from the second chapter of Acts in the New Testament of the Christian Bible, which described how early Christian communities were organized.

Koinonia was financed by capital from supporters and the mobilization of members' savings. This covered the required purchase of assets (land and machinery) to operate the community enterprise and increase the farm's crop yields. Koinonia's interpretation of radical hospitality, which included racial integration and providing hospitality to conscientious objectors, not only led to social ostracism but also resulted in them becoming the targets of a local economic boycott and acts of domestic terrorism. These actions forced them to modify their earned income strategy to include the use of mail-order catalogues to ship their products to supporters across the United States. The members of this community continued to raise funds from these supporters to finance new social ventures.

One of these ventures was the Fund for Humanity which sought to purchase land for lease or sale to African American families so that they could establish their own farms and improve their housing conditions. Clarence Jordan's untimely death in 1969 meant that this agrarian model of reparations did not come to fruition as planned. However, the idea of a Fund for Humanity led to the design and growth of Habitat for Humanity. The same concept has also found life in the model followed by the Fuller Center for Housing. By focusing on affordable home ownership, these two social enterprises have allowed low-income households to acquire an asset which meets their shelter needs and provide the opportunity for inter-generational wealth creation and transfer. They have also created a partnership model which continues to mobilize support across social divides. While the local partnerships that these organizations continue to generate still need to fully reckon with the effects of institutional racism and implicit bias in the United States, Koinonia Partners continues to serve as a model – a demonstration plot – of how social enterprises can facilitate both economic and social justice.

While the tenets of Clarence Jordan's practical theology were informed by his Christian faith and his study of Jesus' Sermon on the Mount, his authentic blend of faith and action serves as a model for anyone – irrespective of their faith or motivation – to start and lead a social enterprise.

Our second source is Francois van Niekerk, author of *Doing Business with Purpose – Beyond success to significance*; he is also the founder and former CEO of the Mergon Group in SA. Facing insolvency in 1980, Francois made a vow that he would give 30% of the business for the expansion of the Kingdom of God if the Lord helped him. God intervened, the company was saved, and Francois followed through on his 30% commitment by placing the shares in an independent trust. This trust became known as the Mergon Foundation Trust. Francois and the Mergon team went on to establish several successful businesses in partnership with like-minded entrepreneurs. This approach, together with unmerited favor, has resulted in Mergon achieving sustained, above-market returns for nearly 40 years. Today Mergon funds over 130 strategic, impactful initiatives which are committed to transforming the lives of people, from all walks of life both practically and spiritually. Mergon encourages and equips other business leaders to make a difference through its Nation Builder initiative (more about this in Chapter 6) and through workshops aimed at inspiring business leaders to use their own capital, influence and business platforms in a practical way that also has both spiritual and social impact.

Social enterprises which trace their origins to a religious tradition need to reflect that tradition's values and teachings in their mission statements and in the way that they engage their human capital to create valued products. Failing to reflect these values increases the likelihood that these social enterprises will lose their soul over time. While we are painfully aware that faith traditions have often been used to justify violence and oppression, and that congregations and faith-based organizations have often covered up abuses perpetrated by their leaders, we have also found the spiritual dimension to be a critical part of a social enterprise. It is wise for leaders of social enterprises to periodically lead their social enterprises through a process of metanoia (repentance and renewal) to ensure that they remain true to their core values.

In conclusion of this chapter, please note that the holons we have listed are not exhaustive, nor are they exclusive. We advocate that leaders and managers of social enterprises should employ this holon framework (whole and inter-related holons), to better understand their organizations and shape their organizational practices. This includes all areas of organizational practice, from planning, deciding on what products and services to offer and how to offer them, to marketing, risk management, governance, management, and operations.

Chapter 2

PLANNING FOR SOCIAL ENTERPRISES

Every social enterprise, from its start-up to beyond, wants not only to survive but thrive. The picture of a thriving (sustainable) enterprise may be described as having healthy, satisfied employees and customers, a management team and board that makes good business decisions and avoids unnecessary waste of human and enterprise resources (especially time and money), keeps up with the times, grows, and constantly evolves to the next level. This is an enterprise that is not found sleeping, but one that is on the alert: ready, keeping watch and ready to take on whatever comes their way; vigilant of their political, social, financial, and environmental surroundings. In essence, a sustainable social enterprise engages with all Six Capitals in an efficient and unique manner.

For this picture to become a reality, there is need for regular planning, and continuous, structured evaluation to obtain feedback on how they are doing. There are several tools and insights that help the leaders of a social enterprise to plan for and evaluate their program and its impact and enable them to take advantage of opportunities for growth. We have selected a few that have influenced our practice and that we have found highly effective. These include Theory of Change, Systems Thinking, Sigmoid Curves (S-Curves) and Business Plans, and we have provided a brief introduction to each one in this chapter. The tools can be used separately or combined as there are several crossovers.

Planning with a Purpose – The Planning Process

A definition of planning is to decide in advance what to do and how to do it so that certain desirable goals can be met. Planning is not just a process of setting goals, developing strategies, and outlining activities and timelines to accomplish these goals. It also gives an enterprise a future direction whilst honoring its values, vision, mission, and culture. Without a plan, no valuable information would be gathered. Management needs this to make effective decisions and allocate the available resources in a way that will enable the enterprise to reach its goals.

Planning is a basic managerial function that brings value to your enterprise in the following ways:

Direction: To plan effectively, you must determine where the enterprise is headed and identify its priorities. Establishing this gives the enterprise a sense of direction and ensures that the right development happens in the right place at the right time.

Efficiency: If you know what to focus on, you will spend less time on tasks that get in the way of your goal. Productivity is maximized and resources are focused on tasks and activities that have a good chance of success.

Accountability and governance: Creating a detailed plan with checks and balances in place helps you to anticipate problems and cope with change; it reduces the chance of errors and places you in the decision-making seat with options, rather than leaving things to chance or, even worse, letting others make decisions for you.

Creativity: The more you think and engage in planning, the more likely you are to come up with a variety of ideas and options.

Engagement: Planning establishes a basis for teamwork and co-operation, especially if it is a joint process between management and employees. It also serves as a prerequisite to employing all other management functions.

Steps in the Planning Process

Planning is an intellectual process and needs to remain flexible or open to change. It is a future focused, goal orientated and continuous activity, and best explained by a 6-step process:

- Gather information.
- Set objectives - determine what is to be accomplished.
- Develop premises – identify problems and opportunities and evaluate alternatives.
- Identify resources and how these are to be assigned.
- Plan and implement tasks; include timelines and task/role assignments.
- Decide on monitoring and evaluation methods.

Good planning begins with gathering the right information and then strategically thinking about what to do with that information in the context of your environment. The aim is to improve and grow the enterprise. Good planning helps you to anticipate possible scenarios so that you can avoid unnecessary problems and take advantage of great opportunities. Poor planning results in a directionless enterprise where no one has a clear picture of where to go or of what is expected of them. Planning – before you take action, while you are taking action, and after you have taken action – pays off.

Systems Thinking

A Systems Approach to Understanding Enterprises

The belief that "if you can anticipate what will happen in your enterprise, you can start to shape the outcomes you want" is something that resonates with us. However, a deep understanding and knowledge of your enterprise is essential before you can realistically anticipate what might happen. Applying a Systems Approach and Systems Thinking is one way of gaining this understanding and knowledge.

We introduced you to the term holon in Chapter 1, where holon refers to the whole system as well as to its components. Williams (2019) refers to the system and its components as several sub-systems or smaller systems operating within the context of a larger system. Regardless of the size of your enterprise, it will contain multiple systems and sub-systems which need to work together to achieve its objectives. When these mutually dependent systems and sub-systems continuously and effectively work together, the whole enterprise functions properly and grows. Gitterman and Germain (1980) state that enterprises evolve and adapt through transactions with all of the elements in their environment (or the larger system in which they find themselves). In these adaptive processes, the enterprise and the environment reciprocally shape each other.

If they wish to grow and develop, then all systems must be open to receiving input from the other systems with which they interact. Compton and Galaway (1989) conclude that a system must be open to interact with the smaller systems that make up the whole, as well as the larger system of which it is a part. Thus, any action within a system may affect the whole system as well as the smaller divisions of the system. Building on the term holon (or "holism") leads to the understanding that there are two dimensions to Systems Thinking. The static dimension involves mapping the distinct parts of a system, while the dynamic dimension focuses on the interactions and inter-relationships between these parts. Taken together, these two dimensions constitute the Systems Approach to understanding enterprises.

Dimensions to Systems Thinking

The Static Dimension

The Systems Approach demystifies the business process. In this Approach, enterprises convert the inputs they gather from the external environment into outputs which consist of valued products, services, and waste. Internal and inter-related sub-systems such as people, technology and machinery are an integral part in that conversion process. Holism and ubuntu contribute the insight that there are (sub)systems within larger systems. Therefore, an enterprise is a whole that is comprised of smaller sub-systems. It is simultaneously a sub-system within a larger system or external environment. Each sub-system enjoys a permeable boundary and although this boundary is a reality, the ease with which there are harmonious flows through these boundaries will vary. In some cases, flows may be smooth while in other situations and circumstances they may be characterized by conflict and disorder.

The Systems Approach uses the acronym PESTAL to order the external environment of the enterprise. This order consists of several inter-related spheres (along with the types of actors in each sphere) which impact the operations and success of any enterprise.

- *Political:* This includes actors whose role it is to make decisions about the common good. These actors are regulated by political constitutions and boundaries. When applied to enterprises, the political sphere encompasses all elected and appointed officials whose policies and regulations directly and indirectly govern these enterprises. An example in point is the growing international consensus to reduce greenhouse emissions to slow the rate of climate change. Decisions made in this international realm will impact every enterprise.
- *Economic:* This includes all actors in the economic sphere whose decisions and actions impact on the enterprise. These actors include the enterprise's financiers, competitors, suppliers, and customers who exist and operate in close physical and virtual proximity to it. There are also economic actors who are further afield; these include central banks and other economic sectors whose (mis)fortunes may, or may not, impact the enterprise. This sphere also includes the micro-economic realities of households to fit their level of prosperity and purchasing power.
- *Social:* These include the communities and larger societies within which enterprises operate. This sphere is concerned with households, community organizations and local institutions and how they are affected by demographic shifts and changes in values and tastes. The quantity, quality and resilience of households and voluntary community structures fit into this sphere, along with organized local institutions such as those responsible for health, education, and the arts.
- *Technological:* This sphere includes those actors responsible for introducing new technologies as well as the technologies themselves. Technologies may facilitate the work of an enterprise, or they may disrupt or revolutionize not only the products and services it delivers, but also the very rationale and basis for doing so. Technology cycles can introduce incremental or episodic change (see Chapter 10). Episodic cycles

arise when new technologies are introduced which transform the ways in which households, communities and societies operate. Incremental cycles are calmer, more predictable and are controlled by the enterprise as it improves the technologies in use.

- *Legal:* The legal sphere starts with the legislation that outlines the different forms that enterprises can assume, how they are to be governed, and their responsibilities towards the wider system. It includes the rules created by regulatory agencies, given their responsibility for enacting legislation through specific regulations. This sphere also includes those areas of civil law that govern how the enterprise interacts "civilly" with those parties with whom it enters legally binding contracts. Actors in this sphere include the judicial system and the mechanisms that enterprises follow when resolving any conflicts.

The Dynamic Dimension

Systems are dynamic. This dynamism flows from the inter-relationships between their constituent parts or sub-systems. These different sub-systems influence one other with this observed behavior of action and reaction (or cause and effect) and generate the energy which propels the broader system (Senge, 1990: 75). System theorists refer to these energy flows as feedback loops. Beukes (1989) writes that Jan Smuts understood these two feedback loops as being the inner factor (evolution) and the outer factor (holism).

When applying this dynamic dimension to enterprises, Senge (1990:79) states that there are two types of feedback loops. Reinforcing feedback loops amplify the effects of actions or the failure to act. They may be productive (virtuous) or unproductive (destructive) to an enterprise. In the latter case, they may be caused by sub-optimization where the sub-systems strive to increase their efficiency without realizing that their actions are creating problems and inefficiencies elsewhere in the enterprise. Reinforcing feedback loops are present when enterprises are experiencing periods of growth as well as periods of decline.

Balancing, or maintenance, feedback loops arise when an enterprises' actions run into natural constraints, or they reach a goal or boundary standard that the enterprise has set for itself. These feedback loops therefore help to keep the organization stable and the related stresses manageable. They also show up when enterprise-level change is being resisted.

Senge (1990:80) concludes his introduction to feedback loops by introducing the concept of delays. He defines delays as "…interruptions in the flow of influence which make the consequences of actions occur gradually." When applying the Systems Approach, part of the art of managing is to be patient and remember that delays are inevitable in any system and to understand when they are likely to happen, given the unique characteristics of each enterprise.

Tools and techniques to assist in the application of Systems Thinking

Even though no two enterprises are ever the same (this includes their systems and sub-systems), there are Systems Thinking tools and approaches that can be applied universally and we have selected a few that we have found most useful.

A popular tool used for guiding Systemic Thinking is the Iceberg Model. Thanks to Steven Spielberg's movie, Titanic, we have a clear picture of the danger that icebergs pose. With only a fraction of its total mass appearing above the waterline, it's the invisible bulk that lies underwater that poses the greatest risk. Similarly, for enterprises, what is visible can easily be dealt with. It's what's invisible that causes the greatest damage.

The Iceberg Model contains four levels of thinking as seen in the diagram below. The event level is the part of the iceberg above the waterline; this is concerned with what we can see and it is openly visible to all. We can easily fix what we see wrong and it often just requires simple adjustments and surface level, first-order changes. Once we go below the waterline, we encounter the pattern level. Even though we try not to, people and enterprises alike find comfort in operating in routine and structure, and this leads to the development of patterns of behaviour and operation. The pattern level focuses on observing similar events and behaviour that have been taking place over time which are either constructive or problematic. Once we know the patterns, we are better able to predict events as well possibly prevent them from happening.

It is not enough to just be aware of patterns; you must drill deeper to know what is causing those patterns. This occurs at the the third level, or structure level, and it is usually the structures themselves (e.g. environmental factors, policies, rules and how they shape behavioural patterns).

The final level, the mental model level, is concerned with the attitudes, beliefs, morals, expectations and values that allow structures to continue functioning as they are. These factors need to be validated and understood in order to work towards the necessary systemic change.

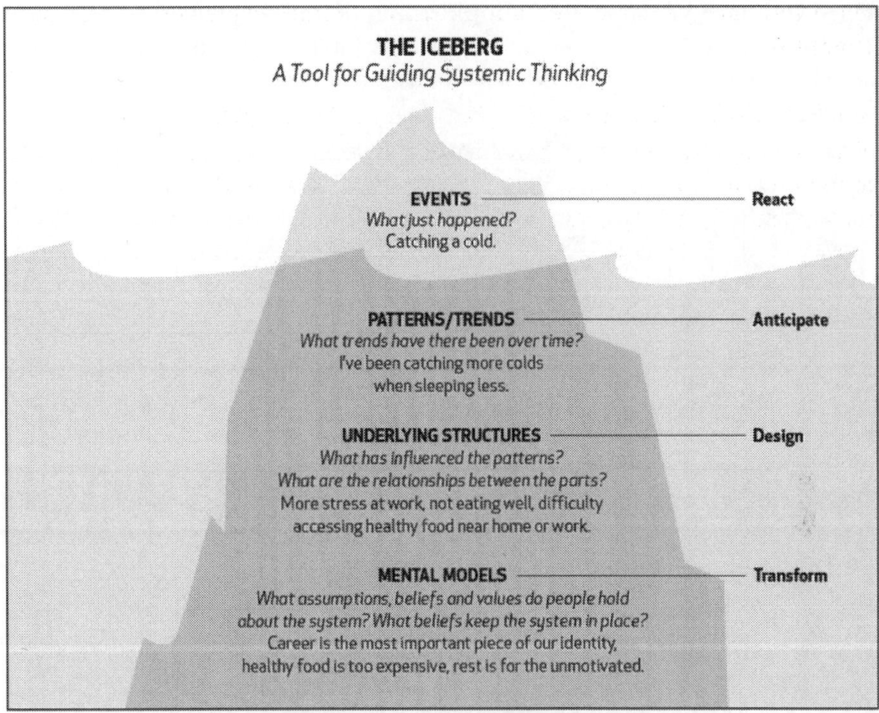

(Source: Kohei Nishizuka)

Another way to apply a Systems Thinking process would be to *begin with identifying the problem or issue that needs solving*. This first step involves looking at the whole system and not just its sub-systems so that we can gain a holistic view or deeper understanding of the true cause of a problem in an enterprise and address it effectively.

The best way to gain a holistic view or deeper understanding is to meet with all the stakeholders (systems and sub-systems) involved and invite them to share their perception of the problem. We all see problems from a different point of view and our awareness of these differences can lead us on two possible journeys: to a place of conflict or to a place of discovery. We get to that place of discovery by creating the right context or space where people can think and share openly. Some of the tools which can be used to create that context have been provided in this chapter.

When people are allowed to openly share what is on their minds without fear of judgment and with the intention of gaining a genuine understanding of a situation, problems can be examined more completely and accurately. This leads to intentional actions rather than reactions because listeners are less likely to jump to premature conclusions. Later, with all viewpoints represented on a problem, there is a greater buy-in and acceptance of solutions by all who need to implement them.

Once you have gathered all the information on the problem, it is helpful to formulate a *focus statement* so that all stakeholders (systems and sub-systems) have a clear idea of the issue. A useful tip is to present the statement in such a way that it is open to question and not viewed as a conclusive statement. A clear problem or focus statement makes it easier to start examining what is happening in the here and now. The system structure should be described in terms of the relationships and connections that make up the dynamics of the whole. As systems and sub-systems connect and interact over time, behavior patterns develop. Identifying these patterns helps us to gain a deeper understanding of the problem, what reinforces it, and ultimately how to better manage and/or change it.

The second part of the process involves *brainstorming for solutions and planning for intervention* for the entire system. If we only address one part of the problem in a system, any solutions we implement are likely to be short-term. As with identifying the problem, it is helpful to involve all the stakeholders (systems and sub-systems) in the brainstorming of solutions as well as the consequences of implementing them.

The third part of the process is to complete a *reality check*. Now that we have a better understanding of the problem or change needed, as well as some good ideas for solving it, there is always the temptation to run ahead and implement solutions. We would caution against this and to rather spend some time evaluating as to whether these solutions are realistic, as well as perhaps conducting a few tests to check initial results of the change.

Tool | Thinking Environments

In her book *Time to Think*, Kline (1999) highlights the importance of people being able to think for themselves and to think well collectively. She lays out a set of conditions that create what she calls Thinking Environments. When people are placed in the right environment, they begin to think for themselves. This involves creating a space where the principles of quality listening and freedom of expression are practiced. Everyone gets a turn to think properly, express their feelings and be heard. This is especially important in times of heated debates, tense relationships, crises, and stress. Practicing a Thinking Environment in your enterprise is a great way to solve problems and using its principles and components in all your meetings, presentations, supervision, and peer mentorship will certainly contribute towards the enterprise's creativity, dynamic interconnectedness, improved synthesis and, ultimately, its growth.

The components of a Thinking Environment and its application can be found in more detail in Kline's book, *Time to Think*. For easy reference, we have included the components in the table below.

Attention	Listening with respect, interest and fascination.
Incisive Questions	Removing assumptions that limit ideas.
Equality	Treating each other as thinking peers; giving equal turns and attention; keeping agreements and boundaries.
Appreciation	Practicing a five-to-one ration of appreciation to criticism.
Ease	Offering freedom from rush or urgency.
Encouragement	Moving beyond competition.
Feelings	Allowing sufficient emotional release to restore thinking.
Information	Providing a full and accurate picture of reality.
Place	Creating a physical environment that say back to people, "you matter'.
Diversity	Adding quality because of the differences between us.

Table 1: Components of Thinking Environment

Tool | Systems Mapping

Systems mapping allows for a visual representation of all the elements within a system. A visual representation makes it easier for all stakeholders

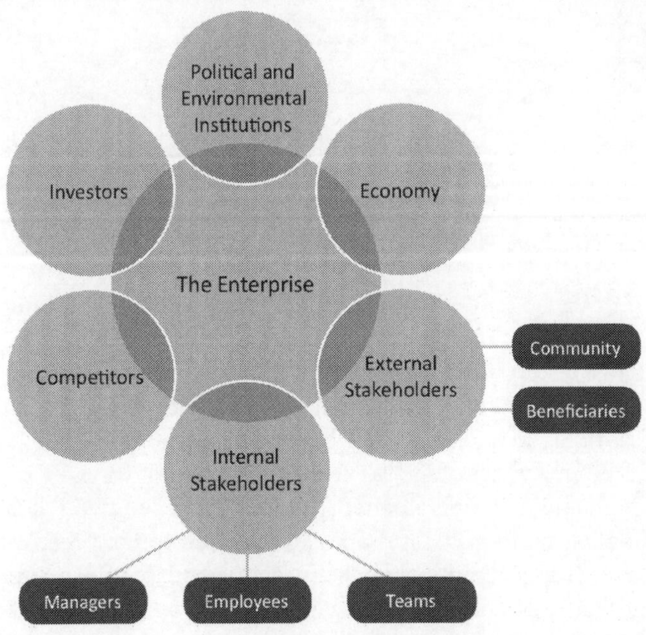

Fig.1: Systems Mapping

to understand exactly what the elements are and how they interconnect, relate and act in a system. Insights gained from the representation are then used to develop interventions that will help to change the system in the most effective way.

Tool | Behavior Over Time (BOT) Graphs

Although Systems Thinking predominantly focuses on what is happening in the 'here and now', if something is an entrenched problem, it has happened over time. The problem should thus be tracked accordingly, and a Behavior Over Time (BOT) graph is the perfect tool for this. Showing a curve that presents a specific behavior (Y) through time (X), a BOT graph helps us to see the bigger picture: from observing events, to identifying patterns of behavior over time, as well as the structures that drive those events and patterns. This big picture view makes it easier to identify potential solutions that can drive second-order change.

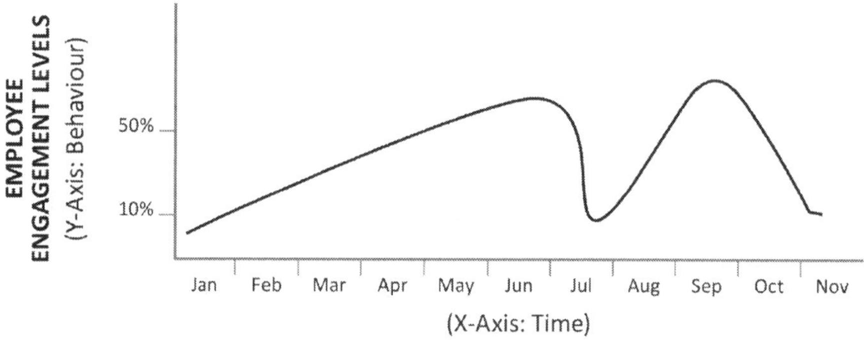

Fig.2: Behavior Over Time (BOT) Graphs

Tool | A causal loop diagram (CLD)

Causality or cause and effect are concepts in Systems Thinking that look at the way things influence each other in a system. A causal loop diagram (CLD) is essentially a storytelling tool used to introduce a number of elements in a system, and the relationships between the different elements, in a way that stimulates dialogue and creativity between stakeholders. The aim would be to encourage the stakeholders to come up with new ways of seeing the current problem and thus find a better solution. There are two types of feedback at play in a causal loop diagram. Positive or reinforcing feedback results in homeostasis (stable equilibrium between system parts), while negative or balancing feedback shows up the gaps between what is desired and what is really happening. As the gap widens, corrective actions are needed to adjust the actual level so that the gap decreases.

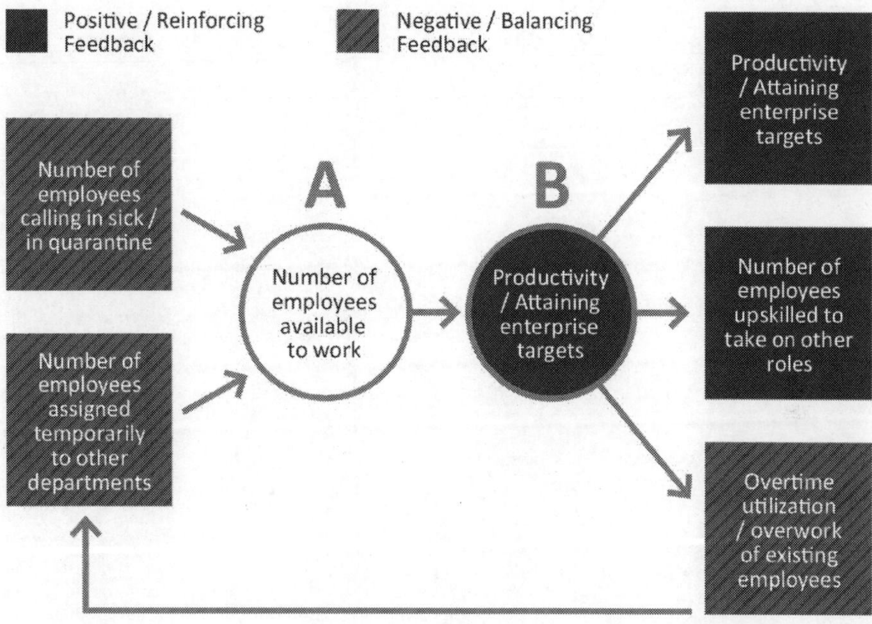

Fig.3: A causal loop diagram (CLD)

Tool | Questioning

Effective questioning is an extremely important tool in systemic practice and, when used with appropriate timing, can be helpful in revealing information that benefits the system (Starr, 2003, p. 163). Following a systemic line of questioning allows a system to go beyond what is made evident, probe deeply, unlock blockages, expand the horizon of perception, and help create a new frame in which new solutions emerge.

SYSTEMIC questions are used to:	***Examples:***
▪ Facilitate change ▪ Help a system develop a systemic perspective on their issues rather than seeing them purely as personal concerns. ▪ Help systems become aware of some of the patterns of interaction, which they habitually repeat.	▪ *How do you experience the enterprise at present?* ▪ *What do you think is going well and what is not going so well?* ▪ *What would have to happen to improve...?*
CIRCULAR questions are used to:	***Examples:***
▪ Find patterns that connect persons, objects, actions, perceptions, ideas, feelings, events and beliefs. ▪ Look at differences and therefore are a way of introducing new information into the system. ▪ Illuminate the interconnectedness of the system, sub-system and ideas. ▪ Shift perspective – questions are asked to all members or stakeholders of the system, and all receive feedback from the answered questions.	▪ *What do you think is the biggest challenge this board is facing?* ▪ *If A was more supportive, what would you see A doing?* ▪ *Who might be the one who has the best... in your team?* ▪ *What do you do when...?*
FUTURE-ORIENTATED questions are used to:	***Examples:***
▪ Change perspective. ▪ Focus on possibilities the system would like to see. ▪ Get the system to stop repeating all the reasons why a problem cannot be solved. ▪ Connect past and present and future and present. ▪ Move a system forward from a problem to a solution (Goal and solution orientated).	▪ *You mentioned things were different when you joined the enterprise. How would it be if we still did things that way?* ▪ *How would you recognize a successful outcome?*

Table 2: Questioning

The advantages of applying Systems Thinking in your enterprise are numerous and can help take it from ordinary to dynamic and uber-efficient. When enterprises change in response to internal and external factors in order to survive, they can do this best by applying a Systems Perspective (a complete understanding of the entire enterprise) to systems and sub-systems and their interconnectedness.

Applying a Systems Perspective enables an enterprise to:

- Make good business decisions, as each decision is analyzed according to its potential systematic consequences.
- Optimize business processes by removing unnecessary steps and finding effective short cuts; this can end up saving time, money, and other resources.
- Gain a holistic understanding of the entire ecosystem; this can lead to increased creativity and to discovery of new ways of thinking, problem-solving and goal setting.
- Understand the concept of systemic interrelatedness and the value of teamwork, and apply tools to integrate interconnectivity, creativity, and productivity into your workplace – employees need each other to achieve enterprise success.
- See problems as opportunities and potential ways to innovate and develop the enterprise.

Authors Corner: Systems Thinking and the Systems Approach has been the preferred coaching and theory model of one of the authors. In the earlier part of their career much emphasis was placed on first-order change, where individual behavior change takes place without impacting the structure of the system of which the individual is a part. However, the years spent engaging in grassroots work resulted in the author valuing and appreciating second-order change far more, as second-order change results in real understanding and knowledge of where and with whom one is working.

The Systems Approach and Systems Thinking is holistic and realistic. No one is an island – we are continuously affecting and being affected by our environment and the people in it and, as such, we cannot understand the behavior and thoughts of people and/or enterprises in isolation from the system in which they function. There is also no one truth in the life of a system or sub-system; therefore, to promote understanding, change and growth, we need to engage in open scrutiny and examination of all systems beliefs and interactions.

Systems Thinking helps us look at the heart of the matter – at the real core issues – and then focus on what needs to be done in order to get to where we want to go. Take-away nuggets for practicing Systems Thinking include:

- *Focus on the present:* Concern yourself less with why something is happening (how things got to be this way) and place more focus on what is happening in the here and now.

- *Process is more important than content:* There is less interest in what is being said, and more on how these messages are communicated.
- *Problem locus is rooted in the system(s) rather than an individual:* Frame problems in terms of relationships within the system (its structure and communication patterns), rather than individuals.
- *Aim for second-order change (transformation of the whole system - i.e., a change in its structure)*: Change in a system's structure contributes to change in the behavior of individual members. Second-order change occurs when the system cannot accommodate a change made by an individual and must therefore make an adjustment to its structure.
- *Invite Feedback:* When you engage in action, there are consequences. These consequences can be seen as feedback regarding the effect you have on others. Feedback keeps a system functioning. No feedback = no system.
- *Cause and effect may not always be connected in time and space.*
- *Factor in time delays.*
- *The easiest solutions are not always the most effective.*
- *Manage transitions carefully:* Although behaviour worsens when change is introduced, it will improve later.

Theories of Change

The word change means to alter, vary, or modify; to make or become different (Merriam-Webster: 2021). A Theory of Change or ToC is used to help promote social change by explaining how the activities undertaken by an initiative (e.g., project, program, or policy) contribute to a chain of results (outcome pathways) that lead to an intended impact. A ToC is applicable to enterprises in the profit, non-profit, and government sector; it is thus appropriate for small and large initiatives and helps to create a framework that describes how change will occur in the short, medium, and long term and achieve the intended impact. Graphically depicted and presented in a narrative format, it helps to explain why a particular way of working will be effective and how the work will be done.

The earliest and perhaps closest example to a ToC is Peter Drucker's concept of Management by Objectives (MBO). In his book, The Practice of Management (first published in 1954), he describes MBO as a joint process between management and employees, whereby they define the specific objectives they want to achieve within their enterprise, how they want to achieve each objective, and in which order this needs to occur. The process of breaking down each objective into activities and timed order helps to make them seem that much more obtainable, thus boosting both management and the employees' morale as they see and measure their accomplishments against the objectives set. This in turn contributes towards a positive work environment, and a greater sense of motivation and productivity within the enterprise.

In the 1980's, Carol Weiss began applying social program theories to evaluation methods. In *New Approaches to Evaluating Community Initiatives* (1995), Weiss noted that while it was possible to evaluate a social program on the overall achievement of its final long-term goals and outcomes, a gap existed as it was not possible to evaluate exactly how the change process occurred. Assumptions of how change might occur were rarely articulated and, if alluded to, were not made clear. Little attention was paid to mapping out the early and mid-term changes needed to reach a long-term goal. This not only hindered the evaluation quality, but also the opportunity to offer guidance and direction to make any necessary and timely changes to reach the intended impact. *New Approaches to Evaluating Community Initiatives* challenged developers of social programs to adopt a ToC process to guide their work and, in so doing, improve their overall evaluation plans, and thus their programs. Over the years, ToC has gained traction amongst programs, initiatives and enterprises working for social and political change.

Change as a Journey

We find it helpful when setting up a ToC to use the analogy of preparing a journey to your dream destination. This analogy provides a good understanding of the ToC terminology. All good journeys begin with a plan: the normal process is to decide on your dream destination and the mode of travel, and then plot the desired route. You'll include all those must-see and -do activities or stopovers along the way and tie them to an itinerary to ensure you reach each destination on time. Next, you'll decide who to take along with you on this journey. This step is essential, as choosing the wrong travel partner(s) can cause many a headache and spoil the experience. Careful consideration and wisdom must be applied in how you sell them the journey experience – they need to know what they are in for. Finally, a journey of this undertaking could not happen without necessary resources; thus, planning has to take into account the resources you have at your disposal, whether these be your own or those of the chosen travel partners coming along on the journey. In this analogy, the only twist to this journey preparation is that you flip the planning process around and start at the end of your journey then work your way backwards to the starting point, but this will be explained in more detail in the next few paragraphs.

Defined in ToC language, the roadmap is the ToC framework or process you will follow (and against which you will test assumptions about what activities will best produce the outcomes in the model). The mode of transport for this journey is the type of intervention used (i.e., a single program or coordinated initiative). The desired destination you hope to reach is referred to as **impact** or an **impact statement** and this is the starting point of the ToC / journey. Once this is clear, it is easier to set specific **outcomes** to make this impact a reality. Outcomes are the must-see or stopover places that cannot be missed on the journey. These are the steps you take to make the impact become a reality. Indicators **(outputs)** are the activities that must be completed at each must-see or stopover place. Indicators operationalize the outcomes, giving you a clear plan and purpose of exactly what needs to be done at the stopover. The people you take along on the journey are your target audience (the direct beneficiaries of your impact statement) and your stakeholders. Lastly, a ToC advocates that it is important to identify various human, material, or financial resources (referred to as **inputs**) to help you to bring about the outcomes you have identified. Once all this is firmly in place, the roadmap can be depicted in a **ToC diagram** which you use to motivate and compel your audience to join you on the journey.

When plotting a ToC, practical steps include conducting a situation analysis; identifying target groups, intended impact, outcomes, activities, change mechanisms, stakeholders, and assumptions; sequencing; and ToC diagrams. To simplify the process, we like to plot the roadmap or ToC process in three phases, each with their own specific actions.

Phase 1: Setting the Context

Every journey begins with a reason or desire to do something. A ToC is no different - you are placing the vision in context and providing a motivation for change. It's the first action you take. While the overarching purpose of a social enterprise is to bring about some form of social change, exactly what it wants to change and why (impact) needs to be defined as explicitly as possible. The more comprehensive your understanding of what you want to address (and why), the more effectively you will be able to plan for your impact. This comprehensive understanding is gained by gathering evidence that is not limited to the specific requirements of the intended beneficiaries and the systemic landscape in which the change will take place. This evidence will include an analysis of the resources (human, material, financial) you have at your disposal, as well as other service providers available to assist the beneficiaries. It is also helpful to research whether the desired change (impact) – or something similar – has been attempted before, and whether this was effective.

Identifying the intended beneficiaries is the next action in the context phase. Referred to as target groups or key agents of change, this includes the people or institutions you want to work with directly. Whether you choose to work with singular or multiple target groups, it is very important to define them clearly in terms of demographics (e.g., age, location, education, gender, race), characteristics (e.g., knowledge, attitudes, behaviors) and needs (e.g., strengths, assets, challenges).

ToCs can be developmental or descriptive in nature, and part of setting the context phase is deciding which of these two processes to follow. A developmental ToC process is best used when planning a new initiative, whilst a descriptive ToC process is a tool to improve existing work. In this way you can evaluate the effectiveness of a particular initiative, especially when there is potential to scale it up or copy it elsewhere. You will probably find yourself between these two processes. Either way, as long as you are engaging in reflective questioning around the 'what, why and who' during this phase, you will find the right process for your purpose. It is helpful to involve a variety of stakeholders in this reflective questioning process to gain a more comprehensive understanding of the identified beneficiaries, their needs, and what you are able to provide. If you are following a developmental ToC process, include stakeholders such as the key decision makers in your enterprise, your employees, intended beneficiaries and selected external stakeholders. For a descriptive ToC process, it is helpful to involve the people who already have experience with your intervention. These would include front-line employees and the current beneficiaries.

Phase 2: Planning for Action

Once the context is set, an **impact statement** *(1*)* must be defined. This is a clear, articulated statement about exactly what you hope to achieve overall, and for each target group (if there is more than one). The impact statement must describe the long-term change you want to see in your target group and ideally should be one or two sentences at most. The comprehensive work done in the context phase on your target groups (beneficiaries) will result in good insight into their needs, thus placing you in the best position to develop an impact statement that reflects the desired change.

Next, realistic, achievable **outcomes** *(2*)* need to be set in order to make the impact statement a reality. Outcomes can be long, medium, or short-term to make them that much more achievable and measurable. Indicators **(outputs)** *(3*)* are those activities that need to be done to achieve the outcome, and must be clearly articulated in concrete, observable, and measurable terms (e.g., "I'll know [outcome reached] when I see [indicator]"). Desired outcomes motivate people, so be sure that all beneficiaries and stakeholders clearly understand how the intended impact and associated changes will benefit them, as well as what is required from them. Application of the "twist" or "backward mapping" *(4*)* occurs in the action phase. Beginning with your long-term outcome, work back toward the earliest changes that need to occur by considering which pre-conditions must be in place for this outcome to be reached, and repeat this for each outcome set. Pre-conditions are things that need to change before your long-term impact can happen.

All the identified changes are then mapped as "**outcomes pathways**"*(5*)* showing each outcome in a logical relationship with all the others. Pathways represent a causal logic, in that a chain of outcomes must come into being before the next outcome in the chain can be achieved. Most initiatives have more than one pathway that leads to the long-term outcome. All pathways also represent a chronological flow, indicating when activities and outputs should occur. The change-order is referred to as **sequencing a**nd remains fluid throughout the ToC process. Sequencing is helpful when it comes to managing beneficiary and stakeholder expectations and makes for more efficient planning, especially when managing resources.

Knowing what needs to be achieved (and when) helps you allocate activities and resources or **inputs** *(6*)* and set a budget for the initiative. Beginning with a single outcome, consider what is needed to make that outcome happen. This will likely include what the intended beneficiaries will be thinking, feeling, and doing during the initiative; key features of the planned activities and their frequency of occurrence; and the services or resources that the identified stakeholders would contribute toward the initiative.

The gathered and collated information creates a compelling case of the 'why and how' for your intended impact and must be presented to all the beneficiaries and stakeholders – present and future – so that they totally understand and completely buy into it. The best way to present this would be to first write up a comprehensive narrative of the overall vision and purpose, some of the context gathered in phase 1, the process followed in developing the ToC, the major pathways of change, assumptions (to be discussed in phase 3), and interventions. Secondly, the action phase can be represented on a ToC diagram (made up of numbers 1 – 6*) as depicted below.

The narrative and diagram are useful communication tools that quickly and easily convey your vision; this facilitates easy understanding especially for those who have not been involved in developing the ToC, and as a quick reminder of the original intention.

Phase 3: Evaluation

In *New Approaches to Evaluating Community Initiatives* Weiss (1995) defines a ToC as a "set of assumptions" that explain a series of steps taken to reach the main goal and the intended impact, as well as the connections between the activities and outcomes that occur during these steps. She argued that the more specific your ToC is, the easier it is to implement, monitor and evaluate it. As such, a ToC is rooted in assumptions, monitoring and evaluation.

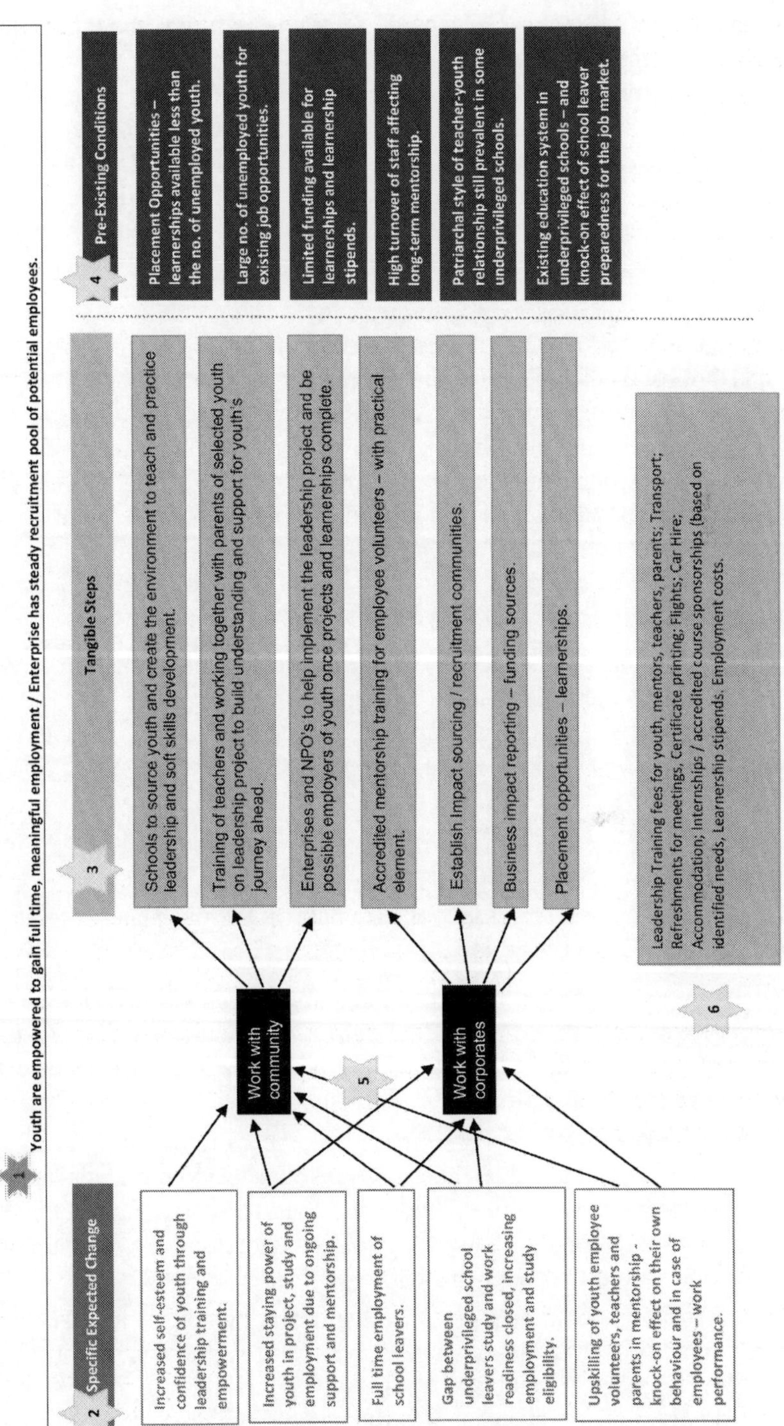

Diagram 4: Theories of Change (ToC)

An assumption is a willingness to accept something as true without question or proof (Cambridge Dictionary: 2021). The causal links and pathways in a ToC all rest on assumptions that a particular output will lead to an outcome, or that only the achievement of one outcome can lead to the achievement of another one and so on. For the ToC to be effective, all identified assumptions must be verified by finding evidence to support them. This evidence can be found in organizational reports (internal and external), academic research or literature, as well as in the expertise and experience of the stakeholders involved.

As mentioned previously, Weiss placed great importance on setting clear outcomes and indicators by mapping the entire change process though short, medium, and long-term goal achievement. **Monitoring and evaluating** the entire change process through these outcomes and indicators allow for the gathering and assessment of valuable information which over time can be extremely beneficial. Without this information, it would be impossible to determine whether an initiative has met or will meet its intended impact, where adjustments need to be made (or could have been made) to get better results, or whether the initiative has scalability and the best way to proceed with that.

This information and the evaluation thereof will also have an impact on the target audience and stakeholders and, just as development of a ToC is a participatory process, monitoring and evaluation should be conducted in a participatory way. It is important to remember that a ToC is a living document and should be revised as new evidence emerges, or as you develop new ways of working. The best practice is to revise the ToC during the enterprise's yearly strategic review.

A comprehensive, well-thought-out ToC can have numerous benefits to your enterprise, employees, stakeholders, and clients.

- It serves as an effective communication and engagement tool that helps employees, stakeholders and clients gain a clear understanding of the long-term goals and intended impact, as well as their specific roles and functions in the change process.
- It helps an enterprise to become more specific in terms of what, why and how they intend to achieve their purpose for the whole organization or specific initiatives within it. The value is in the detail, and potential risks can be spotted in the change process and addressed as you share the underlying assumptions in each step.
- The emphasis on monitoring and evaluation is beneficial in assessing impact in areas such as governance, capacity strengthening and institutional development. Accountability is also key, and all role players need to be held accountable for what they did and did not do.

Sigmoid or S-Curves

The Sigmoid or S-curve can be used to map the natural life cycle of an individual, enterprise, product, or idea. This concept has been employed in both the "hard" sciences, such as mathematics and biology, as well as the "soft" social sciences. It also surfaces in management textbooks to help students understand how technology changes drive innovation. The S-Curve is an ideal learning tool and metaphor which compliments the systems thinking model and tools we introduced earlier in the chapter. It is always wise for an individual or team to engage an external consultant and facilitator when they use this tool, as this person will ask the right and often difficult questions that hold the team accountable. The success of any planning and after-action review session that employs the S-Curve is proportional to the extent to which the group members are willing to be vulnerable, intellectually rigorous, and honest in their research and assessment. This tool is useful both when an enterprise is in crisis as well as in anticipatory planning. The application of the S-Curve tool indicates that the leadership team and the external facilitator are concerned about the sustainability of the enterprise, and with the new strategy, products, and services they need to introduce to ensure that sustainability.

When using a S-Curve, the life cycle of the subject being studied is plotted along a two-dimensional scale. Time is represented along the X-axis whilst the maturity, productivity and value of the item being analyzed is depicted along the Y-axis. In the S-Curve, the letter *S* is rotated 90 degrees to the right as depicted in the following graphic.

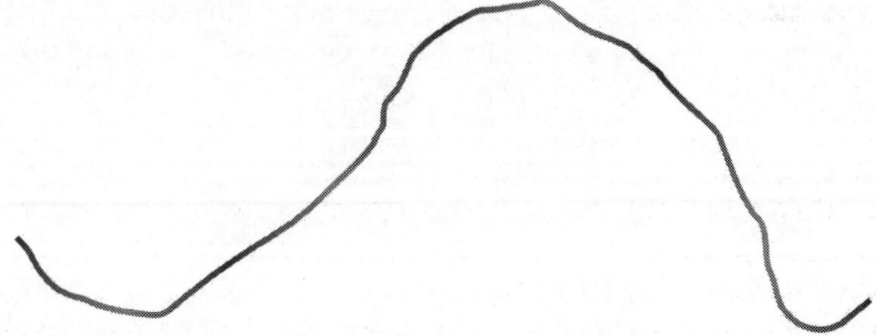

Fig.5: Sigmoid or S-Curves

Practitioners such as Handy (1989) and Avery (2017) describe how, while applying the S-Curve at various enterprises, they discovered that the natural life cycle had sequential phases. The first phase is the birth/start up phase of an enterprise or new product. Just as with humans, this is a time of mastering new skills and learning from mistakes, and working long and hard hours. During this phase the enterprise has a small number of employees, and people learn by reflecting on their mistakes and incorporating these lessons into how they produce or deliver a product or service. This phase is characterized by initial hopes and excitement, followed by a drop in morale as the enterprise encounters some early setbacks. This is represented by the first dip on the S-curve. The founder and managers interact more with the rest of the employees to solve problems and keep the enterprise's processes moving forward. New Zealand farmer, Doug Avery, uses the metaphor of a fruit tree to describe the different phases of the S-Curve. He compares this start-up phase to a person who climbs and reaches towards the outside branches of a young fruit tree. Just like the tree climber who has to weigh the risk of where to place their feet so that they do not fall, the entrepreneurial manager has to decide how to incorporate feedback received by the enterprise into subsequent actions.

Assuming that their perseverance pays off, the enterprise begins to experience sustained growth. This is reflected by the number of products or services that are sold and consumed, along with an increase in its revenues. At this point, the enterprise enters the middle or "growth" phase of the S-Curve. Regular patterns emerge in terms of customer expectations and orders and this certainty allows the enterprise to regularize its operations. The leadership team, managers and employees understand and adapt to these regular organizational rhythms. Policies and procedures are put in place and the relative calm that prevails allows the enterprise to enjoy the sweet fruit of its labors.

But the S-Curve carries a warning. While this is not a tranquil phase – the enterprise remains hard at work – it can also herald the "calm before the storm" if the enterprise is unattuned to changes in its larger environment. The third phase of the S-Curve is inevitable and is referred to as the "decline" or "death" phase. If an enterprise continues to offer the same product or service or becomes complacent and fails to embrace innovation, then it will decline and eventually cease to exist. Signs that an enterprise is entering this phase include its gradual loss of market share as customers start to use products and services offered by its competitors. The enterprise realizes diminishing returns as revenue steadily declines while customers and employees register less satisfaction with the enterprise's products, services or performance. Leaders and managers of the enterprise employ the phrase "this is how we have always done it" or a variation thereof when questioned about the way they operate or their lackluster results. Members, either through implicit or explicit actions or words, resist any changes being made to the status quo of the enterprise. Another warning sign is internal complacency and bureaucratic infighting amongst its senior leadership. Morale declines as more forward-thinking leaders and employees leave the organization. The enterprise fails to invest in its human and manufacturing capital and an air of benign neglect surrounds its facilities and people.

These 3 sequential phases are reflected in the image which follows.

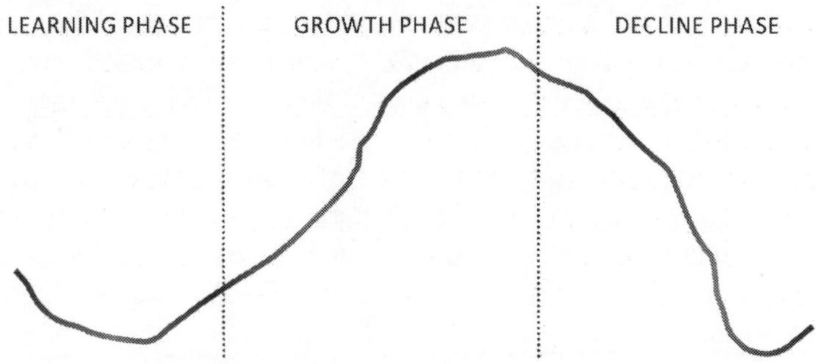

Fig.6: Phases in the Sigmoid Curve

So, what can an enterprise do to minimize or avoid the third phase of the S-Curve? Its leaders and senior managers need to understand this natural life cycle and how it applies to their enterprise. They should use its insights to anticipate when they will need to introduce change in the form of new products, services, and strategies.

As the next image demonstrates, these changes should be introduced during the growth phase, at the point that the enterprise begins to enjoy the fruit of its labor and initial investment. The leadership group should display maturity by committing to and providing employee training schemes early in the enterprises' existence and including this in their budget. They should gradually increase their investment of time and finances as the enterprise enters the growth phase. This change is therefore funded from a portion of the social enterprise's early profits or surplus revenue. Ideally, this investment and change needs to be made before the enterprise reaches the zenith, or peak, of its life cycle.

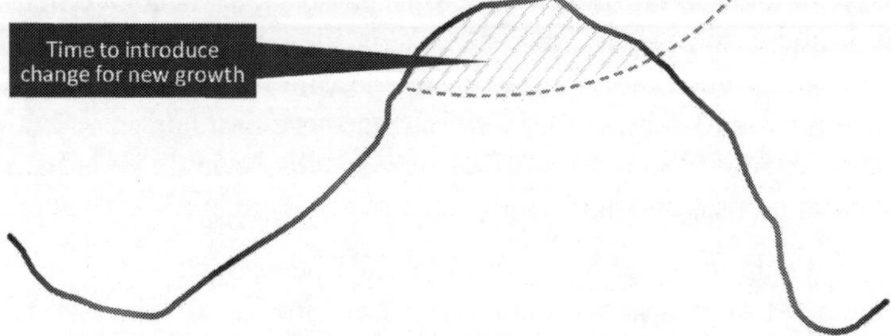

Fig.7: Intervention in the Sigmoid Curve

As we wrote earlier in this section, a wise leadership team employs a competent external facilitator to lead them through any learning process, including when they employ the S-Curve to understand and respond to their unique circumstances. There are several steps associated with employing this tool. First, the team must agree on which part of the enterprise they want to analyze and understand. Is it the entire organization or is it just a particular product or process? Once they have agreed on this, they should consider the length of their timeline as this will determine the amount of information they ought to collect and analyze. After allowing for sufficient time to collect this information, the team then participates in a facilitated session where they consider all the information they have gathered. They discern trends and lessons before looking at which of these they can influence or control. An important question to consider at this point is what they can do differently in the future. They may have more than one option to consider, and it is wise to subject each of these to a thorough review before deciding how to move forward. Once they reach this point, the final step in the process is to develop a strategic plan with action steps. This plan must include accountability milestones and an explicit process to compare the planned objectives with the actions taken.

It has been our experience that S-Curves are not as widely used within social enterprises as they should be. One reason for this is the frequent turnover of leaders and managers, both at the staff level and amongst the Board of Directors. The enterprise's failure to retain or re-engage this institutional memory means that it continues to face the same challenges on a regular basis which, in turn, undermines its impact and results in an under-utilization of capitals.

Creating a Structured Business Plan

Process for creating and writing a plan

Based on our professional experiences (both successes and failures), the conversations we have had with our peers and clients, and what we have observed in other enterprises, we have learnt that the best time to start thinking about writing a business plan is when the enterprise's founder and/or executive team conceive the idea for a new product or service. An idea emerges as an eureka moment. When we conceive a new idea, we are animated. We feel alive. It triggers our limbic brain and we become emotionally attached to it. But we will need to subject that idea to rigorous examination and flesh it out if we are to bring it "to market". The way in which we do so is by using the discipline of a business plan.

So where do these ideas come from? It has been our experience that they come about through the combination of two processes. The first process is a well-conceived strategic planning process which takes place over several sessions and months and relies on good questions, team research and structured interactions with the enterprise's stakeholders.

Author's Corner: In 2012, one of the authors used these practices while working with their local Habitat for Humanity affiliate to create a five-year strategic plan. This was to guide both their neighborhood revitalization work and to position themselves as a recognized player in the local affordable housing space. The feedback they received from their stakeholders, along with the financial and impact data they collected from their records, revealed both future trends and untapped internal capacity. This allowed them to create a vision of what success would look like for the neighborhood they were partnering with on a revitalization initiative. They were able to set quantifiable objectives to realize that vision. However, this vision required them to develop new approaches and services.

Comments made during some of the early sessions led to various eureka moments amongst members of this Habitat affiliate. One idea was to reduce the number of blighted and abandoned houses in the neighborhood by deconstructing them with local labor, and this was provided by hard-to-employ residents. Materials salvaged from these houses were either recycled or resold and the land on which houses had stood became available to serve as a greenspace or for new housing units. The idea was a radical departure from the traditional products and services offered by this Habitat for Humanity affiliate. Turning that idea into practice required that the enterprise write a business plan so that it could attract the necessary capital and create the operational structure it needed to bring these products to market.

The second process occurs when an idea for a new product or service is brought in from the outside. The founder or members of an enterprise identify a local, unmet need and find a product or service which has been successfully employed in another community. They decide to introduce the same, or a variant, of that product or service in their own community. They may choose to do so under a franchise arrangement or take advantage of an open-source approach by customizing it to their market and its unique needs.

While we know that the leaders and managers of social enterprises can feel overwhelmed by the daily pressures they face, the failure to set aside time and resources to think strategically and to employ the discipline of creating and revising business plans will negatively impact their enterprise's medium- to long-term viability.

The benefits and pre-requisites of a successful Business Plan

Benefits	Pre-Requisites
• Business Plan team develops a shared language based on the terms and structure of the business plan template they decide to employ. • The team develops the intellectual discipline necessary to bring an idea to practical fruition. • Creating a business plan is a team building exercise. • It forces the enterprise to look to the future. • It puts the enterprise's strategic plan into action rather than leaving it on the bookshelf to gather dust. • Promotes intentional engagement with stakeholders and uses their feedback to ensure that the enterprise's products and services continue to be relevant, valued and add to its bottom line.	• A diverse, yet manageable team to research and create the business plan is crucial. • The enterprise deliberately engages with its customers and stakeholders. • The team must employ intellectual honesty when analyzing the pros and cons of the product and service it proposes to deliver. • Engage an external consultant and subject matter experts where appropriate. This is critical. A process consultant will keep the team accountable to their timeline to complete the business plan. External experts can share valuable insights and research to help the team fine-tune its product or service. The team can also benefit from the robust criticism offered by the external expert. • Engage potential funders early in the process. Their initial reactions can be invaluable as positive feedback will provide the team with confidence to proceed. A timid or negative response from those funders will save the team from wasting time on a venture that will not come to fruition.

When creating a business plan, start by writing down what success will look like and how your enterprise will describe, measure and report on the impact which this new product or service delivers. We challenge your enterprise to consider how it will describe in its integrated annual report the ways its unique mixture of the Six Capitals was employed to produce this new product or service.

The Structure of Business Plans

While there are many templates for business plans, depending on the industry or sector in which a social enterprise operates, we have found that they generally include the following areas:

Executive Summary

The Executive Summary provides the reader with an overview of the business plan. It offers an overview of the social enterprise and the product and service it plans to provide. The executive summary answers five questions.

- Who is the enterprise and its customers?
- Why is this product and service needed and what positive impact will it have?
- What is the proposed product and service?
- How will the product and service be created and at what cost?
- By when will the product and service be available for distribution and sale?

There is widespread consensus that the executive summary is one of the last sections of the business plan to be finalized. It provides readers and funders with their first impression of the social enterprise as it invites them to read more about the impactful service or product that the enterprise proposes to deliver. The business plan thus needs to be accurate, inviting, and succinct.

However, this does not mean that we (as the team writing the business plan) should delay working on this summary. Developing succinct answers to these non-linear questions is deceptively complex but in reality, the answers will emerge as the team works through the sections of the business plan that follow the summary. Placing these questions in front of the team will provide us with the intellectual discipline we need to arrive at a plan which most likely will be funded, will result in the purchase of the product or service, and will have a positive benefit on the enterprise's financial and social impact.

Overview of the Social Enterprise and its External environment

Whenever we write this section of the business plan, we introduce the reader to the social enterprise and the reason for its existence. We describe the specific environment within which it operates by providing a brief introduction to the five external stakeholders to whom all enterprises, including ours, are accountable. These stakeholders are its customers, competitors, suppliers, governmental entities that regulate its operations, and the interested parties within the community it serves. Pertinent demographic and economic information will be shared at this point.

Products and Services

Here we describe the products and/or service that the social enterprise plans to produce and sell. We discuss the value that this product or service will add to community and look at its competitive attributes.

Operations

This section of the business plan describes how the social enterprise converts inputs (resources) into the desired output (product or service). It prudently reflects the process the enterprise will follow whilst converting input to output. The term "prudent" means that this section of the business plan should provide the reader with enough information to know that the team has thought through its "manufacturing" process. However, it does so without disclosing sensitive and potentially patented intellectual property which is proprietary to the enterprise and which it needs to produce the product or service. This section speaks to the manufacturing capital the social enterprise must procure and use to produce the products or service, and it shows how the social enterprise will source its inputs. We conclude by demonstrating how the social enterprise will produce, distribute, and market the proposed product or service.

Target Market and Marketing

In this part of the business plan, we focus on how the proposed product or service will meet the market need, and we provide demographic information about the intended consumer. We set this need in the context of the wider market/community problem our enterprise is seeking to address. As we write this section, we include the results of our market surveys and outline the methodologies we employed while conducting those surveys. The plan should answer the key question: What is the price of the proposed goods or service? The research should also show that the target market can indeed afford to purchase this product. This section includes a description of their competitors and the products they deliver. It also compares the social enterprise's product or service with that of their competitors. The section ends with an overview of the strategy the enterprise will follow to publicize its product and services amongst the target market. Identifying the most effective mediums of communication (billboards, radio, social media, in-person) can only be done once the social enterprise understands its potential customers and the information platforms they use.

Strategy

The social enterprise will describe its short and long-term strategy and then, within that strategic framework, locate the particular product or service described in this plan to show that it will add value and have the desired impact. When we write out this strategy, this part of the plan should allude to how the strategy, product and service will allow the enterprise to be both sustainable and impactful in a way that furthers its core values. Social enterprises should use this section of the business plan to include their Theory of Change and show how their product or service will positively impact the markets they are serving.

This section of the plan should also speak to the enterprise's risk management and mitigation strategy and outline the opportunities available to the enterprise. It must outline the envisaged risks and the steps it will take to mitigate them. These risks can include a scarcity of resources amongst its Six Capitals as well as their contingency plans should the enterprise lose key personnel. While it is impossible for an enterprise to anticipate every risk that it will encounter, completing this exercise allows it to demonstrate to its funders that it has the maturity and contingency plans in place to deal with risks and threats when these arise.

Governance and Management structure

Governance and Management provide funders with the assurance that the social enterprise is legally incorporated and that it is well led and professionally managed. When we write this section of the business plan, we describe the enterprise's board of directors and executive team and how they include, engage with, and reflect the values and insights of the enterprise's internal and external stakeholders. If the social enterprise is structured as a cooperative or worker-owned enterprise, then we are required to demonstrate how its members participate in the governing and management structures. This description is of particular interest to funders who specialize in funding this type of organization.

Sources of Financing and Financial Forecasts and documents

The business plan concludes with pertinent information on the projected earnings from the sale of the product or service it proposes to deliver and how much it will cost to produce. Since start up costs are incurred prior to the first sale of the product or service being produced, and since it will take time before the business recoups those costs and begins to show operating profit, the business plan pinpoints the date the social enterprise expects to reach its financial breakeven point and begins to realize a profit or surplus.

When we compose this section we make sure we include the sources of capital the social enterprise will access (i.e., who it will approach for funding) as well as the type of capital it will solicit from them. Social enterprises rely on three types of financial capital. These include owners' equity (which could be provided by members if this is a cooperative or a worker-owned business); debt (i.e., loans which the enterprise solicits from banks, credit unions or grants) and equity (which takes the form of shares which local and affinity group investors purchase in the enterprise and from which these investors expect some return).

The financial section of the business plan uses a variety of financial statements to project the growth of the enterprise over a five-year period. These statements are included as exhibits at the end of the business plan. Common statements include a balance sheet, profit and loss statement, cash flow statement, and a spreadsheet that informs the funder when the social enterprise will break even with the sale of the proposed product or service. More information about these sheets will be provided in Chapter 4, Financing the Social Enterprise.

Concluding Remarks

Business plans are detailed road maps which outline the strategy that the social enterprise will follow to develop, produce, distribute, and market its product or service which, when consumed, will add value to the community that is benefiting from its work.

Funders fund people as much as they fund new products and services. They want to be assured that the social enterprise has the necessary human capital in place, and that the enterprise is well-led and professionally managed. To this end, the funder will be interested in the collective experience of the leadership team and the degree to which they engage with those who have different skills and experience.

Authors Corner: We always encourage our clients to ask potential funders to provide their preferred business plan format. The team can then drop the boiler plate answers they've developed (in response to the eight sections above) into that template and customize it accordingly.

Chapter 3

STRUCTURING A SOCIAL ENTERPRISE

Deciding which legal form to adopt for your social enterprise

In Chapter 2 we established that a business plan's executive summary answers the five categories of questions that begin with the words "Who, What, Why, How and When". In the case of a social enterprise startup, once its founders have determined the reason and purpose for the enterprise, it is essential that they answer another important question: "*What legal structure should we adopt?*"

The sequence of the foundational questions tell us how to answer this question. Once the founders agree on their purpose and core values, the next logical step is to determine which legal form to adopt. It is important that they balance realistic expediency with the values of the social enterprise and embrace the tension that exists between those values and what the founders can do under the prevailing corporate law.

The enterprise's purpose and values will determine its form. Choosing a legal form is therefore a strategic decision which is informed by the values of the enterprise and where it will source its capital. The founders must also consider whether the legal form they select is the best form to source the capital for the social enterprise's start up and also later on when it needs an infusion of capital to scale up its operations. This chapter will focus on the different legal forms, their tax obligations and how they are governed. Chapter 4 will address how the choice of legal form will affect/ influence the social enterprise's access to capital.

Consider the following scenarios:

Two social enterprises committed to selling fair trade coffee in their communities share a common commitment to intermediating an enduring and profitable relationship between the small farmers who grow the coffee beans and their local coffee shop patrons. The founders of the first social enterprise enjoy access to a group of angel investors and decide to pursue a more traditional for-profit legal form. They incorporate their social enterprise as a *Limited Liability Corporation.*

In contrast, the second social enterprise emerges from a group of individuals whose values and shared commitment to pool their capital leads them to incorporate their coffee shop as a *cooperative*. They decide to partner with coffee producer cooperatives. They also use their individual memberships of local credit unions to access additional start up and operating capital. Their coffee shop is legally structured so that employees can become vested members of the cooperative.

Thus, the choice of legal form is also determined by the range of stakeholders to whom the enterprise's founders feel accountable. The enterprise may decide to accord some stakeholders more prominence and priority than others; the founders of the first social enterprise use a structure that protects their interests and those of their investors, while the second social enterprise is structured to protect and attract pooled capital from identified affinity groups.

The legal form a social enterprise adopts will help it to address the following seven areas. It will:

- Determine how the social enterprise structures and practices governance.
- Stipulate the degree of transparency towards its stakeholders. The legal form will outline the minimum reporting standards that the enterprise must adhere to.
- Regulate the level of support it can expect from the public (beyond its customers) as well as the degree of involvement it can expect from elected officials and government agencies.
- Dictate the social enterprise's tax obligations.
- Outline the legal liability to be borne by the social enterprise's owners and managers.
- Indicate how the social enterprise will manage and distribute its profit or surplus.
- Provide for the dissolution of the said enterprise.

The field of legal institutionalism argues that legal status permits a corporation to acquire and own assets, to enter contracts to procure and sell goods and services, and allow its creditors redress should the corporation violate contractual obligations or cause harm.

The evolving social enterprise landscape

The interplay between capitalism, industrial methods of production and colonialism gave rise to economic prosperity for some people and unintended socio-economic consequences for others. These factors continue to shape our communities, countries, and planet. The unintended socio-economic consequences, often present in the form of inequalities and historic tensions, informed the introductory chapter of this book. These tensions gave rise to a dichotomous social bargain which, in turn, gave rise to three sets of organizations whose presence and influence continue to this day. Firstly, there were industrial-size businesses whose profits generated revenue and spread prosperity, albeit unequally. The primary responsibility of this type of business was to be a good steward of the invested capital, and to deliver a good return in exchange. The second player was the state, with the extent of its involvement in these services being determined by how much political authority was granted to it to do so, and by the ideology which elected officials embraced. Lastly, there were charities whose purpose it was to address the negative social consequences of this business activity. Economic growth and prosperity were still accompanied by persistent poverty while the proverbial rising tide was not lifting all boats. These charities focused on meeting the immediate basic needs of people who had been made landless, homeless, or unemployed. Given their social focus, the operations of these charities were not necessarily held to the same rigorous standards that their for-profit counterparts were expected to meet.

While organized as charities, some of the early non-profits and NGOs created business lines to finance their operations and mission. Goodwill Industries, Communicare and the Salvation Army are three such organizations. In addition to these organizations, faith and community leaders helped to organize members from marginalized communities so that they pooled their social and financial capital to begin enterprises which could furnish them with basic products and credit. The traditional business, charity and cooperative tracks resulted in changes to corporate law and practices. However, all three of these tracks remained largely separate from one another with little crossover between them. We refer to this as Social Enterprise 1.0.

Social Enterprise 2.0 has been driven by the rise of post-graduate education since the early 1970's. Socially conscious scholars and students began to question whether business discipline could help the charity model to realize greater impact. These scholars also questioned whether the charity model was indeed still viable and whether it was contributing to persistent poverty and inequality. The limited success of political revolutions, armed conflict, and the failure of socialism in the former Communist bloc proved that the state was generally no better at creating socio-economic prosperity than the private sector. In response to changing social values, business schools began to introduce their students to the concept of socially responsible business. In essence, this concept sought to minimize the harmful impacts and actions of business, often by having them introduce new products and changing their technologies, so that they could continue to generate maximum returns to their investors. Patagonia is one example of a business that was an early advocate of socially responsible business. Other business schools went further and refined practices in cooperative management and worker-owned businesses.

Social enterprise 2.0 is therefore the merging of social activism and business discipline into new businesses and charities as well as re-imagined charities and businesses. This version views social enterprises as well-organized and competently managed corporations, irrespective of whether they are legally incorporated as for-profits or non-profits and irrespective of how broadly or narrowly they define the stakeholders to whom they are accountable. Corporations are characterized by the following:

- They are legally incorporated as an entity which exists independently of their founder. Their continued existence is therefore not solely dependent on the fortunes and life of their founders.
- Corporations include business, non-profit and governmental entities as well as all related enterprises.
- All corporations are responsible for creating value and impact.
- Corporations are accountable to the stakeholders from whom they receive their Six Capitals.

> Legal context for the terms Corporation and Company: In the United States, the legal term "corporation" applies to both for-profit and non-profit ventures. Given the federal form of government that is practiced in the United States, corporations are registered at both the federal (national) level as well as in the state(s) where they are based and/or operate. In South Africa, the legal term "company" applies to for-profit and non-profit companies and cooperatives. South African cooperatives are governed by the Cooperatives Act of 2005, while companies are governed by the Companies Act of 2008. South African law distinguishes between non-profit companies (NPCs) which can make a profit which accrues to the company, and is not distributed, and the non-profit organizations (NPOs) which are voluntary organizations and traditional charities.

Legal forms of social enterprises

Here are some examples of social enterprises which used either a for-profit or non-profit legal form to structure themselves or their subsidiaries and fund their mission.

- The former *Shore Bank* in Chicago, USA is an example of a social enterprise that was incorporated as a for-profit business to make small loans available in historically disadvantaged and under-banked Chicago suburbs. It drew funds from a small group of 75 investors who represented the faith community, non-profit partners, trusted individuals, banks, and insurance companies.
- *Goodwill Industries* is an entrepreneurial non-profit/NGO that removes barriers to employment through job-based training. While undergoing

their training, trainees work in one of Goodwill's many business units such as contract cleaning and retail operations. Goodwill funds its training through its earned income, traditional fundraising methods and by securing government contracts to provide education and other services.

- Social enterprises can also be set up as traditional businesses. One example is *Newman's Own* which was founded by the actor, Paul Newman. All its after-tax profits are channeled through the Newman's Own Foundation to the charitable causes it supports.

Some scholars and practitioners argue that social enterprises represent the fourth sector, with the other three being traditional for-profits, non-profits or NGOs, and the state (CGC, 2019). However, social enterprises are constituted under the same legal code that governs for-profits and their non-profit counterparts. Social enterprises are thus legally organized as either for- or non-profits <u>and</u> they adhere to voluntary codes which govern their social and environmental behavior. This dichotomous legal framework makes provision for an array of legal sub-forms that social enterprises can use; nevertheless, their choice will depend on their unique requirements as well as the permitted legislation which regulates corporations in their country (and their local state if their country is a federation).

Disclaimer: The following sections on legal forms are for educational and information purposes only. They do not constitute legal advice.

<u>Non-Profit Organizations or For-Profit Corporations</u>

Social enterprises can be incorporated as non-profit organizations. In South Africa they are governed by the Non-Profit Organizations Act of 1997, while in the United States of America they are governed as non-profit corporations. Non-profits are institutions that are organized for charitable purposes; these broadly include (amongst others) religious, educational, scientific, and literary purposes.

Since the United States is a federal form of government, US non-profits register with the Federal Internal Revenue Service by filing IRS Form 1023. Once their application is approved, they receive their 501(c)3 status and unique identification number which allows them to accept tax-deductible donations. Federal US law, which governs non-profits, categorizes them according to the industry sectors they serve and the purpose for which they were created. It will be of interest to social enterprises that the US non-profit code allows traditional non-profits to establish subsidiaries. It also permits the creation of private foundations which can serve as trusts (more on this later in the chapter). In addition to registering with the Federal Government, US non-profits are incorporated in their state of origin. They do so by registering with their respective Secretary of State. US non-profits are required to file annual registrations and returns with their Secretary of State and the Internal Revenue Service respectively.

South African Non-Profit Organizations (NPOs) register with the Non-Profit Organizations Directorate. They are mandated by law to file an annual report with this Directorate.

Non-profits are organized to meet a social or community benefit. They are mandated to have a Board of Directors to oversee their operations. In exchange for fulfilling their charitable purpose for which they were created, they are exempted from federal taxes. Non-profits are not owned by their members and therefore do not pay dividends or issue shares.

South African common law provides for the formation and incorporation of voluntary associations. These associations can be formed by a small group of citizens to fulfill a public or social purpose and can achieve their specific purpose through income-generating projects. Incorporated voluntary associations register with the Bureau of Heraldry by filing a constitution with this office which is housed at South Africa's National Archives. Their application can be denied if their purpose runs contrary to the public interest. Voluntary Associations can serve as an initial legal form for a social enterprise.

Private For-Profit Companies or Corporations

Social Enterprises can be incorporated as private, for-profit companies in South Africa or as corporations in the United States. If the social enterprise is small in scale and if it is being incorporated by an individual, then it may be set up as a Sole Proprietorship in South Africa. If an individual is incorporating a social enterprise in the United States, their state law generally permits them to choose between being a Sole Proprietorship or a Limited Liability Corporation (LLC). In both countries, sole proprietorships are taxed at the individual tax rate, and they are generally ineligible for grant funding. Furthermore, the individual's personal assets are not protected from their enterprise's creditors. LLCs can be organized by, and consist of, a small number of members.

By incorporating their social enterprise as a private company or corporation, the founders are now granted liability protections under law. The enterprise now has its own legal status, and its legal liabilities protect its individual directors from lawsuits filed against the enterprise – if they have not transgressed the law. Private companies and corporations continue to exist beyond their incorporator's lifespan. They can raise capital by issuing shares. Their board of directors is elected by, and generally represent, those individuals and entities who own shares in the corporation. There is no statutory limit on the number of shareholders that companies and corporations can have.

Meat Naturally Africa is an example of a South African social enterprise that has been organized as a private company. This company is operated by conservation-oriented staff, with the company being owned by the farmers who participate and practice holistic range management. Based in Mpumalanga Province, this enterprise works with pastoral households whose livestock graze on communally owned land. Since these households lack ready access to markets for their animals, Meat Naturally provides this access and also provides these households with veterinary services and training in the practice of holistic range management. There are professional conservationists on staff who use technology to monitor the range or veldt to ensure that holistic range management is implemented. The enterprise markets the meat once it is harvested from the slaughter of these herds, and shares the proceeds and profits with the participating farmers.

Joint Ventures

A joint venture is a separate legal entity that is created by two existing corporations. This new entity is created for a single and unique purpose: to allow them to realize a profit. Its creation permits these existing corporations to collaborate on a new product. This collaboration is formalized through incorporating documents and contracts to address areas such as shared resources, distribution of risk, losses and profits, decision-making, and dispute resolution processes.

Negotiation will take place to decide whether both corporations are equal partners (often referred to as co-principals) in the joint venture, or whether one of them will be the lead while the other serves as its agent. In the latter instance, the joint venture will include a contingent management agreement to govern this relationship. The partners need to decide if and how this entity will be reflected on their financial statements. Both corporations must ensure that the joint venture will not only result in new and valued products or markets, but that this formal partnership also will honor their distinct organizational values.

Joint ventures are most common amongst for-profit corporations and therefore may be a viable option for those social enterprises which are incorporated as for-profit corporations. Joint ventures are less common in the non-profit sector and rare between a non-profit and for-profit corporation. A 2010 study by the Georgia Center of Non-profits found that only 5% of joint ventures which Georgia non-profits entered were with for-profit partners (Georgia Center for Non-profits: 2010). The reasons for this include the length of time and professional fees associated with their creation; the potential negative tax impact that they may have on their parent corporations; and their ability to attract sufficient capital since they will initially depend on assets which are held by their parent corporations and these may be pledged as collateral for other projects.

> One example of a joint venture between a for-profit company and a social enterprise is Liva in France. VINCI, the for-profit company, owns 51% of the joint venture with the remaining 49% being held by the Association pour la Réinsertion Economique et Sociale which also serves as Liva's executive manager. ARES is an amalgamation of 12 social enterprises that provide social integration services for marginalized individuals and communities. VINCI is active around the world by providing turnkey services for public infrastructure projects such as airports. Liva employs individuals who are trained and supported by ARES at French public facilities that are owned and managed by VINCI.

Benefit Corporations (B-Corps)

The Benefit Corporation or B-Corp is a variant of the traditional for-profit corporate model that is gaining in popularity. For-profit corporations who seek this designation will pay a fee of up to US$50,000 to B-Labs, a non-profit accrediting agency, which then audits their operations to assess their social and environmental impact. B-Corps are encouraged to modify their articles of incorporation by naming their stakeholders so that the interests of these groups are protected should the business be sold or experience economic stress. The completed audit measures the corporation in areas such as governance, community, workers, customers, and the environment. B-Corps are recertified annually.

B-Corps seek to simultaneously deliver profits and positive impacts to their stakeholders. An increasing number of B-Corps are becoming employee-owned or have made verified improvements to their labor and environmental practices. As of February 2021, B-Lab East Africa reports that there are 3,725 certified B-Corps around the world, with 11 of them being South African. Certified B-Corps in the USA include the King Arthur Baking Company and Ben & Jerry's. Two certified South African B-Corps are Zoona and Lubanzi Wines.

Employee Stock Ownership Plans (ESOPs)

As part of their marketing strategy to become a B-Corp, for-profit corporations can employ the tactic of giving their employees a significant ownership stake in the business. The Employee Retirement Income Security Act (ERISA) of 1974 permits US employees to have a majority ownership stake in their employer's enterprise. New employees become eligible to participate in the ESOP after they have met certain service requirements. These requirements constitute a vesting process. The shares then serve as a qualified retirement program for vested employees. The ownership option is known as an Employee Stock Ownership Plan (ESOP).

ESOPs have been used when a for-profit founder wishes to sell their company and retire. In some cases, they may wish to see their loyal employees continue their legacy. ESOPs permit these employees to collectively purchase the corporation, thereby preventing it from closing or being bought by outside interests.

While not all ESOPs are social enterprises, they do provide a legal and tested method for enterprises to expand their ownership structure to include their employees. They may also provide mature corporations with the opportunity to migrate more into the social enterprise space. ESOPs are not to be confused with employee profit-sharing plans or ones that offer employees the option of purchasing shares. Care needs to be taken that, when ESOPs are formed, employees are given meaningful decision-making power and that they are represented during the selection of the ESOP's Trustee and the subsequent interaction with this person.

ESOPs do not require for-profits corporations to change their legal status. They can continue as for-profit C-Corporations.

According to the National Center for Employee Ownership, there were 6,416 ESOPs in the USA in 2018. These ESOPs had approximately 14 million participants and had a collective worth of over $1.4 trillion (National Center for Employee Ownership, 2020). Examples of ESOPs in the USA include Publix Super Markets, Thrifty White Pharmacy, McNaughton-McKay, and Terracon. These four examples span the grocery, pharmaceutical, wholesale and engineering sectors.

Employee Share Ownership Plans (ESOPs) first rose to prominence in South Africa in the late eighties, only to fall out of favor a few years later. They experienced a re-emergence with the process of Broad-Based Black Economic Empowerment (B-BBEE) (Mail and Guardian, 1997). Regarded as an important transformation or empowerment tool to right the wrongs of apartheid, B-BBEE aims to:

- Promote commercial entity ownership and control by Black SA citizens, defined as Colored, Indian, and African (Broad-Based Black Economic Empowerment Act 53 of 2003).
- Promote human resource and skills development of black SA citizens.
- Empower black SA citizens through procurement from black/high B-BBEE score entities, black enterprise development and corporate social responsibility initiatives.

An enterprise's B-BBEE compliance is measured against a B-BBEE Scorecard with 8 compliancy ratings (levels). A Level 2 B-BBEE rating is often a must-have criterion to do business with local enterprises (e.g., a Level 2 rating makes an enterprise a more desirable and lucrative service provider/supplier in the chain of preferential procurement, as any spending on products or services is recognized at a higher % rating, which equals more points towards B-BBEE Level attainments). A compliancy rating of 8 or above is a necessity if an enterprise is to qualify for government grants from the Department of Trade and Industry (DTI). It is also a minimum requirement when enterprises respond to Requests for Proposals (RFPs); this is when most major corporations solicit bids for new business. The only way that a social enterprise can secure a Level 2 rating, after maximizing its scores on all the B-BBEE elements (Ownership, Management Control/Employment Equity, Preferential Procurement, Enterprise and Supplier Development, and Corporate Social Investment), is via Ownership. This means that it must obtain 25.,01% in this element. 25.01% translates to 25% black shareholding plus one vote. An ESOP is one way of attaining a Level 2 rating.

Hybrids as legal forms for Social Enterprises

L3Cs in the United States

Section 501(c)3 of the IRS Code permits the formation of low-profit limited liability corporations or L3Cs. To be eligible for this designation, these social enterprises must perform a charitable, educational, scientific, or literary mission but they are also allowed to generate a profit as a secondary purpose. Unlike traditional non-profits, they are permitted to have members and raise equity from the same capital markets as their for-profit peers. They are also permitted to receive donations and grants from individuals and foundations, although the uncertainty about whether these donations are tax-deductible makes L3Cs a less popular choice for social enterprises. L3Cs pay income tax on their profits. If all their members are exempt, then they can be exempted from paying corporate taxes. This means that non-profits can create a subsidiary as a L3C.

Federal law permits L3Cs to operate in all 50 states. However, only 11 states and 2 Native-American nations allow for their incorporation in their territories. Although it is technically possible for members in other states to incorporate their L3C in one of these states and then register it as an out-of-state entity within their own state, doing so imposes additional transaction costs on the social enterprise.

Non-Profit Companies (NPC) in South Africa

The South African Companies Act of 2008 makes provision for the formation of non-profit companies (NPC). These companies can state that they have both a profit and a social purpose in their Memorandum of Incorporation (MOI). If a NPC does not automatically invest profits into its social mission, then it is taxed on those profits at the South African corporate tax rate.

NPCs can also apply to the Non-Profit Organization Directorate to be classified as a NPO. If they receive this designation, then they are eligible to apply for government grants. In addition to this, they can apply to become a Public Benefit Organization (PBO), which allows the NPC to accept donations. These donations are tax-deductible for the donor.

NPCs do not offer equity. They can have for-profit companies as members whose donations to the NPC reduce their corporate tax obligations to the South African Revenue Service.

NPCs can be incorporated by three directors. They are managed by a Board of Directors. While its directors and members can receive reasonable remuneration and reimbursement for expenses, they do not own the NPC's assets and income. These must be applied towards meeting the NPC's social purpose.

NPCs are responsible for filing annual returns under the Companies Act and annual reports under the NPO Act. They are required to comply with all financial and other statutory requirements laid down in the Company's Act.

Trusts

In both South Africa and the United States, company and corporate law permits social enterprises to establish trusts, irrespective of whether they have been incorporated as for-profits or non-profits. Trusts are tools to consider when an enterprise seeks to protect key assets, such as land and investment capital, from expropriation by creditors or other entities and to ensure that these assets remain available in perpetuity. Trusts can be created by an individual founder or a non-profit organization, with the latter being the trust's sole beneficiary. In the United States, such trusts are organized as private foundations that can be operating or non-operating. Non-operating trusts merely transfer the income they realize from their managed investments to the organization that they have designated as their beneficiary.

If the trusts are operating concerns, then they are actively involved in supporting the efforts of their non-profit or for-profit arms. In this case, the Trust creates non-profit and for-profit subsidiaries. For-profit subsidiaries can then also attract outside capital by issuing debt and equity while a non-profit arm can attract private philanthropy. The Trust retains the majority ownership stake in that private company and receives a proportionate share of the profits realized by the private company. The Trust then passes these profits through to its non-profit subsidiary.

A trust can be established with a minimum of three separate persons. They need a founder who provides the assets that the Trust will hold, a trustee to serve as the steward of these assets and to fulfill all the administration required by law, and a beneficiary. Active or operating Trusts require a mature Board of Directors, whose individual members bring diverse skills that allow it to understand the enterprise's complex operations and govern it accordingly. A South African example of an operating trust is LifeCo UnLtd SA.

Cooperatives

Founded in 1895, the International Cooperative Alliance defines a cooperative as "... people-centred enterprises owned, controlled and run by and for their members to realise their common economic, social, and cultural needs and aspirations" (International Cooperative Alliance). Today, it is estimated that over 1 billion people worldwide belong to one or more cooperatives.

Modern cooperatives trace their origins to the Rochdale Equitable Pioneers Society which was established by 28 weavers and textile workers in Rochdale in the United Kingdom in 1844. Inspired to put social justice into action and combat the monopolistic practices of company-owned stores, these workers pooled their savings to purchase products for resale at their own store. Their business model was based on seven principles which have become the hallmarks of cooperatives worldwide. Membership was open to anyone who paid a membership fee. Members' purchases at the store were tracked and they received a proportional share of the store's annual profits. The original Rochdale cooperative grew in profitability and membership and today cooperatives are found throughout the wholesale, agricultural, banking and manufacturing sectors. The Basque region in Spain is home to Mondragon Corporation which consists of 96 cooperatives, 14 research and development centers and 81,000 members. These cooperatives span the financial, retail, manufacturing, and educational sectors (Mondragon Corporation, 2021).

All cooperatives adhere to the following seven principles:

- Membership is open to everyone who wishes to join. Members contribute a small membership fee upon joining.
- Cooperatives are democratically controlled by their members. Every member has the same standing and is accorded one vote when the members gather to make decisions. This means that cooperatives differ from traditional corporations where the number of votes held by a shareholder is proportional to the number of shares that they own in that corporation.
- The level of an individual member's economic participation in the cooperative determines their share of profits when these are distributed.
- Membership is voluntary. No one is forced to become a member of a cooperative. This means that cooperatives are only sustainable if they are voluntarily created and enthusiastically supported by their members. State or outside coercion of individuals or communities to form cooperatives is therefore contrary to this principle.
- Cooperatives are concerned with local community issues with this concern translating into financial support for local efforts, such as education

for local communities.

- Cooperatives commit to support and cooperate with other cooperatives.
- Cooperatives commit to educate and train their members.

Law in most states in the United States and national law in South Africa permit their citizens to create cooperatives. Both countries grant cooperatives their own legal standing. In a nutshell, a cooperative is a member-owned for-profit entity whose goal is to meet the economic and social purpose for which it was intended and to generate value in that area for its members.

In both countries, cooperatives trace their origins to the agricultural sectors where farmers used this legal entity to procure inputs and market their produce. Cooperatives came to the fore in the United States in the late 18th Century and were a response to the monopolistic form of capitalism that resulted in a landmark anti-trust legislation known as the Sherman Act. In the United States, cooperatives are governed by laws particular to their state of origin. There is no over-arching Federal legislation governing cooperatives, although parts of Federal legislation address some aspects of their operation. One such piece of legislation is the Capper-Volstead Act of 1922 which established certain guidelines for cooperative marketing efforts so that they did not transgress Federal anti-trust law.

South African cooperatives are governed by the Cooperatives Act of 2005. Since cooperatives are permitted to generate and distribute profits to their members, they are ineligible to become non-profit or public benefit organizations.

In order to remain sustainable, cooperatives must adhere to the same business practices and discipline as a for-profit company or corporation. The difference between them is that ownership in a cooperative is limited to its members. It is not available to outside shareholders. The decision to dissolve a cooperative is therefore in the hands of its membership.

A worker-owned cooperative's articles of incorporation and bylaws will also address the following issues:

- The number of stock and membership available for sale.
- Limit eligibility to purchase stock to members of the cooperative.
- Outline the rights and duties of Directors.
- Adhere to the democratic principle which means that decisions regarding management, policies and use of capital will be based on one member, one vote and not in proportion to the number of shares that each member holds.
- Profits and losses are equitably shared amongst members.
- Membership and meetings are open to all members of the cooperative.

- Members will make the decision to dissolve the cooperative with all assets being distributed amongst them.

Corporate Governance in Theory and Practice

Governance is an area that continues to interest us. We enjoy asking and answering the question, "*Why do enterprises need to have Boards of Directors to govern their operations*?" The answer is that all institutions that are organized to benefit a community and which use other people's money are mandated to have Boards. Political bodies use taxpayer's money and are held accountable by elected officials. For-profits and non-profits leverage the financial resources of investors and donors. The State requires that they have Boards in place to (at a minimum) protect these financial investments. Boards are democratic institutions with the extent of that democracy being reflected in their bylaws.

These insights illuminate a vigorous intellectual discussion within the field of corporate governance. On the one hand, this insight has given rise to the shareholder model of governance which argues that the Board of Directors' responsibility is limited to protecting the financial investment made to the enterprise by third parties. Boards should prioritize these financial stakeholders (investors and donors) over all other issues. As a proxy of these shareholders, they must hold the chief executive accountable for managing the corporation to ensure that they receive a growing return on their investment.

The other school of thought is termed the stakeholder approach to governance. Drawing from the Systems Approach used by organizations, it argues that Boards of Directors should balance the interests of the organization's multiple internal and external stakeholders. These include its investors, employees, customers, business partners and local community. Thanks to the insights from the field of ecology, the stakeholder model has been broadened to also include the organization's impact on the natural environment. It is clear from this description that the stakeholder model allows organizations to account for their triple bottom line and how they employ the Six Capitals.

We argue that social enterprises need to adopt structures and practices which represent the stakeholder approach to governance. We draw from four intellectual sources when it comes to the way in which social enterprises should structure and operationalize their governance. By "operationalize" we mean how the founders of social enterprises, their Boards of Directors and their executive management interact with one another. The quality of this interaction matters. It is not only to fulfil their legal obligations, but to also ensure that the social enterprise is delivering value to the communities in which it is based and in which it purports to serve.

These four sources are:

- The legal framework and process the social enterprise followed to become incorporated as a legal entity. Although discussed previously in this chapter, we conclude it here again because the same legislation and administrative rules that guide the choice of legal form also set out certain expectations about how the social enterprise must be governed.
- Robert's Rules of Order created a standard parliamentary procedure for governing bodies (outside of legislative bodies) to conduct their meetings and arrive at their decisions.
- The King Code of Corporate Governance, in particular the 4th Edition of this Code released in 2016, modernizes the role and responsibility of the Board of Directors by locating these in the context of the Stakeholder Model, the Triple Bottom Line, and the concept of the Six Capitals.
- The Aligned Influence® approach to governance focuses on the way the respective and complimentary roles of Boards and Executive management are brought and locked into alignment.

Governance matters. It is the one area that the founders and key decision makers of the enterprise can control. Within this space of checks and balances they fulfill their fiduciary duty to their stakeholders (however these are defined) and define and monitor the economic and social value the social enterprise generates. It is from this space that social enterprises give public account of how they have employed the Six Capitals to produce a valued product and how this has impacted their triple bottom line.

If the previous paragraph sounds too idealistic, then consider the following strategic and practical benefits that flow to social enterprises when they practice good governance.

The King IV report references six benefits:

- A well-governed social enterprise is more likely to enjoy a good reputation amongst the public and those from whom it sources it capital. Its reputation is its brand. Safeguarding and growing its brand is therefore critical to its sustainability.
- A solid reputation allows social enterprises to recruit and retain employees who are motivated by the congruency between its mission, its operating practices, and its impact. Good governance ensures that this congruency is maintained. Research findings demonstrate how important this congruency is to the younger generations who now account for the bulk of the labor force.
- Good governance facilitates a social enterprise's access to markets and customers by holding its management responsible for developing and implementing efficient marketing strategies.

- Effective governance sets the broad strategic direction for the social enterprise and then keeps the enterprise focused on the ongoing strategy development.
- Practicing good governance assures the social enterprise's stakeholders that it has effective internal controls in place and that these allow it to reduce its risk. These procedures will prevent the mismanagement of the Six Capitals it has mobilized and been entrusted with.
- Governance is responsible for ensuring that the social enterprise has the necessary policies and plans in place for succession planning. This refers to how it will replace key decision makers on its board, the chief executive, and key staff when they retire, come to the end of their terms in office, or accept positions outside the enterprise (The Institute of Directors of Southern Africa NPC, 2016).

These benefits translate into a social enterprise whose brand is trusted and which is regarded as legitimate because its values and behavior are ethically congruent, and they are accounted for in a way that is transparent to its stakeholders.

One governance question that social enterprises will need to answer – and periodically revisit – is how many Board members they should have. The principle of precedent suggests a look at the relevant government legislation governing corporations, as well as the common industry practice. Another way to answer this question is to ask how many Board members the enterprise requires to (a) safeguard stakeholders' interests, (b) adequately monitor the enterprise's managers and operations, and (c) ensure that the enterprise is healthy and growing.

Robert's Rules of Order

Robert's Rules of Order, now in their 12th edition, trace their origins to Henry Robert. (More information about Henry Robert can be found by visiting the Robert's Rules Association at www.robertsrules.com.) In 1863, Robert was asked to chair a church body in San Francisco. His experiences of doing so led him to realize that creating a standard parliamentary procedure would help meetings and governing bodies arrive at decisions in a more efficient manner. In 1876 he published the first edition of what became known as Robert's Rules of Order. In compiling these rules, Robert relied on the process followed by the US House of Representatives. They, in turn, borrowed from the English parliamentary tradition which has also influenced how Boards and meetings make decisions in South Africa.

Robert's Rules of Order speak both to organizational structure and to how meetings are conducted. By organizational structure, we mean that they address the need for bylaws that outline the purpose for which the organization was created, the election, structure, role and duties of its Board of

Directors, officers, and committees, as well as operating and dissolution procedures. The second part of these rules address how meetings are to be conducted and, more importantly, how those at the meeting arrive at binding decisions. This includes the use of agendas to structure and conduct the meeting as well as procedures for introducing, debating, and deciding on subjects that the meeting is to consider. These Rules reflect values of democratic discourse by allowing for all opinions to be heard, with final decisions being made by majority vote.

Robert's Rules of Order are generally followed by social enterprises that have Boards of Directors and which are required to give an account of their activities to outside agencies. These outside agencies can include their parent bodies as well as government agencies.

Duties of Members of the Board of Directors or Trustees

The Board of Directors or Trustees bear ultimate responsibility for the governance and performance of the organization. It is widely accepted that Boards execute a minimum of three duties on behalf of the enterprise.

- The *Duty of Care* means that members act in good faith by sharing their skills with the organization through their active participation on the Board as well as Board committees.
- The *Duty of Obedience* means that board members will ensure that the organization operates in accordance with all applicable laws and regulations and remains true to the intent and mission listed in its incorporating documents.
- The *Duty of Loyalty* means that their primary allegiance is to the organization on whose board they are serving. Board members are required to avoid conflicts of interest by not abusing their position on the Board to further their own individual interests.

A series of major corporate scandals, the growing popularity of the stakeholder approach, the environmental crisis and the rise of social enterprises has forced corporate leaders and governments to reconsider what is meant by governance. The King Report and Code on Corporate Governance, and the Aligned Influence® model of governance are two exciting, complimentary, and innovative approaches to governance, especially when applied to social enterprises.

The King Report and King Code on Corporate Governance and Aligned Influence®

The King Report on Corporate Governance (also referred to as the King Code) emerged in South Africa in 1994. The Code is a set of voluntary principles and best practices for corporate governance. Its provisions are being adopted by countries in Europe and around the Pacific Rim. Aligned Influence® has surfaced over the past decade in the United States in response to the related problems of underperforming boards and organizations as well as the persistent role conflict between Boards and their Chief Executives.

Background

In 1993, the Institute of Directors of South Africa commissioned Mervyn King, a former Judge of South Africa's Supreme Court, to lead a task group to modernize South Africa's corporate governance principles. As King has said and written, he viewed this Commission as an opportunity to both modernize governance and educate the wider South African population about its importance (ecoDA/PwC: 2018).

The King Report and King Code on Corporate Governance emerged from this conference. The document has undergone further revisions with the fourth edition (King IV) being released in 2016. These revisions reflect the growing influence of environmental sustainability in business thought and practice. It extends the governance principles and practices to include not only for-profit entities, but also non-profit and government sectors. King IV provides all these corporate institutions with sixteen principles and best practices of governance. The seventeenth principle applies only to the Boards of Trustees responsible for managing pensions. These sixteen principles address both the structure and behavior of the institution's governance.

The Aligned Influence® model of governance addresses a critical shortcoming in the major governance codes. Codes such as the Cadbury Code, the King Code, and International Policy Governance focus almost exclusively on the role and duties of the Board of Directors. They pay little attention to the role of the Chief Executive, except to tell Boards to recruit them, monitor their performance and hold them accountable for organizational outcomes. Aligned Influence® speaks to the unique, yet complimentary, roles of both the Board of Directors and the Chief Executive. Their individual and collective effectiveness depends on these roles being locked into alignment through governing and operating (administrative) policy sets and regular monitoring of calendars.

Separating, yet interlocking the Roles of Board Chair and Chief Executive

Social enterprises, which are required to have Boards of Directors, must separate the roles of Board Chair and Chief Executive and give the roles to separate persons. The Board of Directors appoints, evaluates and, when necessary, replaces the Chief Executive Officer. The Board, and not the Chief Executive officer, is responsible for recruiting, orienting, and evaluating board members. The Board Chair is responsible for ensuring that the Board operates effectively and efficiently. Neither the Board nor the Board Chair micro-manages the organization.

The Chief Executive is responsible for how the enterprise operationalizes its Six Capitals. The Chief Executive, who has the authority to lead the organization in accordance with its board-approved strategic direction and plans, manages its work and stakeholders within the parameters set and monitored by the Board. The Chief Executive also accomplishes the work by mobilizing staff, who create value by enacting tactical plans to support the enterprise's strategy and reflect its organizational values (Schuetz, 2020). Chief Executives and their staff fulfill these roles when they apply the principles and practices that are covered in this book.

Board Committees

The complimentary influence of the Board Chairperson and the Chief Executive radiates out through separate Board Committees (which allow the Board to fulfill its governance duties) and staff committees (which are concerned with daily operational issues). In the Aligned Influence model, Board Committees help the Board to direct, protect (monitor) and enable the organization in a disciplined way, and to ensure accountability to the organization's stakeholders. Operational committees are run by staff to lead, manage, and accomplish the work of the organization so that it delivers a valued product to its clients. (Schuetz, 2020).

In order to function effectively and to distribute power amongst the board members, Boards create specialized committees to help monitor the enterprise's financial and social performance, engage with stakeholders, and ensure that the Board itself is a viable subset of the organization. These committees are made up solely of Board members. They assist the Board to fulfill its legal and ethical obligations to the organization's stakeholders. These committees are named in the enterprise's bylaws.

Drawing from our own experience, as well as insights gained while studying the King Code and Aligned Influence, we argue that social enterprises should have an Executive Committee, a Board Development Committee, a Finance and Audit Committee, a Stakeholder Committee, a Risk Committee, and a Technology and Information Committee.

Executive Committee

This committee includes all the key Board officers whose titles and duties are set out in the enterprise's incorporating documents and bylaws. Common board officers include the Board Chair, Vice-Chair, Finance Chair or Treasurer, and Secretary. This committee manages the Board calendar and creates the agendas which are followed at the Board meetings. The Board often delegates to this committee the discretion and authority to address time-sensitive matters that arise between Board meetings, and which fall within the purview of the Board of Directors. The Executive Committee also supports the Board Chair as they supervise, evaluate and, when necessary, replace the Chief Executive.

Board Development Committee

This committee is charged with recruiting, orienting, and evaluating members of the Board of Directors. In our experience, board development is an ongoing and cyclical process. It is the responsibility of the Board of Directors to recruit the new board members. A key task of this committee is to ensure that its Board recruitment criteria embrace all facets of diversity, given the increasing social expectation that Boards are to represent diverse skills, experiences, and communities, and given the growing evidence that social enterprises which embrace diversity are more sustainable. This committee is also responsible for leading the board through a regular self-evaluation and for enforcing term limits.

Finance and Audit Committee

This committee fulfills a critical oversight function on behalf of the Board. It is responsible for monitoring the social enterprise's financial health. The Finance and Audit committee holds the Chief Executive accountable by monitoring the enterprise's revenue and expenses against the board-approved budget. This committee engages and receives reports from independent auditors who provide the organization and its financing stakeholders with an independent and objective assessment of the enterprise's financial position. The Finance and Audit Committee provides the full Board with regular financial reports, and ensures that the enterprise complies with applicable tax laws. If the enterprise's Board members are remunerated for their service, then this committee, or a sub-committee which it establishes, is responsible for determining the scope of that remuneration, reviewing it on a regular basis, and including its reports on said remuneration to the Board, the enterprise's auditors, and its stakeholders.

Stakeholder Committee

The members of this Board committee are responsible for engaging with the enterprise's primary stakeholders to gather their insights when the enterprise's business strategy is being developed. They are also responsible for helping the Board assess and report on how well the enterprise has discharged its social obligations to its employees, local community, and the environment. One practical way in which this committee handles this reporting is through the annual report. Committee members help the Board to create and update the enterprise's core values and to monitor its adherence to them. The King IV Code also refers to this committee as the Social Ethics Committee. This term is often used in worker-owned enterprises and cooperatives.

Risk Committee

The King IV report raises the importance of assessing and understanding organizational risk to Board level. Part of this committee's responsibility is to help the Board and Executive think strategically about the threats and opportunities that face the organization. These insights are of particular benefit during strategic planning sessions. But, at the very least, the committee must ensure that the enterprise's risk management strategy is explicit. This committee must provide the board with the necessary capacity to regularly review the staff's risk management plan to ensure that it has the necessary safeguards and insurance in place, to mitigate the risks that the enterprise faces.

Technology and Information Committee

This committee is concerned with how the enterprise uses information and technology to create a valued product. Like the Risk Committee, it is concerned with ensuring that the necessary precautions are in place to safeguard the enterprise's intellectual capital (such as patents and processes). It also looks to the future to identify the information and technology the enterprise will need to mobilize so that it can remain sustainable and competitive.

Some concluding remarks about Board Committees

Risk and Technology and Information Committees have been inspired by the forward-looking focus of the King Report and Code. Rather than merely respond with remedies to past Board (in)action and corporate scandals, the King Code also points to the landscape that social enterprises are encountering in the 21st Century. Our collective awareness of the impact of climate change on every enterprise and community, and our common reliance on digital technology, make it impossible for social enterprises to ignore the erratic and transformational impacts these areas have on them and their operations. The King IV report raises this awareness to the Board level. It assigns responsibility to the Board to ensure that their enterprises are prepared to address them and action when necessary.

If the size and youth of a social enterprise results in it only having a few board members, then these committee responsibilities need to be allocated between the core Board Committees.

Our experience is that Boards do not utilize their committees effectively and efficiently. They fail to do so because they do not understand their purpose. Rather than being viewed as a waste of time, committees provide venues for individual Board Members to bring their necessary skills and insights to help the Board and staff ensure the enterprise's long-term sustainability. It is our experience that the failure to distinguish between long-term sustainability and short-term tactical planning lies at the root of much of the conflict we have witnessed between Boards of Directors and their Chief Executives. This plays into the confusion over the role of Board Committees. In summary, Board Committees have a duty to remind the Board to focus on the way the enterprise accounts for its triple bottom line and how it employs the Six Capitals.

Common themes from the King Code and Aligned Influence

The ethical behavior of any enterprise begins with its Board of Directors. From there, it radiates throughout the enterprise to include its internal and external stakeholders. The Board of Directors of a social enterprise are its center of gravity. It is here that its strategic focus originates and that the enterprise's efforts are monitored. It is from here that the enterprise operates with trust and is trusted in turn by its stakeholders.

The Board of Directors expresses its long-term mindset through developing strategy; by planning for succession; by ensuring that the enterprise offers competitive compensation to attract employees; and by safeguarding the enterprise's reputation. This means that Board members have a systems-level understanding of the social enterprise they govern. They must have a long-term focus and restrain themselves from becoming involved in daily operations. Staff are responsible for those operations and for ensuring that the organization's products are created and delivered. The Aligned Influence model refers to the staff's roles as being to "lead, manage and accomplish" the work of the enterprise so that it delivers a product that adds value to the enterprise's customer and client (Schuetz, 2020).

Both Aligned Influence and the King Code institutionalize checks and balances within the enterprise. They do so by separating the roles of Board Chair and Chief Executive, by delineating the roles and responsibilities of the boards and executive staff, and by judiciously using committees to fulfill all the Board's obligations. They elucidate the Board's duty to engage with stakeholders. The Board is responsible for hiring and monitoring the Chief Executive. It is also responsible for recruiting and orientating skilled, independent Board Members by means of term limits and classes, to ensure that Boards change to reflect intellectual and demographic trends in the communities they serve. Another beneficial practice is for Boards to adhere to the King IV requirement that all boards subject themselves to regular self-evaluation, and that they document having done so.

Both the King Code and Aligned Influence remind Boards that they set the enterprise's strategic direction. Boards answer the strategic "why" which speaks to the enterprise's purpose. Aligned Influence tells them to reflect these answers in its Direct Policy. Boards monitor the way in which the enterprise's management and staff develop and implement a strategy to mobilize the Six Capitals and thereby create and deliver a unique product. The Board monitors the work of the organization in the areas of strategy; finances; treatment of, and accountability to, internal and external stakeholders; risk; information; and technology. Aligned Influence captures this monitoring role in what it terms the Protect Policy. This policy provides the Chief Executive and staff with a framework to create administrative and operational policies. It also serves as checklist the Board can use to fulfill its legal reporting mandates.

Finally, the Board has a responsibility to engage with its stakeholders to provide an account of the enterprise's performance and impact. It needs to engage in a disciplined manner with its stakeholders and the Chief Executive. The Board ensures that the enterprise remains in compliance with government regulations, its incorporating documents, and bylaws. Aligned Influence calls on Boards to capture this discipline and accountability in its Enable Policy.

When taken together, the King IV Code on Corporate Governance and Aligned Influence are an exhaustive, exciting, and practical guide to what Board service should look like in a 21st Century sustainable social enterprise.

Chapter 4

FINANCING SOCIAL ENTERPRISES

The social enterprise stratosphere

While non-profits and, in some cases, cooperatives, do not use the term "profit" in their financial statements, they do use the term "surplus". Taken together, profits and surpluses are necessary to ensure that the enterprise is sustainable.

Financial capital makes it possible for the social enterprise to deliver social impact and to do so profitably. It does so in the following ways:

- Finances are a universally accepted way of measuring the social enterprise's success or failure.
- Sharing financial information with its internal stakeholders can motivate them to ensure that the enterprise remains relevant and sustainable.
- Financial data quantifies plans and helps to surface the assumptions the social enterprise is making about its future operations.
- Financial data that is captured in budgets promotes accountability to internal and external stakeholders.
- Wise stewardship and growth of a social enterprise's financial capital is the only way in which it can achieve its social mission.

Social enterprises can only achieve their mission if they are raising capital (from investors, by selling products and by using that revenue to build cash reserves) <u>and</u> if they are employing their financial capital in an efficient manner. While it is important that social enterprises see their capital increase, it is equally important that they employ this capital efficiently.

The rise of the social enterprise phenomenon has also fueled the emergence of social impact investing, social venture capital funds, and impact bonds. These funding opportunities have been made possible through the investments that large philanthropic foundations (e.g., Rockefeller and Ford Foundations), have made into non-profit social venture funds such as the Acumen Fund. These funds invest in initiatives that drive large-scale social change, with investors being repaid over longer time frames in the form of social impact and possibly below-market returns. Social and Development Impact Bonds allow private investors to invest in social enterprises with their investment being repaid by either a governmental entity or a private foundation, but only if the enterprise achieves its social goals.

Recoverable grants are another innovative financial instrument introduced by these entities to reduce the financial barriers that social enterprises face during startup. Recoverable grants help to bring encouragement and discipline to the social enterprise. Social enterprises that qualify for such a grant use it to assist them with their startup or expansion. Once they meet their agreed targets and become profitable, then this grant converts to a loan with little to no interest being charged. The social enterprises repay the loan into a revolving loan fund, which can be used to finance the startup or expansion activities of other social enterprises.

Most social enterprises may find it challenging to access these sources of funding, as these funders may not have a visible presence in their communities or their regions, nor may they include these geographic areas in their service area. Furthermore, the particular social mission and business product these enterprises pursue might not fall within the parameters funded by these initiatives. This may further discourage local social entrepreneurs and groups from starting or growing their initiatives. The purpose of this chapter is to provide the reader with an overview of the varied financing options that are available to social enterprises and to encourage them to persist in their efforts to attract and grow the financial capital that they need to deliver social impact and profitability. This chapter may also spur regional philanthropies to consider offering these financing products.

Financing for Social Business

<u>Non-profit Social Enterprises and Non-profit Corporations</u>

Social enterprises that are organized as traditional non-profits use their tax status to attract donations from individuals and businesses. In exchange, they provide these donors with the documentation that they need to deduct these donations from their taxes. Donors to non-profit causes are motivated by a sense of altruism which flows from the social return they receive from their investment. They also benefit from a reduced tax obligation. Unlike many of their for-profit peers, non-profits do not issue shares and therefore shareholders do not expect a financial return on their investment.

However, when donors are not forthcoming or when they need access to large sums of capital, established non-profit social enterprises may need to resort to debt financing instruments to finance their expansion. They may qualify for a loan from a commercial bank or a state financing authority, or they may qualify for bond financing offered by governmental authorities or social venture groups. As with their for-profit peers, non-profit social enterprises repay these loans and bonds through fundraising campaigns or from a portion of their earnings. They may also self-finance their growth by tapping into cash reserves that have been restricted for this purpose.

The South African Animal Sanctuaries Alliance (SAASA) is a Public Benefit Organization (PBO) and Non-Profit Organization (NPO) that oversees the wellbeing of several wildlife sanctuaries in SA, one of them being Monkeyland. An award-winning sanctuary and leading major tourist attraction (Skål International's 2019 Sustainable Tourism Awards), Monkeyland is located in Plettenberg Bay, South Africa, and provides a safe environment for previously captive primates (monkeys, lemurs, and gibbons). It is not practical to release these primates into the wild locally as most of them have been rescued from the pet trade and are not all indigenous to South Africa. Meeting the day-to-day needs of the animals is a costly business, and tourism has always been a vital part of the Monkeyland business model as the income it generates keeps the animals fed and in good health.

The advent of COVID-19 and its negative impact on the SA tourism industry forced Monkeyland founder and CEO, Tony Blignaut, to rethink their business model and how it might be sustained. His concern was that future generations of stakeholders might not have the same passion for the animals that the current ones do. He began thinking about how to ensure Monkeyland's future for the time when he and his team would no longer be there. Apart from the animals, Monkeyland also employs several members of the local community, and the enterprise attracts tourists to the area. He and his team subsequently came up with the idea of literally giving the animals rights over their own land: they did this by placing the primates' rights in a trust with SAASA.

Monkeyland operates on land belonging to a proprietary limited company (in this case a farm), but the welfare of its animals remains the responsibility of SAASA. The owners of the farm agreed to sell the land to SAASA, and SAASA in turn has set up its *'Buy a square meter of land for primates'*[1] campaign so that members of the public can help fund the purchase by donating as little as a single square meter to the cause, at a cost of only R 90.00 per square meter. With a total of 216,000 square meters available, the campaign will hopefully raise more than the required amount, and the balance will go into an emergency fund to protect the animals' food bill until such time as tourism returns to normal. SAASA has both PBO and NPO registration numbers, making all donations tax-deductible in terms of section 18A of the Income Tax Act 58 of 1962.

The *'Buy a square meter of land for primates'* campaign is currently underway and if successful, will hopefully be rolled out to the other sanctuaries in the SAASA fold.

For-Profit Social Enterprises

Equity and bond markets are the largest source of capital available to social enterprises. Unlike their non-profit peers, for-profit social enterprises enjoy wide access to these markets. They can issue shares and offer their investors a return on that investment. However, there are transaction costs that come with equities, and public offerings take time to create and they require the assistance of reputable financial professionals. Even when public offerings are done professionally, there may be little to no public interest in the shares when they are offered.

Their for-profit status affords these social enterprises access to the mainstream, traditional capital markets. This means that for-profit social enterprises do not generally attract donations or grants from the philanthropic community and government. While they can accept donations, their donors cannot deduct these donations from their taxes. Despite this broad disqualification, for-profit social enterprises may enjoy access to government grants and low-interest loans that target those enterprises which serve distressed neighborhoods, under-served populations and rural areas. Minority- and women-owned social enterprises may also qualify for government startup grants for small business development, given the historic barriers these groups have encountered when seeking access to capital and markets. In South Africa, for-profit social enterprises that are 51% Black-owned and whose annual turnover (the number of times a year that an enterprise generates revenue using its assets) falls below a certain threshold are eligible for startup grants from the South African Government.

Another source of capital for social entrepreneurs and small social enterprises may be from registered and regulated micro-lending institutions. Most micro-lenders offer loan products to small and medium-sized enterprises that serve economically marginalized communities.

For-profit social enterprises may attract angel investors who invest in start-ups in exchange for equity or debt. Some communities or regions might have local angel networks. Cortese (2011) writes about the Local Investment Opportunity Network (LION) which consists of local investors who reside in Port Townsend in Washington State in the United States. Since the US Security and Exchange Commission rules permit nonpublic offerings of debt and equity to a small number of closely related persons, LION uses social gatherings to bring local businesses and investors together. These interactions allow investors to make individual investments in the businesses. Most of these investments take the form of loans. It is possible for a non-profit social enterprise to take advantage of local angel investors by seeking debt financing from them.

Social enterprises can follow a related approach which is to appeal to their local neighborhood or community for financing. The enterprise can offer equity investments to larger investors and can, if necessary, diversify this support with a layer of debt financing. Forms of debt and equity repayment can include cash as well as in-kind coupons that can be redeemed for goods and services which the social enterprise produces. For example, a social enterprise which sells sandwiches and whose employees are drawn from a marginalized population could offer coupons to their investors which can be redeemed for sandwiches after the enterprise has been in operation for a certain time. Cortese (2011) shares the example of the Greenlight Bookstore in Brooklyn NY. This enterprise raised its startup capital from friends, family, and customers, and these investors were offered promissory notes in exchange for their investment. They could choose their interest rate and they received quarterly interest payments during the store's first and fifth year of operation. This bookstore has subsequently used this model to grow its operations. The owners also created an advisory board, drawn from their investors, to help the business remain disciplined and connected to its local community.

Local banks are another source of debt financing for non- and for- profit social enterprises. In the United States, these banks are referred to as *community banks,* with this moniker applying to private banks that hold less than $1B in assets. These banks mobilize local deposits and then lend that money locally. In many cases, these banks are owned by local families and investors who have a keen appreciation of local economic conditions. They are aware of the reputation of those residents who are involved in the social enterprise. However, because community banks are often part of the local power structure, they may be hesitant to lend to a social enterprise whose social mission challenges the status quo.

Employee Stock Ownership Plans (ESOPs)

There is a favorable policy environment for ESOPs in the United States and, as was noted in the previous chapter, the number of US companies that are ESOPs continues to grow. South African law permits ESOPs and, due to BBBEE regulations, more South African companies are starting to adopt this model to broaden ownership and increase productivity.

There are five players who are involved when creating an ESOP. These include:

- The owner of the company.
- The employees of the company who wish to purchase it from that owner.
- The company itself.
- The ESOP Trust.
- A bank that is willing to finance the transaction.

Once the owner and employees agree on a sales price for the company, they create a trust in the name of the ESOP. This secures a loan from the bank which has agreed to finance the transaction. The company issues stock to cover the loan amount and exchanges the stock for the loan proceeds. The employees use that loan to purchase the company from the owner. The Trust serves as both financier and trustee of the stock that secures this loan.

The company makes annual payments on this loan to the Trust and funds these payments from its revenues. The company realizes additional tax relief by deducting all of its loan repayments to the ESOP from its income taxes. This reduces its corporate income tax liability. The Trust uses these annual payments to pay off the loan to the bank. It then releases a proportionate amount of stock to the ESOP which distributes these amongst the employees' individual stock accounts. The bank reduces the loan balance by the amount that it receives from the Trust. There are tax benefits for the bank as well. It can deduct 50% of the interest that it earned on the loan from its tax obligations.

This annual process continues until the loan is paid off. At that point, the remaining players are simply the ESOP and the employees. Once a year, the ESOP engages an independent auditor to appraise the value of its stock. Employees withdraw or sell their stock back to the ESOP when they retire or decide to leave the company for other employment. New employees join the plan once they have met the ESOPs vesting requirements. They then begin to accumulate stock.

Low-profit Limited Liability Corporations (L3Cs)

L3Cs offer investors a tiered system of investing with the option of a lower-risk/lower return to charitable investors and foundations as well as higher-risk/higher-return option to traditional investors. While this tiered system of investing does allow L3Cs the best of both worlds, they will incur the additional transaction costs associated with offering equity to different types of investors.

Non-profit Corporations (NPCs)

While South African non-profit corporations cannot issue equity, they can raise capital in the form of grants from the philanthropic sector and government, donations from for-profit companies, debt financing and revenue sharing agreements. However, to qualify for grants and donations, NPCs must be approved as non-profit and public benefit organizations.

Revenue-Sharing Agreements (RSAs)

Both US and South African law create the space for non-profit and for-profit corporations to use RSAs to finance their growth. The two parties of the RSA are the social enterprise and the investor whose respective rights and responsibilities are captured in a legal contract. The investor agrees to invest an agreed sum in the social enterprise and, in addition, the investor accepts that this sum, along with a portion of the enterprise's profits, will be returned over an agreed period of, for example, five years. If the enterprise is profitable, the investors recoup their investment as well as a portion of the profits. But if the venture fails, they lose their investment as well as any additional income. RSAs include provisions which mandate the enterprise to share their financial statements, income tax returns, and independent audit reports with their investors. Other provisions mandate the investor to keep these statements confidential and to respect the enterprise's intellectual property.

Since RSAs are not equity vehicles, they are not regulated by the US Security and Exchange Commission. Contrary to their initial appearance, RSAs are not loans. They are generally unsecured as the enterprise does not pledge collateral in exchange for the initial investment.

Financing Cooperatives

Cooperatives do not offer outside investors an equity stake in their operations. Instead, their members are the primary source of startup financing for cooperatives. Membership dues are reflected as owner's equity on the cooperative's balance sheet and are then used as a source of working capital. The cooperative's Board of Directors decides how much of its retained earnings are to be distributed amongst its members. They also decide how to reinvest these earnings so that they can expand their operations, markets, and products.

In the United States, credit unions raise capital by lending out members' deposits and reinvesting their earnings. Member deposits are guaranteed by the Federal Government. Credit unions can lend capital to other types of cooperatives as per the seven principles that are internationally accepted by all cooperatives.

Under South African law, credit unions are referred to as Cooperative Banks. While there is a healthy network of informal credit unions or *stokvels*, only two credit unions have been established in South Africa since the South African Parliament passed the Cooperative Bank Act of 2007. Reasons given for this slow rate of adoption include a lack of public awareness. Fewer members result in limited capital being available to start up and grow these Banks, which subsequently suffer further from a lack of capacity and the skills necessary to create and sustain these institutions (Levy, 2017).

In addition to member dues, retained earnings and loans, US law permits cooperatives to offer shares, but only under limited conditions. These conditions include that the shares can only be held by members and that they can only be sold in the cooperative's home state. These shares cannot be sold to non-members and their dividend is generally capped. As is the case with

ESOPs, cooperatives purchase their shares back from those members when they decide to sell them (Cortese, 2011).

Since the cooperative's membership base may be too small to help finance its expansion, a small cooperative may modify its by-laws so that it can adopt a multi-stakeholder model to include members, employees, non-member customers and investors. These stakeholders may receive representation on the cooperative's Board of Directors when they become eligible to purchase a limited number of shares in the cooperative. These shares may come with little or no limited voting power (Cortese, 2011).

Financial Statements, Dashboards and Key Ratios

Social enterprises employ different financial statements to plan, manage and monitor their financial health and performance. These documents are used when the social enterprise creates its initial business, when it prepares its annual budget, and when it releases monthly, quarterly, or annual reports to its stakeholders. Financial statements are included in business plans to project business activity over the next five years. An annual budget provides a financial window into the social enterprise's activities for the upcoming 12 months. Annual financial reports prepared by the social enterprise and its independent auditors, paint a financial picture of what transpired over the previous 12 months.

Types of financial statements

Income and Expense statement

Income and Expense statements list the enterprise's sources of revenue as well as all the expenses it incurs to produce the goods or services that it sells. Its primary revenue source is sales. Other sources include investment income, donations or income realized from the sale of its ancillary products and services. Income and Expense Statements are also referred to as Profit and Loss (P&L) Statements.

Income and Expense statements are closely aligned with the annual sales and program plans developed by the social enterprise. In turn, these plans help the enterprise create its annual budget based on its projected income and expenses for the upcoming 12 months. The revenue and expense line items in the budget help to structure the future monthly Income and Expense Statements. This provides the social enterprise's Board of Directors, management, and staff with the ability to operate, to measure their progress against financial goals, and to take corrective action should this be necessary. Income and Expense Statements provide these internal consumers with an idea of the social enterprise's revenue, expenses, and profitability in the preceding month and help them to plan for any seasonal variations that the enterprise might encounter.

Income and Expense Statement for X Enterprise Month ending (Month & Year)				
LINE ITEMS	BUDGET	ACTUAL	YEAR-TO-DATE	VARIANCE
Revenue:				
Sales				
Investments				
(Revenue Source)				
(Revenue Source)				
Total Revenue				
Expenses:				
Advertising				
Bank Charges				
Professional Fees				
Payroll				
Payroll Taxes				
Utilities				
(Expense Source)				
(Expense Source)				
Total Expenses				
Net Revenue	(Total Revenue - Total Expenses)	(Total Revenue - Total Expenses)	(Total Revenue - Total Expenses)	(Total Revenue - Total Expenses)

Table 1: The following table illustrates the common outline of an income and expenses statement. (Note the number of revenue and expense lines can be increased)

Balance sheet

Balance sheets are sometimes referred to as Statements of Financial Position as they provide their readers with a snapshot of the social enterprise's total financial health and wealth. The numbers on the balance sheet compares the enterprise's current financial position with the position they held 12 months earlier. The basic formula behind the balance sheet can be portrayed as follows:

Assets = Liabilities + Owner's' Equity

The social enterprise's assets are divided between current assets (cash, accounts receivable, and assets which can be liquidated quickly) and fixed assets which include the items it owns and uses to produce a valued product. Common examples of fixed assets include equipment, land, and intellectual property.

Liabilities are the short and long-term expenses that the social enterprise has incurred and for which they are indebted to others. If these liabilities need to be paid during the upcoming 12 months, then they are classified as current liabilities. If they will become due later than that, then they are treated as long-term liabilities. An example of this is when an enterprise has borrowed money from a bank to finance its purchase of equipment and has begun to repay this loan. The portion of the loan that will be repaid over the next 12 months will fall under the current liabilities. The remaining balance will fall under its long-term liabilities.

The difference which remains after the total liabilities are subtracted from the total assets is known as owner's equity. Common accounts under the heading of owner's equity include the enterprise's stock and retained earnings. In other words, "owner's equity" reflects the net worth of the social enterprise. In the case of ESOPs and cooperatives, the owner's equity belongs to their respective members rather than to outside investors.

Balance sheets provide investors, donors, and lenders with the information they need when they underwrite their investment or loan to the social enterprise. This financial statement also provides the enterprise and its stakeholders with the information to assess its financial health by using the ratios which will be discussed later in this section.

Cash-flow Statement

Social enterprises have the option to record transactions on a cash or accrual basis. The cash approach sees a sale or purchase being recorded at the point the cash is exchanged for goods or services. Under the accrual approach, a sale or purchase occurs as soon as it is invoiced. Since Income and Expense Statements generally reflect accrued transactions, another statement is required to indicate when the enterprise anticipates receiving or spending its cash. This statement is referred to as the cash flow statement and it is completed by answering the questions:

- How much cash do we project we will receive over the next period?
- How much cash do we anticipate paying out to vendors over the same period?

The cash flow statement follows the same structure as the Income and Expense Statement. Since business models and cash flow cycles are unique to each enterprise, their managers must understand these cycles so that they can create a realistic cash flow for their enterprise. While an annual cash flow forecast is included as part of the annual budget, managers also need a short-term cash flow statement that covers anywhere from 6 to 13 weeks. This rolling cash flow forecast is updated weekly, and the activity forces managers to examine their cash position for the current week, as well as what it is projected for several weeks in the future.

Cash Management

No-one likes to see their vehicle leaking lubricants onto the ground, because this automatically signifies a costly mechanical problem. The loss of those lubricants will result in the vehicle becoming inoperable and eventually lead to its demise. In the same vein, a social enterprise that uses more cash than it receives is unlikely to survive. Keeping a careful eye on the enterprise's cash position is therefore a critical function that must be fulfilled by its management and its Board.

In order to safeguard their cash, social enterprises need to not only use their cash wisely, but to also invest it prudently. The rule of thumb is that a social enterprise wants to keep as much cash on hand as it can to meet both foreseen and unforeseen circumstances. It wants to limit the amount of time that its customers owe money to the enterprise. One canny way to do this is to negotiate longer repayment terms with its suppliers while pressing customers to pay for their purchases as soon as possible after they receive the enterprise's product. This allows the social enterprise to build up its cash reserves.

Cash is a critical part of the enterprise's working capital since this allows it to finance its daily operations and production over a set period. Cash reserves allow the social enterprise to attract the financing it needs to upgrade or expand its operations. It is unacceptable for social enterprises to simply have large cash reserves on hand without a plan to invest them prudently into new initiatives that increase the enterprise's social impact.

Inventory Budget and Statement

When a social enterprise purchases and uses materials to produce goods or services, they need to track that inventory on their financial statements. To do so, they should create an inventory management system and statement which reflects the receipt and disbursement of materials from the enterprise's inventory. The inventory statement allows procurement and production managers to be good stewards of these resources by ensuring that materials are sourced and used in a timely and efficient manner.

Capital Budget

Most social enterprises will purchase equipment and physical property at some point in their existence. The initial purchase of these items, along with their subsequent replacement, must be included in the enterprise's long-term strategic plans. Failure to do so will inhibit the enterprise's growth. Social enterprises build a Capital Budget by forecasting what physical assets they will need and when they will need them. They reserve a portion of their retained earnings for this purpose and then use these savings to make these investments at the appropriate time. Social enterprises often use the depreciation schedule provided by their accountants and auditors to calculate how much they should reserve for their ongoing capital needs.

Personnel Budget

With regards to personnel, social enterprises are no different than any other organization. They depend on their human capital to transform materials and knowledge into valued products and services. Like for-profit organizations, their human capital is a significant cost to the enterprise. In the traditional for-profit and capitalist corporation, human capital, or labor, is viewed as a variable cost as its workforce grows or is downsized based on the market and the economic conditions in which the firm finds itself. In the case of cooperatives, especially those that are worker-owned, labor is viewed as a fixed cost. Consequently, layoffs are viewed as one of the last solutions to be implemented when the firm encounters market volatility and economic hardships.

Personnel costs include wages or payroll, the employer portion of payroll taxes, and benefits such as health insurance and retirement. For example, US employers are responsible for contributing the equivalent of 7.65% of their employees' wages to the Federal Government. This is known as FICA – the acronym for Federal Insurance Contribution Act. This money helps to fund the Social Security and Medicare programs. The South African Revenue Service levies a 1% tax on employers whose annual payroll exceeds R500,000. This tax helps to fund job and skills training.

Key Ratios

To monitor and measure the financial health of their social enterprise, the managers, executives, and Boards of Directors, along with their stakeholders, will employ all, or combinations of, the following five financial ratios. In accounting and financial management, the term *current period* refers to the upcoming 12 months.

Liquidity ratios

These ratios allow an enterprise to determine how much cash it has on hand to cover its expenses and to meet the demands of its creditors for prompt payment. The most common liquidity ratio is the current ratio. This is calculated as follows:

Current Assets/Current Liabilities: In a healthy enterprise, current assets exceed current liabilities by a 2:1 ratio. This means that the enterprise has double the assets on hand to meet its short-term obligations. Liquidity ratios are of special interest to managers and Boards of Directors.

Leverage ratios

These ratios are largely the preserve of donors and lenders, who use these ratios when a social enterprise approaches them to request financing for growth and expansion of operations. Knowledge of these ratios will also be of use to the senior management and Boards of social enterprises when they create business plans to expand operations. Leverage ratios provide both internal and external stakeholders with an idea of how much the enterprise is indebted to its funders. The most common leverage ratio is the debt-to-equity ratio which is calculated as follows:

Total Liabilities/Total Equity – The lower its debt, the more likely it is that the social enterprise's request for financing will be approved. However, lenders and donors will also consider the industry sector in which the social enterprise operates, as this will also have an impact on its ratio.

Activity or efficiency ratios

These ratios measure the enterprise's ability to use its assets and manage its liabilities over the current period. Efficiency ratios measure the rate of productivity when an enterprise converts (turns over) its assets into revenue by selling its products. These ratios can be applied to areas such as the enterprise's inventory, customers (accounts receivable) and suppliers (accounts payable), and can also be used to identify risks to the enterprise's viability. The human resources department can use an efficiency ratio to calculate staff turnover. A high turnover in personnel results in increased recruitment and training costs, and points to potential problems within the management structure itself. The enterprise will also experience lower revenue income as a result of lost productivity.

A common efficiency ratio in the housing financing sector is a delinquency ratio. This allows a housing enterprise that offers mortgages to monitor how much income it is failing to collect from its borrowers. The enterprise can use the following ratio to calculate delinquency:

Number # of delinquent mortgages/total number # of mortgages held

Managers can use this ratio and the details behind it to develop an aged analysis of the enterprise's delinquents. This allows them to create an action plan to address the enterprise's problem with those delinquent borrowers.

Profitability ratios

These ratios are used to calculate a social enterprise's overall efficiency in generating profits. The most common ratio relies upon the following formula:

Gross Profit/Total Sales – The higher the result, the greater enterprise's efficiency and profitability. It is good practice for the social enterprise to compare their results to those of their competitors. If the enterprise's margins are lower than those of a similar competitor, it may be an indication that the social enterprise is selling their product too cheaply. When this is the case, they should raise their price to see if the market can sustain it. If it does, a price increase will allow them to increase their profit margin.

Market ratios

These ratios are used by owners and investors to calculate their return on the investment they made in the social enterprise. They can then compare their return to what they would have received had they invested in bonds and the stock market at large. These owners and investors use the following formula to calculate the return on their equity:

Net Income/Owner's Equity

This section has already introduced the reader to the concept and use of financial ratios to calculate the financial health of a social enterprise. The specific form a ratio will take will depend on the nature of the social enterprise and the sector it is in. Given that a social enterprise's financial assets are the lubricant which allows it to deliver its social mission, it is imperative that the enterprise's management, their Board of Directors, and their stakeholders use ratios to monitor their enterprise's financial health and that the enterprise includes relevant ratios on its internal dashboards. It is prudent for these internal consumers to remember not to fixate on them at the expense of the enterprise's social impact ratios. Balance is important.

Ratios are also important when social enterprises adopt and implement the practice of Open Book Management, a topic that we will expand on a little later in this chapter.

Participatory Financial Planning

Social enterprises can greatly enhance their competitive advantage by employing an enterprise-wide process when they create their annual budgets, as well as the financial statements for their business plans. The creation of a participatory annual budget begins when social enterprises include this process in their annual work calendar. By doing so, employees at all levels of the organization know when the annual budget is approaching. The enterprise's employees gather in their work teams to forecast the expenses they will incur over the next 12 months and when these are likely to transpire. They then use the realism which comes from this analysis to set their team and individual goals. These revenue and expense projections flow from the teams to management who compile these projections into a consolidated annual budget, seeking additional clarification where necessary. The budget is then approved by the social enterprise's top management and Board. Management should ensure that all employees are provided with a copy of the budget as well as its subsequent monthly income and expense statements. These documents will provide employees with the numbers specific to their department so that they know how well they are performing. The statements should also reflect how their performance relates to the enterprise's overall financial position.

Open Book Management

Open Book Management (OBM) is a participatory management tool which improves employee engagement with the purpose of increasing the enterprise's retained earnings. It takes the participatory financial planning process (detailed in the previous section) and turns that process into a powerful tool for employee ownership. John Case (1995) studied how US businesses from different sectors and of different sizes used a combination of four principles to implement OBM. In the United States, the bootstrap story of how the managers of Springfield Remanufacturing Corporation (SRC) purchased their plant and then applied the principles of Open Book Management to ensure that this corporation survived and grew, is truly inspirational. SRC's Founder, President and CEO, Jack Stack, has written several books which detail their successes as well as the lessons they learnt along the way. SRC has spun off multiple businesses which are now owned by former employees. SRC employees set their goals and, in consultation with the Board of Directors, determine what their bonus goals will be. Stack traces SRC's profitable growth, low employee turnover and high level of employee satisfaction to its implementation of Open Book Management (Stack, 2013).

The practices of OBM can be summarized as follows:

- Managers determine the enterprise's key revenue and cost drivers.
- The enterprise provides training to all employees to help them understand basic personal and business finances.
- Managers and employees understand how the enterprise's finances tie the different parts of its operations together.
- Everyone understands that they have a role to play to keep operating costs down, while also seeking out new markets.
- Managers practice financial transparency by sharing all the enterprise's financial information with employees. Financial information is no longer the sole preserve of management. Management sets the direction and then provides the necessary information and resources. The employees prepare and implement plans, monitor their implementation, and take corrective action where necessary, based on the financial and operational information they receive.
- Employees are empowered to make necessary changes to keep costs down.
- All employees have a financial stake in the enterprise's success through a well-designed and transparent bonus system. SRC has reinforced this by also converting their company into an ESOP.

The benefits which OBM brings to employees are that of pride, an ownership interest in the success of the enterprise, and the ability to build their household wealth. The enterprise benefits from motivated employees who have a vested interest in continually keeping the enterprise competitive, lower personnel turnover, and a consistent market share. Some of these benefits are captured in the virtuous cycle below.

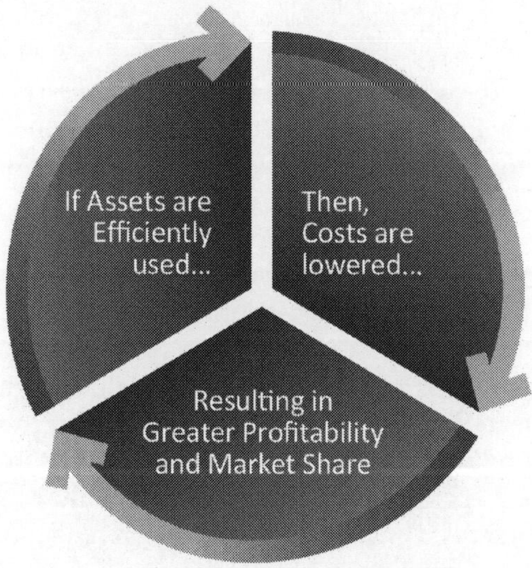

Fig.1: The benefits of Open Book Management

In the last section of this chapter, we will focus on some principles and practices of corporate financial literacy and transparent financial statements. The principles of employee financial rewards and employee empowerment will be addressed in the chapters on Human Capital and Operations Management.

Building a Financially Literate Workforce

Our experience has been that most managers and employees do not fully understand the financial side of the enterprises where they are employed. In fact, many Board members fail to understand the business model and financial conditions as well. It is therefore imperative that social enterprises build a financially literate workforce from their start-up phase, and that they include business literacy training as part of their human resource management system.

Building a financially literate workforce begins with the top management. They must understand how the enterprise's financial capital lubricates its operations. Furthermore, they should identify their enterprise's unique revenue and cost drivers. It is essential that top management provide explicit pivotal numbers, and ensure that all employees not only understand them conceptually, but also instinctively understand how their individual and collective efforts impact those numbers. Managers should reinforce this knowledge on a regular basis.

Social enterprises can employ external organizations or use internal managers to equip all employees with the financial literacy tools that they need, to fully understand how the enterprise's finances impact its operations and their jobs. This training should have the related objective of showing each employee how their best efforts contribute to both their, and the enterprise's, success. Any literacy training must be based on the principles and practices of adult education, by using a combination of basic lecturing and experiential learning techniques such as role plays and small case studies. Case (1995) shares how one company that practiced OBM had new employees begin their orientation by creating a personal balance sheet for their household. They were then tasked with creating their own fictitious home-based cookie company. Creating this company introduced them to exactly how their decisions about strategy, operations, and marketing impacted its finances and their personal balance sheet. Once they had mastered this scenario, the employees used what they had learnt to understand how finances flowed through the company that employed them. This training equipped them with the skills and insights they required to practice Open Book Management at their company.

Transparent Financial Statements

By *transparent*, we mean that financial statements and dashboards must reflect the circumstances facing the areas where the employees who are reading them work and which they control. This means that employees are presented with the financial data for their unit or department. This data shows how much they have earned and spent. These financial statements take the form of weekly and monthly income and expense statements, as well as the rolling cash flow analysis. The level of financial detail contained in these statements depends on the organizational level where the employee is engaged.

These financial statements must allow their readers to see any variances between the projected income and expenses which were included in the annual budget, and those which have recently occurred. They then have the knowledge they need to implement corrective actions. Employees and managers can thus use this information to determine whether they are likely to earn their bonuses.

The key numbers from these financial statements should be regularly updated and posted on public notice boards throughout the enterprise. This serves to update and remind all employees about their goals and how well the enterprise is performing.

Authors Corner: In an enterprise where one of the authors implemented OBM, a department began to track their daily sales revenue. Those numbers were updated daily and posted in the breakroom, so that department's employees could review them and act accordingly. These sales numbers allowed them to know whether they were on track to meet the monthly sales goal and thereby secure their bonus.

In conclusion, social enterprises face tough competition as they balance their mission with profitability and growth. If they are to succeed at this, they require an enabling environment within which to operate. This means that the communities and societies that surround them adhere to the rule of law which promotes safety and social order. It is important that the rule of law protects property rights and allows for the creation and enforcement of contracts. It is also important that social enterprises enjoy the opportunity to access credit, whether this be informally, from micro-credit lenders, foundations, government, or the conventional banking sector.

OBM helps to improve the operational efficiency, quality of work life, and financial health of the enterprise. It is not a substitute for the core requirements of an effective strategy, a solid reputation, or the delivery of a superior service and product. OBM cannot be enforced from outside the enterprise. Instead, it needs to emerge from within, and reflect the enterprise's unique business. However, we feel strongly that OBM is a critical component of any successful and sustainable social enterprise.

Chapter 5

A SOCIAL ENTERPRISE AND ITS HUMAN CAPITAL

Human Resources and Human Resource Management

The term Human Resources (HR) refers to the employees who work for an enterprise. Human Resource Management (HRM) is the term used to describe the formal systems and structures (consistent set of practices, policies, and codes of conduct) devised for the management of employees within an enterprise. Human Resource Professionals and/or the HR department are responsible for establishing a positive work environment and managing all matters related to employees from creating, managing, and cultivating the employer-employee relationship, to devising and implementing all workplace policies, procedures and programs. Since the size of HR departments are proportional to the size of the enterprise itself, their founding entrepreneurs and managers need to step up and fulfill the HRM role at their enterprise.

The fundamental principle of HRM is that human resources are the most important assets of an enterprise and that without effectively acquiring, managing and optimizing the effectiveness of this resource, the enterprise cannot be successful (Gubman, 1996). Personnel policies and procedures should be linked to the enterprise's overall objectives and strategies. Essentially, employees who are subject to effective human resource management are more aligned to their enterprise's goals and objectives, and are more likely to achieve them (Armstrong, 2014).

Whatever the size of your business, corporation or social enterprise, the importance of HRM cannot be overemphasized. Human resource issues do not discriminate between enterprise sizes and, if not handled correctly, can have a devastating impact on business health. Recruiting, training and retaining the right people for the job contributes to steady enterprise growth; conversely, employing the wrong people will hamper growth (Irving Burstiner, 1989). This is the value and function of HR and HRM.

The Changing field of Human Resource Management

Previously, HRM was known as personnel management, where their primary role was the hiring and firing of employees. Today, that is just one aspect of HRM. In recent years, a number of business trends, such as flattened management structures, people analytics, digital HR, agile ways of working, and hybrid business models (employee work-from-home and work-from-office models) have had a significant impact on the field of HRM. This has led to fundamental reassessments of HR structures and positions, most notably that HR is now a major role player in the business processes of any enterprise (Johnston, 2018). Being charged with the strategic utilization of all employees, as well as managing and measuring their productivity and development, has given the HR department a voice in cost/benefit justifications and other operational aspects of the enterprise. Members of the HR team are often assigned to various departments of an enterprise and are known as that particular department's HR Business Partner (HRBP). This ongoing business partnering relationship enables both Operations and HRM to build a better understanding of what goes on in each of their departments and thus develop mutually beneficial long-term strategies and solutions for people issues before these arise. Business partnering has resulted in better HR support offered to Operations and a positive impact on the bottom line.

The function of HR has definitely become more fluid in recent years. A more agile and personal employer-employee approach has replaced outdated procedures and paperwork. Competitive and successful enterprises promote workplace cultures where employees feel heard, supported, trained, appraised, and adequately compensated. The advent of digital HR has done much to further the employer-employee relationship. Continuous and direct access to their HR support system enables employees to voice their needs and wishes and, in turn, get results. It's direct, time-saving, at the point of work and does not distract from everyday tasks; this is in contrast to booking an appointment and waiting for instructions.

By employing the latest HR technologies, HRM are better able to engage with employees on issues like payroll, leave, access to benefits, and work-life balance. New HR technology also ushers in a sense of fairness as HRM are able to track and evaluate employees in real time more easily, and thus measure performance efficiently. This allows for a more complete view on which employees are deserving of payment increases and bonuses. Freeing up HRM from paper-heavy tasks, means that more time can be spent on developing HRM and enterprise strategies. The benefits all round include happier employees and cost saving to the enterprise.

Components of today's Human Resource Management System

Whilst HRM structures may vary widely due to the size, nature and governing philosophies of the enterprises they serve, today most HR departments focus their efforts on six critical areas/functions in relation to the people they look after. These six functions include:

<u>The employee life cycle</u>

The employee life cycle constitutes the employment life span of an employee from start to finish at an enterprise. HR plays a role in every step of this cycle, whether it be recruiting competent employees in a fair manner, educating or developing, disciplining or rewarding, and retaining or exiting employees.

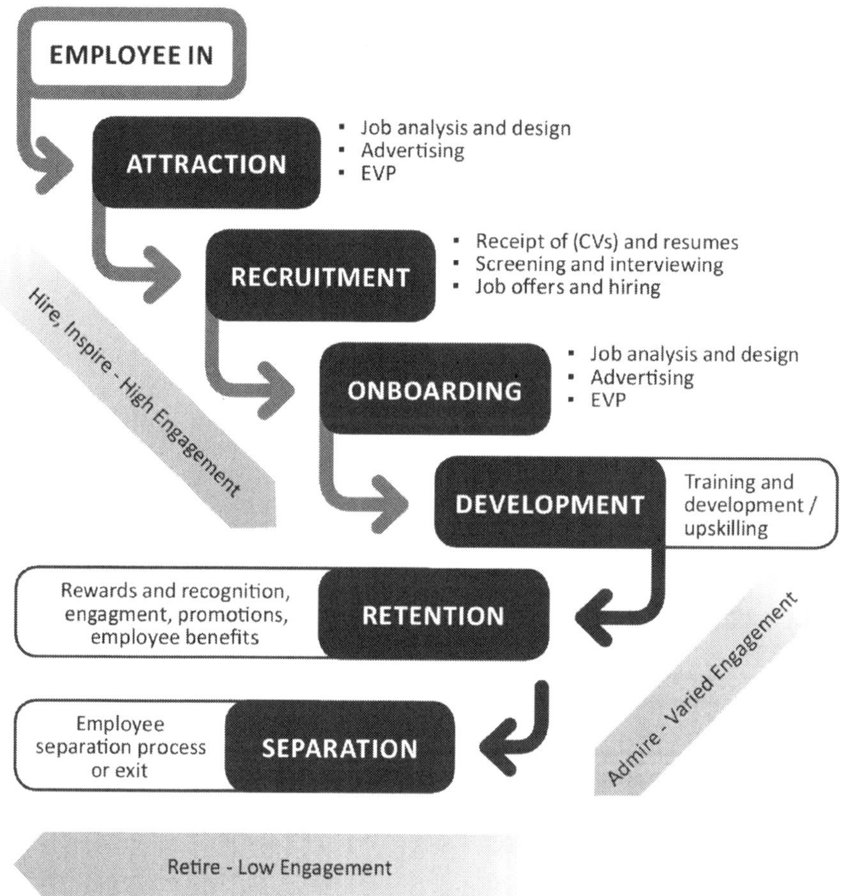

Fig.1: The Employee Life Cycle

Job analysis and Job design: Job analysis is essential to HRM practice and is used to make important decisions around job domains and descriptions, new hire selection processes, compensation plans and reasonable accommodation or incapacity should it occur. It also assists HRM in developing performance appraisals and promotion criteria and in determining training needs (Bateman & Zeithaml, 1990). As we have mentioned in previous chapters, planning is everything. The biggest mistake an enterprise can make is to employ people with the wrong skills, and at the wrong time. Working together with Management and Operations, the HR department is best suited to perform a job analysis to determine the necessary skills and experience required from an employee to successfully fill a position. Conducting a job analysis also ensures that the enterprise keeps abreast of the job and industry trends and enables the HR department to make projections about future employment levels and skill requirements so that the enterprise can reach its goals and outcomes. Once the job domain, description, necessary skills and experience required from an employee to perform in a position have been established, HRM engages in job design. This involves the organization of all the tasks, duties and responsibilities needed to satisfy organizational requirements into a unit of work with set objectives.

Resource planning: At any given time, a HR department should be able to give an account of not only the current number of employees in the enterprise, but also their skills, qualifications, job positions, benefits, and performance levels. HR is also responsible for forecasting future requirements for employees, especially in times of enterprise growth or restructuring, and setting plans in place to fill any identified gaps.

Staffing / Recruitment: Managing the flow of employees into, within and out of an enterprise remains an HRM staple.

» *Into the enterprise*: HR is responsible for the full hiring process, from the advertising of positions and the receipt of applications and curriculum vitaes (CVs) and resumes, and the subsequent screening and interviewing, to the point of job offers and hiring. When hiring an employee, HR should ensure that the hiring process is open and fair, and that it adheres to all the applicable labor laws. Once an employee is hired, HR places them on Induction or Onboarding programs, with the aim of helping them to settle in, learn the 'lay-of-the-land' and feel supported. This goes a long way in creating a positive first-time experience and contributes towards building enterprise loyalty from day one.

» *Within the enterprise:* The organization, utilization, and maintenance of employees is another HRM staple. For an enterprise to be efficient, effective and profitable, its employees should be organized in such a way as to maximize the utilization of their time, skills and experience.

» *Out of the enterprise:* Whether an employee resigns, is dismissed, or retrenched, the HR department must oversee the employee separation process or exit. This entails completing the necessary paperwork and legalities, settling any outstanding remuneration and benefits, retaining all company assets, and severing access to all company resources.

A common mistake made by small enterprises (and sometimes social enterprises themselves), especially when building their business is to think that they do not need to apply or implement any initial HRM. Whether you have two employees or 1000+ employees, it is always wise to:

- » Implement and document policies regarding HR issues (recruitment and selection, compensation plans and employee benefits, training, promotions and terminations). In business, one is dealing with humans and issues are bound to appear at some time, for the right or wrong reasons. Being prepared upfront allows the enterprise owner to hold problems to a minimum, and stave off any legal issues.
- » Conduct a proper job analysis. Questions you may want to ask yourself as an enterprise owner include: What kind of person is needed to do the job at hand? How many people are needed? How should these people work to achieve the vision and mission of the enterprise? What skills are needed? Can some of the services be outsourced to various stakeholders?
- » Engage in proper recruitment processes. Jobs need to be defined accurately and the talents of prospective employees matched with the enterprise's needs.
- » Actively take part in the recruitment process. A small enterprise owner is likely to work very closely with his/her employees and it is thus essential to choose the right person who will not only fit the job, but also within the culture the owner is trying to achieve.

Measurement and appraisal of work force performance

A performance appraisal involves assessing an employees' job performance and then providing feedback on how well (or not) that employee is performing in their job. Whilst actual appraisals take place between employees and their direct managers, HR are responsible for the development and management of, as well as training on, all policies that deal with all matters relating to performance issues at the workplace. Whether it be the yearly performance review, a probationary evaluation for a new employee or a special performance review, performance measurements are very important for both the enterprise and the employee. Without assessing an employee's job performance, there would be no way of telling how they were performing. The enterprise has a responsibility to guide employees on their professional development and to provide opportunities for growth and improvement. A performance review will be able to show if an employee is struggling to meet their job requirements and the reasons why. This allows HR to make an informed decision on whether to provide the employee with additional training and development, or if they need to let the employee go. In keeping with fair labor practices and company policies on compensation and benefits, performance appraisals are a fair way to determine salary increases and promotions. Performance appraisals are also a great way to improve communication and working relationships in the enterprise. Providing regular, honest and constructive feedback to employees boosts their motivation and develops open and trustworthy patterns of communications between employees and managers. It also increases productivity when good work is recognized and areas that need improvement are addressed in a constructive manner.

Learning and Development

Learning and Development (L&D) is vital to any enterprise if they want to remain competitive and retain employees. To remain competitive, an enterprise must equip their employees with continuous on-the-job training. Investing in training and development of employees goes a long way to ensuring long-term business profitability (Roberts, Seldon & Roberts, 1993). As mentioned in the previous chapter, the HRM should ensure that business literacy training is an essential part of L&D. All employees need to work from a solid, practical foundation in that they understand business terminology, statements and concepts, that they understand their enterprise and how they can make an impact. The added benefits of training and developing employees include increased productivity and efficiency and positive sentiments towards the enterprise, and thus increased employee retention.

HR is the department responsible for determining an enterprise's L&D needs and supplying the programs necessary to meet those needs. A distinction should be made between Learning and Development. Development focuses on preparing employees for future roles and responsibilities in the enterprise. Learning, using a variety of techniques and activities (e.g. job rotation, discussions, and work-based learning), focuses on meeting current employee needs or competency gaps. The aim is to bring about a change in employee's attitudes, skills or increased knowledge of their tasks and activities. It must be remembered that although People or Human Capital development is a long-term process and takes time, commitment, and energy, it benefits the health of the enterprise in the long term, as opposed to tactical hiring or short term courses here and there (Russell, 2019).

Employee morale and motivation: Rewards and Recognition | Engagement | Communication

HRM has the immense task of ensuring that an enterprise's workforce remains motivated. High employee motivation and morale has a favorable impact on people's behavior and performance, which in turn translates into greater success and revenue for the enterprise. Rewards and Recognition, Employee

Engagement and Communication are the best tools at HR's disposal to do this.

Rewards and recognition: We have yet to come across a person who does not enjoy acknowledgment or appreciation for something that they have worked hard to accomplish. While it is motivating to receive words of affirmation or appreciation of this effort, it is even sweeter to receive some sort of tangible gift or reward. In the world of work, this acknowledgement or appreciation, known as Rewards and Recognition, can be a very effective tool in encouraging and motivating employees to do their best, and this in turn benefits the enterprise. The golden rule remains that when employees feel valued, their dedication and enthusiasm grows for their jobs, colleagues and organization. This in turn increases their retention, performance and productivity levels. Managed by the HR department, Rewards and Recognition are awarded to employees not only for good performance, but also for helping to create a positive work environment. An employee might be excellent at doing their job, but if their behavior is contrary to the enterprise's culture, ethics, code of conduct or workplace policies and programs, then it will hamper their chances of receiving a reward. As mentioned, acknowledgment and recognition of a job well done goes a long way to create personal satisfaction for an employee. However, tangible rewards, including financial rewards (bonus and pay increases), promotions, extra leave, and celebrations maximize employee motivation and commitment, and help to create and maintain a good company culture.

Employee engagement: Employee engagement, not to be confused with employee satisfaction, is the extent to which an employee feels connected to the enterprise in which they work. It includes feeling passionate and committed to the work they do and what the enterprise stands for. They are the enterprise's biggest promoters, and participate or get fully involved in all it has to offer. HRM enhances or aids employee engagement by creating a positive climate or workplace culture through proper communication, fairness in all execution of policies and procedures, rewards and recognition, engagement or fun activities, promotion of health and well-being etc. The challenge to the HRM is in deciding which solutions will be the best for the employee, the enterprise and the culture. Good engagement not only improves an enterprise's outcomes, but also contributes to the employee's well-being.

Employee communications: The benefits of effective communication can never be overemphasized and the results speak for themselves. When a person is able to speak freely and engage in dialogues about issues that concern them, when they feel heard and are kept updated with what is happening within their own world and around them, then their communication, engagement, morale and positive sentiments flow at an all-time high. The same applies for effective communication within an enterprise, referred to as Internal or Employee Communications. These include:

- Regular one-on-one meetings between managers and employees.
- Building strong lines of communication within teams.
- Implementing self-service applications for convenience and speed.
- Updating employees on all changes and activities within the enterprise.
- Acknowledging accomplishments, birthdays and good performance.
- Promoting health, wellness and engagement activities.

Creating a culture for open dialogue, where employees are able to express their opinions without fear and where management actually listens and applies this input in future decision-making, will reverberate positively across the whole enterprise. The benefits will include positive attitudes, higher morale, good company culture, lower turnover and absenteeism rates, greater loyalty, and excellent productivity.

Supporting line managers

With the changes in HRM functions and roles, many core HR delivery functions have been shifted onto line managers. For example, the determining of increases and bonuses are now the responsibility of line managers; these are the actual people who have regular one-on-ones with their team members, determine if their key performance indicators (KPI's) are being met, and help set their Personal Development Plans. Although line managers have the most say in how their team members are performing, the HR department serves as a check on managers to ensure that they are not making biased decisions when awarding increases and bonuses and that they remain within the enterprise's allocated budgets for this. Apart from determining increases and bonuses, other HR activities such as maintaining attendance records, managing staffing requests, booking training and submitting payroll information are also devolved to line managers.

Thus, line managers not only manage people and day-to-day operations, but also help implement HR and other organizational policies, including people development. Good line managers impact their team members positively, resulting in engaged, committed, innovative and productive employees. In contrast, poorly performing line managers bring about demotivation and demoralization in their teams. These managers often create disharmony and conflict not only in their own teams, but also across the organization; this causes much tension in employee relationships and creates a blame and silencing culture, all of which leads to an increase in staff turnover.

Often referred to as a coach, mentor, facilitator, trainer or role model, a line manager wears a number of additional hats to their main function, which is to carry out the operational requirements of the enterprise. Consequently it is not uncommon for line managers to at times feel overwhelmed and in need of support. In many enterprises, line managers are often promoted to their management position despite the lack of management experience or education at the time of their appointment. They may have performed well in their operational functions and are rising through the enterprise's ranks, and this would be the next logical career progression for them. However, a line manager in such a position needs extensive training and support. Due to their symbiotic relationship with line managers, HRM is in the best position to support, assist and develop employees who are recently appointed into line management roles. This could take the form of:

Onboarding line managers: HRM needs to make sure that all line managers know exactly where they fit into the enterprise, including their roles, responsibilities and accountabilities etc. They need to understand what good management and employee engagement looks like so they can model and strive for this. They also need to fully comprehend the enterprise's mission, vision, values and purpose so that they can they share and promote it to their team members.

Recommending best practices: HRM could provide the line manager with thorough training on all relevant employee management systems in the enterprise. This will help them to manage their team members effectively.

Advising line managers: HRM must ensure that line managers are made aware of all relevant legislation and regulations regarding the management of employees. This includes information on how to avoid discrimination and bias in the workplace and instead focus on fairness, transparency and ethical treatment of employees.

Learning and development: Line managers should be made aware of the support tools and services (employee assistance programmes and occupational health services) the enterprise has access to, so that they can offer support and guidance to their own team members, as and when required. HRM needs to ensure that these managers partake in regular management skills and leadership training to ensure that they keep on learning and consciously and diligently apply their management skills.

Creating an "ask for help" culture: It is also helpful for HRM to have regular one-on-one review meetings and group team meets with all line managers so that they can reflect and give feedback on how things are going (what went well – or not – and the reason why) and thus learn from each other. They should be encouraged to ask for assistance in these meetings, and offered proper help. When line management has been carried out well, praise should be freely given.

Obtaining senior management buy-in: For HR – line manager initiatives to be truly successful, full senior management buy-in is essential. HRM needs to make sure that all members of senior management are aware that they serve as role models for their line managers, and that they should provide a proper measure of mentorship and coaching in support of the line managers' career progression. The relationships between line managers and their own managers and above, impacts on how they carry out their own management to the team members below them. Their actions reflect the management culture of the entire enterprise.

Administrative duties

Administrative duties include everything from managing compensation and employee benefits to developing, promoting and enforcing personnel policies. Salaries, bonuses, health-care or medical aid plans, employee investments and pension plans are typical elements found in a compensation and employee benefits package. Since this often makes up most of an enterprise's budget expenditure, and because it is of such importance to the employee, the HR department takes a strategic management approach to this administrative duty.

Once employed, a new hire not only needs to be educated on their role and responsibilities, but also about the company's policies, culture, ethics and rules of conduct. This responsibility falls on the HR department, and it is never a once-off affair. Policy updates and changes to rules of conduct have to be shared as and when they occur. Cracks in employee-employer and employee-employee (same level or manager) relations are bound to occur and HR should take the lead in settling any such conflicts reported to them. This includes dealing with any forms of harassment or situations where an employee feels unsafe or bullied, conducting disciplinary processes, handling grievances related to misconduct, and addressing any other employee concerns.

The HR department is the primary contact for work-site injuries or accidents. Working in conjunction with the Health and Safety manager of the enterprise, HR is responsible for selecting and training health and safety reps, ensuring that the enterprise complies with the laws that protect employees from hazards in the workplace, and that employees know these laws and the processes to follow should they be injured on-duty. The laws that apply to employee health and safety in South Africa include the Occupational Health and Safety Act (OHSA) (85 of 1993) and the Compensation for Occupational Injuries and Diseases Act (COID) (No 130 of 1993). Employee safety in the United States is regulated by the Occupational Safety and Health Administration (OSHA) which was created under the Occupation Safety and Health Act of 1970.

Human Resource Management and HR's Role in the Social Enterprise

Deloitte's 2018 report on Global Human Capital Trends mentions the 'rise of the social enterprise' and the significance of investing in human and social capital as a way of ensuring an enterprise's sustainability. Many people are currently mistrustful of their political and social institutions, and seem instead to place more trust in enterprises which champion causes and issues that are important to them. Cue the social enterprise. Not only are they governed by strict laws and required to be open, transparent and accountable to their stakeholders (and shareholders, if any), but they also invest in building social capital by engaging meaningfully with their all their stakeholders (employees, clients, local communities and society at large) to address social issues.

This aim of social capital, or meaningful engagement with stakeholders, is to produce benefits or resources for a common purpose (a social issue or need). Social capital thus is concerned with building interconnected networks of relationships between individuals and groups who live and work in a particular society. Based on shared identities, norms, values, cooperation, reciprocity, participation and high levels of trust, these relationships produce resources or benefits (value) for the whole of society and enable it to function effectively.

Investing in social capital cannot take place without investing in human capital. Training employees and stakeholders on how to engage meaningfully, facilitating the building of networks of relationships with stakeholders, and attracting and retaining the right stakeholders to build these networks all fall within the scope of the HR department. In the social enterprise, this demands a fundamental rethink of some of the current HR processes, activities, and strategies. We identify some of this rethinking in the following section.

Talent attraction and retention

Talent is everywhere, it just needs to be found. Sir Ken Robinson (2016) has likened human resources to natural resources. Playing on the mining theme, he states that these resources are buried deep and one has to "mine" them to find them. The social enterprise has an advantage over some corporates as their mission statement and focus tends to specifically address or serve some important social issue. This enables HRM to create, sell and market a unique Employee Value Proposition (EVP) that can attract and retain a particular kind of talent or desired target group. If there is one thing we have learnt about HR recruitment, then it is the importance of hiring the right talent. Not just in ability, but also in terms of aptitude and fit. An EVP is an excellent way to promote the enterprise as an employer of choice and for attracting a desired target group.

Some current recruitment practices gaining traction that are particularly suited to the social enterprise include:

Promoting diversity and multiculturalism in the workplace

A social enterprise is required to build its human and social capital and social ecosystem by engaging with its internal and external stakeholders.

These stakeholder demographics will most certainly include individuals from diverse and multicultural backgrounds. Reflecting external stakeholder demographics in the enterprise's workforce will go a long way to promoting it as an inclusive entity that can be trusted and engaged with. Applied to human capital, *diversity* incorporates those differences reflected in race, gender, class, sexual orientation, religion, ability, appearance, neurodiversity, and differing values, attitudes and beliefs. Similarly, multiculturalism recognizes that there are numerous cultures that make up humanity, with multiple norms.

Internally, diversity is important in recruiting and retaining employees. Multicultural and diverse workforces are known to have higher levels of creativity, innovation and problem-solving abilities. A diverse workforce comes with different perspectives and experiences and, if facilitated correctly, can be encouraged to share these openly so that it becomes a peer learning experience. This important facilitation role belongs to HRM. Predominantly done through diversity workshops, HRM can help educate employees on diversity and applicable cultural norms. They could also encourage the practice of respect and open dialogue to promote understanding as a way to eradicate fear, suspicion and the practice of discrimination. Promoting equal opportunity and equal access to development, and in some cases a more flexible work environment (e.g. in the case of a non-able bodied employee), is also a very important role for HRM.

In addition to the *diversity* categories listed previously, the social enterprise's HRM might want to consider paying attention to recruiting from the following groups:

A combination younger and older workers: Younger workers and their particular characteristics tend to breathe fresh life into an enterprise. Challenging rigid or outdated management styles and traditional business culture, the young and upcoming generations are big on diversity policies, flexible work arrangements, flattened management structures, meaningful work and recognition for it. Their use of technology and affinity with the digital world enhances their employability. Intrinsically motivated to succeed, these younger generations have a high uptake on L&D opportunities and, if nurtured properly on their career development path, can bring knowledge and value to the enterprise at which they are employed. This nurturing (in the form of training and mentoring in soft skills such as problem solving, critical thinking and relationship building) is best provided by older generation workers who have proven and necessary skills-sets (particularly soft skills) within the enterprise. The younger generation of workers can reciprocate by training and mentoring their older peers as they learn to use new technologies and re-examine their worldviews and biases. The benefits of this cross-generational learning can also be very cost-effective for the enterprise.

A combination of Paid-staff and Volunteers: A social enterprise is not averse to engaging with volunteers (seen as a stakeholder group) in its mission to carry out its function and purpose. Although unpaid, volunteers still seek after some nonmonetary rewards, which could include altruism, personal enrichment, recognition and community engagement. This personal level of commitment (often from the heart) leads to higher levels of motivation and hard work. When it comes to social enterprises, most volunteers provide a free service in return for an opportunity to gain experience (skills, abilities and knowledge) that will assist them in finding employment. This practice also contributes towards cost-saving for the enterprise and increases employee diversity.

It should be noted that multicultural and diverse workforces give an enterprise a competitive advantage. In addition to the trust and engagement fostered by the internal-external demographic reflection, the cultural sensitivity, local market knowledge, and insight that comes with the employees makes an enterprise more competitive and profitable.

Open Hiring

If COVID-19 has taught us anything, then it is to prepare for the unexpected. Any enterprise and its HR department need to continually engage in contingency recruitment planning and strategies, including integrating and testing alternative recruitment practices to ensure that they weather the unexpected (pandemics, natural disasters) and not so unexpected events (holiday season periods).

One such alternative recruitment method that is gaining traction is Open Hiring. Also known as inclusive or fair-chance hiring, it operates on a kind of first-come, first-served basis and forgoes some of the traditional recruitment practices. Firstly, any person may apply. Whether you have a criminal history, been out of the job market for an extended period of time, have no reference letters or lack appropriate CVs and resumes, come with a history of substance abuse or neurodiverse diagnoses (e.g. Asperger's syndrome or Bipolar Mood Disorder), all applicants are given equal consideration to being hired. As such, Open Hiring gives those people who would be excluded from a more traditional hiring process a much better shot at meaningful employment. Open Hiring does not mean that future applicants forgo screening. This still takes place, but more consideration is given to what the applicant can offer. This brings us to the second principle on which Open Hiring is based, that more emphasis is placed on the *ability* of an applicant to do the job required than their work experience or history. Included in this is the process of determining whether the applicant is the right fit for the enterprise. Skills can always be taught, but the right attitude takes a lot more work, thus making hiring the right fit a necessity from the get-go. Lastly, Open

Hiring embraces the belief that all people can thrive with the right support. Realizing that previously marginalized individuals who apply for work may have a number of barriers to overcome in order to stay in the job, enterprises engaging in Open Hiring often tend to offer employees useful benefits that will make their work-life much easier. These include counseling, child care, time-off for medical check-ups and transportation.

The Open Hiring model was pioneered by Greystone Bakery, a commercial bakery located in New York. Based on the founder's belief that recruitment needs to be conducted in an inclusive and non-judgmental manner, Greyston Bakery hires people without asking for a CV, interview or background check. Mike Brady, CEO of Greyston Bakery believes that everyone has the potential to be successful in the jobs offered at the Bakery, and so offers everyone the equal opportunity to apply.

Since then, many other enterprises, both large and small have championed Open Hiring, citing the biggest benefit as having access to a wide, diverse and readily available applicant pool with overlooked skill sets. Other benefits include cost-savings in recruitment, as the process is faster and requires less time for interviewing and screening. This means that the money saved in the recruiting process can be used elsewhere in the enterprise, for instance for training personnel.

As mentioned in the Introduction of this book, the purpose of the social enterprise is to address specific social issues (often caused by an imbalance between social, community and market forces) by harnessing these very forces to profitably deliver a product or service. We propose that Open Hiring can be used as a potential tool by social enterprises to help address some of these imbalances.

Poverty, and the social issues that tend to accompany it, is very difficult to escape when there are no opportunities afforded to those entrapped in it. A lack of employment opportunities is one thing. The situation becomes dire when the opportunities *do* exist but marginalized people are repeatedly excluded from them due to their prior history. By applying the principles of Open Hiring, enterprises can help to bring about positive changes to the communities where they operate or draw their employees from. The more community members that are employed, the greater the standard of living in that particular community. A working community is able to rise above poverty when it experiences the resultant improvements in areas like health and safety, education, and community services. Improved social capital also helps to reduce mistrust and strengthens civic engagement.

The knock-on effects for the enterprise include a more appreciative and loyal workforce, and this results in improved retention rates. The appreciation and loyalty from a marginalized person who knows they have been given an opportunity to improve their lives because someone (the enterprise) has cared enough to invest in their success, cannot be underestimated. This loyalty extends to the person's family and greater community, and it goes a long way to building trust and brand sentiment. It also will resonate with the social enterprise's external stakeholders beyond the community.

While Open Hiring does come with a lot of positives, there are some risks that enterprises need to be aware of. Despite the good intentions of hiring applicants from marginalized backgrounds, the enterprise could face punitive damages and legal liabilities should that particular employee harm another employee or stakeholder in any way. This would particularly apply in the case of someone with a criminal past. Thus it makes employee support vital once applicants are hired (e.g. counseling support for known problems or vices). When it comes to background checks, HR can individually assess any criminal records for job candidates or even keep a criminal background screening policy and decision matrix to avoid a blanket no-hire policy for those with criminal records. Not everyone in the enterprise may be happy with the Open Hiring policy. Whilst the potential applicant may be a good fit for the enterprise, divisional mangers or supervisors may wish to vet them before including them in their teams. Even when they are hired, it would still be necessary for HR to run diversity and team building workshops to help overcome any bias, fears or discrimination. With Open Hiring, you really need to know your business and the kind of talent you are looking for. Open Hiring does not work for all enterprises. The ones who tend to do better at it are those that have positions or roles that don't require a specific, specialized skill set or many years of experience.

Authors Corner: In the field of Corporated Social Investment, one of the authors has had numerous interactions with Sihle Tshabalala, co-founder and CEO of Quirky 30 NPC and Quirky Innovations Pty/Ltd. Sihle is an ex-offender and ex-gang member, but is also a successful, award winning (2014 LeadSA's Hero, Mail and Guardian 200 Young South Africans award, 2015 Spark Changemaker award, 2016 WSA International Speaker, Juror and Mentor, 2016 TEDx Fellow and a Levi's Pioneer Nation speaker) **social enterprise leader**, and one who is giving back to his community in a massive way. During his time in prison, he became a key member of the Group of Hope programme (a prisoner-initiated project that changed prison rehabilitation in SA), and it was here that he decided that he would spend his life to help others avoid the mistakes he had made. Since leaving prison, he has co-founded Brothers for All, taught himself how to code, and has become a key voice in his community and a game changer in teaching high school drop outs, teenage moms, unemployed youth, ex-offenders and offenders skills such as Computer Programming/

Coding, Entrepreneurship, and Digital Marketing.

Sihle embodies the attitude and forward-thinking we believe more social enterprises, or any enterprise for that matter, should adopt when it comes to HR recruitment strategies and practices. He recognizes that there is an untapped pool of talent in members of society who would usually be excluded from traditional hiring practices (e.g., the group of individuals listed in the previous paragraph) and that with the right attitude and support (and less focus on their history) they can become fully employable, productive members of society. Although his work would be classified as Learning and Development, Sihle's model of business, his successful results and those of his protégés, should be a green light to anyone wanting to engage in Open Hiring.

For more on Sihle's remarkable story and social enterprise Quirky 30, please read the extract from News24 Journalist, Tammy Petersen (12 July 2018) **Ex-con opening windows of opportunity to make tech hubs out of SA townships** https://www.news24.com/news24/SouthAfrica/News/ex-con-opening-windows-of-opportunity-to-make-tech-hubs-out-of-sa-townships-2018071213

Find out more about Quirky Innovations at https://www.quirkyinnovations. Sihle Tshabala's bio can also be found on Wetopia Acadamey's website https://odawetopia.wordpress.com/about/.

Cultivating innovation and collaboration

Build agile teams

The social enterprise serves a much wider range of stakeholders which is not limited to their own employees, clients, shareholders, communities, but also embraces society at large. With this comes a complex set of challenges and opportunities that need to be addressed, and this cannot be done without the innovative, cross-functional collaboration of employees throughout the social enterprise. This cross-functional collaboration can be achieved by building agile networks of teams, made up of employees who can bring the necessary expertise and solutions to those areas needing attention. Building these agile teams is the responsibility of Management, together with their HR counterparts, and it requires giving these employees more autonomy or self-direction to get the job done. To work effectively, self-managing teams need direct access to and support from their HR department as and when needed, and Management must continuously communicate clear direction and vision. In addition, HR software systems and tools can help these employees to manage their day-to-day HR activities effectively and address everyday administrative tasks (e.g. absence, attendance trackers, etc.), so HR need only be contacted for more demanding issues.

Build a culture of continuous learning

Most enterprises are adopting the practice of building continuous learning and usually have dedicated L&D departments that focus on this. This is certainly true for most enterprises in South Africa, as Skills Development is a weighted part of the BBBEE scorecard. However, most of this learning tends to be formal, structured L&D programs that require employees to complete courses within a specified period of time, and where certificates and credits are given in recognition of competency achieved. Programs are likely to focus specifically on the Skills Development Plan depicting the enterprise's upskilling needs and gaps and future competencies.

Social enterprises, because they deal with such a wide variety of stakeholders and due to their dual focus on social issues and profit, tend to take a different approach to L&D. Working with communities, society at large, and the very nature of social issues and social ecosystems themselves, means that employees are often called on to apply flexibility when carrying out their duties. A social enterprise employee who can work within context, be comfortable with change and, at times, ambiguity is a valuable team member who possesses important skills. Moravec (2016) has termed these type of employees as "knowmadic workers" or "knowmads". Knowmads possess the key traits of cultivated book knowledge, developed soft skills, and mature personal knowledge gained through experience. The combined application of these traits will add value to the work they do.

HR and their L&D counterparts in a social enterprise should structure a learning culture that includes a combination of personal and book knowledge and soft skills development. Opportunities for practical soft skills development can be embedded in book knowledge programs. Experiential learning and individual learning journey portfolios need to be a part of every employees' key performance indicators (KPI) as these go a long way in promoting cognitive, affective, and personal assimilation of learning. Time must be set aside for both individual and peer reflection and feedback, the latter promoting the sharing of experiences and group learning.

HR should also focus on measuring the effectiveness of the social enterprise learning programs. An indication of their efficacy is shown by improved employee performance, productivity, and satisfaction, along with enhanced levels of employee-generated innovation and new value.

Rethink Rewards and Recognition and Employee Benefits

Applying the knowmad learning culture in a social enterprise will not only improve employee performance but, more importantly, will increase employee-generated innovation and bring new value to service delivery and operation. This will have a knock-on effect on the way employees get recognized and rewarded, and to what employee benefits they value most.

Knowmad-trained employees are an intuitive lot and it would be hard for any HRM team to try and offer any 'cut-and-paste' rewards and benefits. Employees want rewards and benefits that are meaningful, efficient, practical, and that contribute towards an enhanced employee experience. Two examples of some current rethinking in terms of these rewards and benefits are discussed in the next few paragraphs.

Creating a bonus using Open Book Management (OBM): Structuring a bonus system forms part of the enterprise's annual budgeting system. Once the enterprise has set its sales and cost-cutting goals for the coming year, then its management should determine how the bonus system will be structured, and communicate this to all employees prior to the new fiscal year. They also need to decide how frequently the bonus will be paid out and if the bonus is cumulative. In other words, will any unrealized part of the bonus roll over into the next period if the enterprise fails to meet its stated goal? Will the bonus be paid monthly, quarterly, semiannually or annually? Management must also set aside sufficient funding to cover the bonus for when it is realized. A failure to do so will undermine the credibility of management and the bonus system.

A key difference between traditional bonus structures and OBM is that the financial goals and process whereby it will be paid out are made known to all employees. With reference to our discussion on OBM in Chapter 4, one of its key components is that management must understand the key cost numbers that drive the success or failure of the enterprise. Management must communicate those numbers to all employees. By reducing these cost drivers, enterprises are more profitable. They can share those profits with employees after setting aside a portion of those profits for reinvestment or to fulfill revenue-sharing or dividend obligations to their investors.

This knowledge and reward is not a prize for a few employees, but rather all employees are eligible to receive the bonus, albeit on the proportional basis. Bonuses can be structured in such a way that they reward employees at the lower tiers of the organization. When viewed through this lens, OBM can be a way to provide employees not only rewards in the next twelve months, but it can also be a way to tackle the salary gap as well as social inequality. The bonus needs to be meaningful, and it can only be so if it is sizeable and in proportion to employees' base salaries. The bonus is not an entitlement. It is only paid when it is earned. As mentioned before, when employees know where they stand in terms of performance (through regular performance appraisals), and understand how they stand to benefit from their contribution to the enterprise (open communication, fair play, adherence to policies and HR etc.), their performance, productivity, trust, and loyalty tend to improve.

If the social enterprise is organized as a for-profit, then its owners can decide to offer financial rewards for meeting goals in the form of shares or a cash bonus. If the enterprise pursues the share option, then it will need to consider creating an ESOP to facilitate this. The only option that is open to social enterprises that are organized as non-profits and cooperatives is to pay a cash bonus to employees should they reach the agreed targets.

Financial wellness employee benefits offerings: HRM is currently placing more focus on teaching their employees to handle their finances more competantly. Financial woes are a leading cause of employee health issues and absenteeism, and thus have a large impact on productivity. Seen as an act of good social responsibility, employees should receive training on how to practically increase their financial sustainability (e.g. how to save, invest, and eradicate and/or avoid debt).

Authors Corner: PAYMENOW – A South African 'financial wellness' employee benefit offering.

Operating in the field as Employee Assistance Practitioner, one of the authors has been constantly inundated by employers needing advice on how to help their employees deal with financial issues. Whether through crises, exorbitant increases in cost of living vs. earning potential, mismanagement of finances, or lack of financial know-how, many South African employees are finding themselves in dire financial situations. The situation is made worse by easy access to credit and loans from money-lenders or loan sharks (sometimes these are colleagues operating illegally on business premises). These loan sharks offer easy cash at exorbitant interest rates, at times as much as 40%, which compounds an already dire situation. The employer feels it in the form of absenteeism (ill health due to stress and avoidance of loan sharks – especially if this lending is taking place on the business premises during work hours) and loss of productivity.

PAYMENOW, a new app on the South African market is great example of an app-type service that would be especially beneficial to those employees who perhaps fit the open hire demographics, such as minimum income earners and school and university graduates entering the job market. PAYMENOW is a financial wellness and inclusion platform that allows employees early access to already earned wages, the percentage of which is customized to each particular enterprise. Its working premise rests on easing the burden inflicted by payday and micro lenders through real-time access to already-earned wages through an app that is integrated with the employer's payroll system.

Whilst some enterprises do pay some of their employees weekly or fortnightly, the true value of PAYMENOW is delivered through the attached educational element. Employees receive training and advice on how to migrate from being debt-ridden to debt-free, and to set and reach their financial goals. They are encouraged to engage in responsible financial behavior, which includes saving and budgeting.

Developing Business Vocation-orientated leaders

Originating in Christianity, the term vocation[1] originally referred to an occupation to which a person felt called to or for which they were suited and trained in. Believing that God has bestowed gifts and talents to every person, Christians consider it their duty to use these gifts to serve the greater common good, whether this be in their professional, family or community (church and civic) life. In this context, social enterprises were considered vehicles in which people could exercise their gifts and talents for the greater common good.

In 1908, Frank Parsons established Vocational Guidance and with it came the evolution of the term vocation: it now included the development of talents and abilities in the choice and enjoyment of a career, giving vocation more of an inward focus on personal gain than outward service. It would seem that some enterprises today function just for the personal gain they can afford their owners and shareholders. Some employees work for the these reasons, often finding themselves driven by self-fulfillment and the need to amass and attain personal wealth. This is hardly surprising as, for a long time in the business world, the narrative has been performance at all costs. Cut-throat competition, excessive demands for efficiency, speed and profitability on a daily basis, together with market logic all place intense pressure on enterprises and their leaders. Without these qualities, the enterprise would not survive. However, the downside is the tendency towards greed, corruption, burn-out, and the associated breakdown of family and community life.

In Pope Francis' 2018 address to business and executive leaders at the 26th UNIAPAC World Congress, he advocated for these leaders to take the noble idea of vocation back to its roots, and referred to the biblical verse that much is expected from those who have been given much. In essence, if business leaders were to apply the principle of generosity or the "logic of gift" within normal economic activity and commercial relationships, the benefits could flow towards the good of all. When business is understood by society at large as a vehicle for leaders and employees to serve the common good before serving [their] narrower interests, human dignity and civility is brought back to the business world.

The social enterprise is perhaps the closest model of business we can think of that represents the concept of business as a vocation. If business is seen as a vocation, a leader is tasked with three interconnected goals. However, these goals are already expected from the social enterprise leader. Firstly, leaders are tasked to produce and deliver goods and services of excellence – the "real deal" stuff. Although focused on keeping the enterprise sustainable, these

---

1 Oxford Dictionary: Late Middle English from Old French, or from Latin vocatio(n-), from vocare 'to call'. https://www.lexico.com/definition/vocation

leaders remain vigilant and open to opportunities to servc underprivileged communities in significant need. To be able to work and support oneself and one's family is vital for anyone's dignity and self-respect. A person's level of dignity and self-respect is raised when they are able to work in environments where they feel productive, valued, recognized, and rewarded. Leaders who provide good work opportunities and environments will treat employees as humans and not just as instruments of production, and invest in them as capital expenditure (capex), not operating expenditure (opex), are contributing to the full human development of employees. Lastly, by being good stewards of the resources given to them, leaders not only create sustainable wealth for the enterprise, but also ensure the fair distribution of this wealth to all stakeholders who have made the wealth possible (e.g. employees, customers, investors, suppliers, and communities).

Askinosie (2017) calls on social enterprises to create their own business vocation. This is a collective internal product which is created by its employees. They identify their collective skills and match these to the unmet need which they see in their community and which they feel compelled to address. They then look at how they can incorporate addressing that need into their daily operations. Askinosie reports that implementing this concept at Askinosie Chocolate has increased employee morale and provides the social enterprise with invaluable and genuine opportunities for marketing and advocacy.

In conclusion, good leadership is essential for any enterprise, but even more so for the social enterprise. Employees in a social enterprise place value on seeing their leaders act as roles models in carrying out the enterprise's vision and mission. Leaders need to be seen working in the trenches and getting their hands dirty (i.e., doing visible social good, showing up at community rallies, and handing out food parcels if need be, etc.). Not everyone is cut out to be a leader and it falls to the HR department to make sure that the existing leaders or leadership team remain in possession of the necessary leadership competencies (and timeously upskill when required). In the light of the importance of leadership strategy, HR professionals should also consider leadership competencies when selecting and developing employees for future leadership roles.

Chapter 6

MARKETING SOCIAL ENTERPRISES

Marketing is not limited to the for-profit business sector – it is a process that affects every organization. There are commonalities between traditional for-profit business and social enterprises when it comes to producing and marketing a product (it is understood here to include physical product or service). The product that they produce must be of a superior quality. It must meet a specific need in the market, and be at a price that customers are willing to pay. Customers must enjoy easy access to the product, and they must be aware of its existence and the benefits it will give them.

Business textbooks have termed these requirements as the *marketing mix* or the 4 P's. These refer to *P*roduct, *P*lace, *P*rice and *P*romotion.

Marketing ethics for Social Enterprises

Tama-Rutigliano (2019) shares four unethical marketing practices that are all too common. These include misleading advertising, the invasion of potential customers' privacy without first securing their consent, the use of controversy to raise awareness about a product, and the manipulation of customer's emotions to pressure them to purchase a product. While these practices are not encouraged in the traditional for-profit sector, social enterprises must be especially careful not to engage in them. Practices such as these will harm their reputation and limit the social good they wish to perform.

Social enterprises must set, attain, and maintain the highest standards for the product or service they produce. The reason for this is that their customers often assume that a product from a social enterprise is inferior to one produced by a traditional business. This perception is even stronger when customers are aware that they are purchasing this product from a social enterprise that is also a non-profit. The only way social enterprises can overcome this obstacle is by delivering a product that is superior from its inception, and is accompanied by outstanding customer service. This ethos of quality must be an integral part of the enterprise's organizational philosophy and culture.

Social enterprises generally serve individuals and groups who, for a variety of reasons, find themselves marginalized from the mainstream of society. They engage these discounted groups either as employees or as customers; however, this provides both a strategic marketing opportunity and the opportunity to commit ethical faux pas. Inviting these employees and customers to share their story on marketing materials and product packaging is a powerful way to market the unique product that the enterprise offers. But the enterprise must only do so with the full and voluntary permission of that employee and client. It needs to respect the whole person by naming them and telling their story. Fair Trade products, which often carry the name and story of the households that grew the product being consumed, is an example of this. It is satisfying to know that one's purchase of a box of tea will directly support the household who grew and harvested the tea leaves which are found inside that packaged box. But social enterprises need to be aware that naming the person can be dangerous to their clients as well. For example, enterprises employing or serving victims of domestic violence could decide not to feature photos of their staff and customers on their products. This protects those individuals from further harm.

Social enterprises must always be honest when including stories and statistics about the social impact that they are delivering. Every statement they make needs to be true. While their vision might include effecting large systemic change, social enterprises need to be humble and point to the impact that their specific intervention is making in the lives of those whom they are serving directly. They need to link this individual-level change to larger and positive systems change to remind their audiences that addressing the structural and systemic causes and consequences of inequality requires dedicated work from many social enterprises and other players over the long haul.

Members of the World Fair Trade Organization, a global community of social enterprises, have agreed to adhere to 10 principles to govern all facets of their business operations. Incorporating these principles into their core business philosophy, product, and operation design positions social enterprises to market their product in an ethical and authentic way. By educating their staff and customers about these principles and including them when they deliver the impact and outcome reports to their stakeholders, social enterprises will have a readily available ethical checklist which they can follow when deciding how to market a new product. They can also use this checklist when they consider entering a cause marketing campaign with a traditional for-profit partner.

The World Fair Trade Organization presents these 10 principles as follows.

Source: World Fair Trade Organization.
https://wfto.com/our-fair-trade-system#10-principles-of-fair-trade.

Human and Process Components of a Social Enterprise Marketing Plan.
It has been our experience that marketing plans for social enterprises begin with an idea for a new product (goods or services). Subsequently, a team is built around the idea, and charged to investigate whether the idea is viable and how to bring it to fruition. The basic team structure will look something like Figure 1.

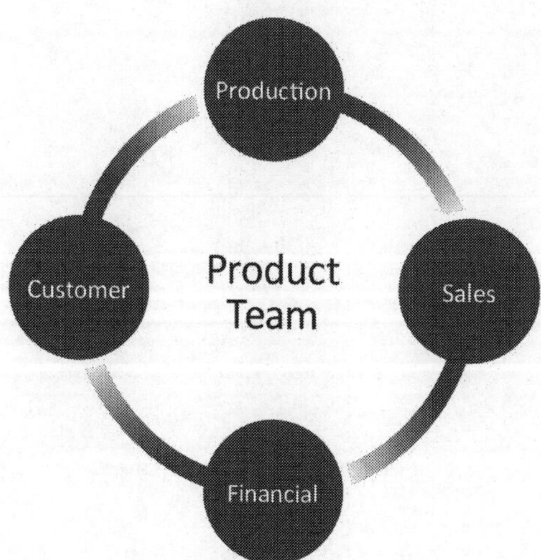

Fig.1: Human and Process Components of a Social Enterprise Marketing Plan

Assembling this team requires adherence to a few principles. Firstly, the team is to consist of no fewer than five people but no more than nine. Secondly, four groups should be represented on the team: those responsible for creating the product, those responsible for its marketing and sales, those responsible for tracking costs and expenses, and those who account for the initial startup investment being made in the idea. Finally, the team should include a reliable customer who will treat this process in confidence, and who believes in the enterprise yet who is authentic enough to provide honest feedback to the rest of the team.

Lynch and Walls (2009) write that every successful marketing plan which is developed and used by a social enterprise contains four components. By employing, and then repeating, these four components in a disciplined way, the social enterprise then creates a virtuous marketing cycle. This virtuous cycle is presented in Figure 2.

Fig.2: A Virtuous Marketing Cycle

A virtuous marketing plan starts with the design, testing and production of quality goods or services. This product can take the form of a consumable such as coffee, condiments, chocolate, clothing, or household products. It can also take the form of an asset such as housing or machinery. An example of services would be loan products or community mediation. The social enterprise creates these goods and services through a reinforcing cycle of research, prototype development, testing and refinement. At the same time as it follows these steps to create a quality product or service, the production team engages closely with its financial counterparts who track the set up and production costs associated with each step. The financial information they collect will help the enterprise to determine whether the total cost of the final product or service is lower than the price consumers will be willing to pay for it. If not, the team either needs to refine the product or stop pursuing it, since the social enterprise cannot run at a loss. The new product or service line must be a profitable one.

The next phase of the virtuous marketing cycle is that of superior service. It is here that the sales team plays a key role by engaging with customers to understand their expectations and to resolve customer complaints when these arise. When social enterprises recruit salespeople, they must look for the following characteristics: individuals who are optimistic, who have a service mindset, and who have an engaging personality. These individuals should be curious about the social enterprise and willing to learn about its mission; they should treat the rest of the enterprise staff as colleagues, and must be able to communicate to the consumer how the purchase of goods or services will allow the enterprise to further its social mission.

While hiring a superior sales team is important, the delivery of superior service is only sustainable when it is baked into the enterprise's culture and where every individual employee visibly exhibits a spirit of service every working day. A culture of superior service is most visible when individuals collaborate across departments (silos) to solve a problem with a customer or when part of the organization experiences a loss of key personnel due to illness or resignation. This culture is particularly apparent if collaboration happens during a critical production or service run. Creating a culture of service begins with the enterprise's founders and leaders.

The third phase of the virtuous marketing cycle is competitive pricing. Superior service and a quality product or service will only be rewarded if the enterprise receives the price they are asking their customer to pay. The customer must be willing to pay a price that consists of cost + margin if the social enterprise is to remain a viable entity. A social enterprise begins to set the price of its goods or services when it first conceptualizes them and when it begins to test them amongst its target market. Some of the early questions to ask consumers when testing the idea and prototype include "*Is this a product that you would find useful?" "Would you be willing to purchase it?" "How much would you pay for it?*" The social enterprise also needs to study similar products to identify their competitors. Learning the prices that these competitors are charging for their products is part of this research phase and will be ongoing throughout the product's life cycle.

The final stage of the virtuous marketing cycle is that of co-creation. This stage occurs where the enterprise engages with its customers. Interaction begins at the research phase when the social enterprise identifies the target market for its proposed product, and conducts focus groups with a representative sample from that market. The feedback gathered from these focus groups helps the enterprise's team to design and produce a quality product. It is this interaction that turns the marketing cycle into a virtuous one. Once these initial customers purchase and consume the product, the enterprise continues to engage them for the purpose of building their loyalty to its brand (mission and product). It creatively and authentically turns them into ambassadors for the enterprise's work and product, through the building of a genuine relationship in which customers feel valued and appreciated.

As this virtuous cycle grows and the customers become more invested in the enterprise and its product, the enterprise can experiment with newer, niche products which allow for different levels of pricing. This is commonly referred to as premium pricing.

Authors Corner: A new product opportunity, owner-occupied repairs, emerged from the strategic planning process undertaken by a Habitat for Humanity affiliate in 2012 (we referred to this strategic process in Chapter 2). Although the long-time homeowners from the neighborhood which Habitat for Humanity was helping to revitalize expressed their appreciation for the new homes that were being built amongst theirs, they also lamented the absence of loan products and construction services they might use to improve their own properties. With the support of the Habitat Board of Directors, one of the authors undertook to work with a group of these homeowners to design and test a product to meet this need. He used the four components in the following way to inform the process of designing an owner-occupied repair program.

1. Habitat for Humanity created a small task force comprising two homeowners and three Habitat staff members who worked in sales, financing, and construction, respectively.
2. The team met at the homes of the homeowners.
3. The task force sampled a cross section of housing in the neighborhood to determine the types of improvements most needed. They also investigated the obstacles that had up until then prevented the residents from addressing these proposed improvements.
4. The Habitat team shared information they had collected from other housing agencies who were engaged in owner-occupied home repairs. It was important to understand their best practices as well as the lessons they had learnt from failures.
5. The information collected in steps 3 and 4 was used to design a pilot loan and construction product.

6. The product was purchased by the first homeowner, the repairs were completed, and the loan repayment scheduled and implemented.
7. Habitat staff who served on the task force remained actively involved with this first customer to solve problems when they arose and use the customer's experiences to help improve the product.
8. The satisfied customer then helped Habitat to promote the use of this product amongst other homeowners who resided in the same neighborhood.

Engaging with a Cause Marketing Partner

Cause marketing occurs when a traditional business approaches a non-profit, or a social enterprise that is incorporated as a non-profit, to request the latter to allow that business to use the enterprise's logo and name on some of their products and promotional materials. The business pays the non-profit for the privilege of doing so because they benefit from having their product or name endorsed by the non-profit, while the association provides the non-profit with a welcome infusion of cash as well as the opportunity to engage and educate new supporters. Cause marketing can allow both organizations to improve their brand.

It has been our experience that social enterprises should approach cause marketing with care. They should consider whether their mission and core values would be compromised if they entertained a cause marketing request. If the answer to this question is "no", then they should create a policy which outlines how they would go about assessing such a request. This policy must include what criteria they would use to assess such a proposal and it must also indicate who in the organization would be responsible for negotiating the terms of a cause marketing contract and with whom the final approval authority rests.

Lynch and Walls (2009) allude to these points when they recommend that social enterprises address the following items during their negotiations with the cause marketer and their client, the traditional business.

- Social enterprises need to do their due diligence to ensure that they are entering into partnership with a reputable business. Social enterprises should remember that a major motivation for that business is the financial and reputational rewards that they will reap from this partnership. The business may also be using this partnership to atone for past practices and products which were found to be unethical and controversial. Therefore, social enterprises must consider how their key stakeholders will respond to such a partnership. They also need to research whether their business partner has run afoul of advocacy groups in other communities or even other countries around the world.

- Both parties should consider whether this partnership is exclusive to the two of them and whether it will restrict them from pursuing partnerships with other businesses who operate in the same sector. There are pros and cons to exclusivity clauses, and these must be carefully weighed on a case-by-case basis.
- Social enterprises need to identify all their interests when they are offered a cause marketing contract. They should remain aware of these short- and long-term interests when they review and negotiate the terms of the contract that will govern the cause marketing partnership.
- Lynch and Walls (2009) recommend that the social enterprise seek a long-term commitment from their cause marketing partner. This makes sense given the amount of work the social enterprise will need to invest in this partnership. However, it also depends on how exclusive the business partner wishes this relationship to be.
- All the negotiations which flow between the social enterprise and its future business partner must be captured in a legal contract. It should cover items such as the conditions and process which both parties will follow when exiting from the partnership. The contract should also stipulate how they will address any disputes which might arise during its implementation.

Authors Corner: While one of the authors was serving as the senior executive at an affordable housing enterprise, the latter participated in a national competition and received a significant financial award from a large national bank to help the enterprise capitalize its expansion. The award was widely publicized through traditional- and social media following a public awards ceremony. Within a few hours, social media posts which were critical of the housing enterprise's decision to accept the award, were made on some of the enterprise's media platforms. The criticism centered around the bank's role in foreclosing on residential properties in the aftermath of the Great Recession of 2008 that was largely fueled by the deceptive lending practices in the subprime mortgage market.

The enterprise's marketing staff analyzed the criticism and then engaged with the critic in a thoughtful and non-escalatory way. Their analysis showed that the critic did not reside in their community and that these posts were not picked up by other visitors to the enterprise's pages. The enterprise's measured response quelled further comments from the critic.

Marketing Tactics for Social Enterprises

Our experience is that the following six categories of marketing tactics produced good sales when used by our social enterprises to promote and advertise their products. These categories are informed by the ten tactics put forward by Lynch and Walls (2009) which are based on their collective experience and that of their peers.

Creating and empowering Brand Ambassadors

The role of ambassador has long been associated with the field and practice of international relations. In that context, the term *ambassador* refers to accredited diplomats who are based in a foreign country where they represent their own country's political and economic interests. The use of this term has migrated to the field of international business since enterprises of all shapes and sizes often source and sell their product in international markets. The adoption, by business management theorists, of the systems approach to organizations has popularized the view that a member of a business who engages in sales, marketing and executive leadership will serve as their company's ambassador. But rather than promoting national interests, these ambassadors promote a particular brand and the products that are associated with it. They also help the social enterprise to manage its relationships with external stakeholders.

Social enterprises are no exception to this practice. However, there are four stakeholders that social enterprises should consider when recruiting their brand ambassadors. These groups include their customers, their suppliers, their employees, and their board members. For those social enterprises who are legally required to have a Board of Directors, the Board members serve as automatic brand ambassadors.

Once they have been recruited and have agreed to serve in this role, Brand Ambassadors need to be trained and equipped with promotional material that enable them to be effective in this role. Our experience has been that there is a direct correlation between how much the enterprise invests in training their ambassadors and how effective these employees are when marketing the social enterprise within their circles of influence and at events. It is also important that the Brand Ambassadors are authentic when they are in these spaces and that they can draw upon their own experiences with the enterprise and its products. This makes it even more important for the social enterprise to consistently deliver a quality product that is supported by exceptional customer service.

Quantifying the Mission

Successful social enterprises use their physical space and packaging to share their social impact with their customers and employees. Visitors to the downtown branch of Z-Beans Coffee, a US-based social enterprise which markets itself as an Ecuadorian coffee importer and roaster (www.zbeanscoffee.com), encounter wall murals which introduce them to the small farmers who grow the coffee sold in the shop.

Another social enterprise that we worked with created a visually appealing notice board near their checkout location. They used this board to share their annual goals and pinned regular updates on it to chart the progress that they had made towards achieving these goals. Some of these goals included the number of houses that they had sold and repaired during the year, as well as the economic impact they had made. By updating this board on a regular basis, the social enterprise kept its customers and employees engaged with, and responsible for, its mission.

Every report and piece of marketing material produced by a social enterprise can quantify its mission and impact. Annual reports are common in the non-profit and for-profit sectors since these groups mobilize capital from the larger public. Issuing an annual report, which uses the principles of integrated reporting to show these stakeholders how the social enterprise has mobilized the Six Capitals to deliver its product, should be part of every social enterprise's annual marketing calendar and practice. Those social enterprises who are organized as non-profits should also embrace the concept of the Six Capitals, re-orient their product and processes to use them, and adopt the integrated reporting approach when preparing their annual reports.

Experiential marketing

Experiential marketing refers to a process whereby a social enterprise's suppliers, supporters and customers co-create its product. While doing so, they become inspired by the mission and the impact the enterprise seeks to realize. These stakeholders become more deliberate and informed consumers of this product and this tangible engagement may even translate into them becoming brand ambassadors for the social enterprise.

We have seen social enterprises use site tours of their operations, team-builds, and pop-up replicas of their products as examples of experiential marketing.

Marketing Jujitsu

People expect social enterprises, especially those that are organized as non-profits, to always have their hands out with the expectation of receiving support while giving little to nothing in return. To counter this belief, social enterprises turn the tables when they engage in marketing jujitsu and provide some of their product at an event or venue where they are traditionally not represented. This may involve purchasing space for a booth at an event or venue, or donating gift certificates which the event attendees can redeem by visiting the social enterprise. By making a strategic investment of this magnitude, the enterprise can reach into a previously untapped market.

Opportunities for Conversations

Creating Brand Ambassadors as well as the collateral material that they will use (e.g., pop-up replicas that intrigue the target customer's visual senses) provides opportunities for conversations. Social enterprises should explore their local media to see how they might be invited to share more about their product and mission on those platforms. These might include local radio and podcast shows and at community events. In addition, COVID-19 has opened the realm of virtual meetings which are inexpensive opportunities for social enterprises to create brand awareness.

Marketing Platforms

The digital revolution has revolutionized the ways in which social enterprises can, and must, market their product. However, the advent of internet sites and social media forums should not lead social enterprises to rely solely on digital marketing to reach their customers and other stakeholders. Factors such as the location of the social enterprise, whether it is marketing a niche product, the demographic and socio-economic profile of its customer base and the literacy rate of those customers, will determine which platforms it should use to reach its desired market.

The choice of platforms begins with identifying the enterprise's intended target market and understanding where this group gets their media information. This information can be sourced by talking with a representative sample from that target market. Another way is to engage with groups and organizations who already work in that space. Once an enterprise knows where its potential customers source their information, they can decide which platforms to use. These can be traditional advertising spaces such as print, radio, television, and billboards. Depending on the product and its market, platforms can include trade and market shows, social media, websites, and promotional giveaways.

An often-overlooked marketing resource are the employees of the social enterprise. Our own example of this comes from our work with Habitat for Humanity. Potential homebuyers would regularly approach the construction staff while they were supervising building on a house. Habitat's homeowner services manager quickly realized that she could increase her marketing team by providing her construction colleagues with some key information. This consisted of a one-page overview of the homebuyer application process, homebuyer qualifications and the manager's contact details.

Inexpensive and valuable marketing tools – such as ensuring that all employees wear a branded uniform, can answer basic questions about the enterprise, its work, and its products, and use the enterprise's physical space to tell its story – should be fully exploited.

Finally, the social enterprise's supporters and funders provide another marketing resource because they have a vested interest in the enterprise's success.

Stakeholder Engagement and Reporting (King Code)

A *stakeholder* is a person or groups of people with a vested interest in an enterprise. Types of stakeholders include investors, employees, customers, suppliers, communities, and governments. Being a stakeholder means that they can impact, or are impacted by, the enterprise's operations and goals. Stakeholders provide financial and practical support, resources, and help grow services etc. Their influence spreads everywhere and, if adequately engaged by the enterprise, can be a wealth of information, loyalty, and support for its future growth. *Stakeholder engagement* is the process by which an enterprise engages with its stakeholders.

Greenwood (2007) defines stakeholder engagement as the practices the organization undertakes to positively involve stakeholders in organizational activities. Positive involvement of stakeholders in organizational activities equates to adequate engagement. For this to happen, an exchange between the enterprise and the stakeholder involving dialogue and communication needs to take place on a regular basis. The more the enterprise communicates openly, honestly, and consistently with their stakeholders, the more comprehensively they will understand what the stakeholders want. The enterprise will also come to understand the stakeholders' timeline for realizing those wants, the extent of their loyalty and buy-in, and the influence of the enterprise's operations and services on the stakeholder. From the stakeholder's perspective being entrusted with information and valued enough to be asked for an opinion, or being included in transparent decision-making, helps to build their sense of involvement, accountability, and loyalty. This perception of influence goes a long way to ensure that stakeholders support the decisions taken to safeguard the enterprise's sustainability and growth.

Stakeholder engagement is a fundamental component of ensuring an enterprise's sustainability. Without input from key stakeholder groups, an enterprise is limited to its own reporting, interpretations, and assessments of how things are going. Without a 360° outward focus, valuable opportunities could be missed to modify or change activities or programs, should anything not be going according to plan. A *stakeholder engagement plan* is required to ensure that all relevant stakeholders are represented and consistently engaged throughout the enterprise's lifespan or that of its particular project or product. This plan ensures that the right people get the right information at the right time and set the rules for how they can contribute towards this information. Owing to their dual mission of ensuring profit and meeting a social need or issue, social enterprises usually have a wide range of stakeholders with diverse and conflicting interests, and thus really need to pay attention to their stakeholder engagement.

Stakeholder engagement begins with mapping (i.e., the process of identifying and prioritizing the enterprise's internal and external stakeholders). Mitchell,

Agle and Wood (1997) identify and prioritize stakeholders according to the three dimensions of power, legitimacy, and urgency. Power is concerned with the physical, financial, or material, and/or symbolic resources a stakeholder can offer an enterprise to help it achieve its outcomes. The priority and influence of the stakeholder will depend on the power they have to help bring about the outcomes. The more legitimate a stakeholder is in terms of its reputation, actions, norms, values, and beliefs, the more desirable they are to work with. Lastly, the urgency of a stakeholder's claim defines how promptly the enterprise will address its concerns.

Then, with long-term focus as the driving force, the plan sets out the engagement logistics and methods to be used, and the expectations of key stakeholders in the engagement process, as well as the rules of engagement. These rules will include how to ensure equitable stakeholder contribution, mitigate tension, and proactively resolve disputes. The final part of the plan states the next actions (as gained from stakeholder interaction and feedback) against goal progress and the plan for the next engagement session. All selected stakeholders are informed upfront of the stakeholder engagement plan.

Stakeholder Mapping is a process and visual tool used to clarify and categorize the various stakeholders within an enterprise so that the enterprise can effectively network and communicate with them. **Figure 3** represents an example of a Stakeholder Map showcasing possible stakeholder groups. **Figure 4** is a power/interest matrix used to map out the interests each stakeholder represents in the enterprise, as well as their expectations. It can also be used to determine the amount of power and influence stakeholders possess and how this could affect the enterprise, either positively or negatively.

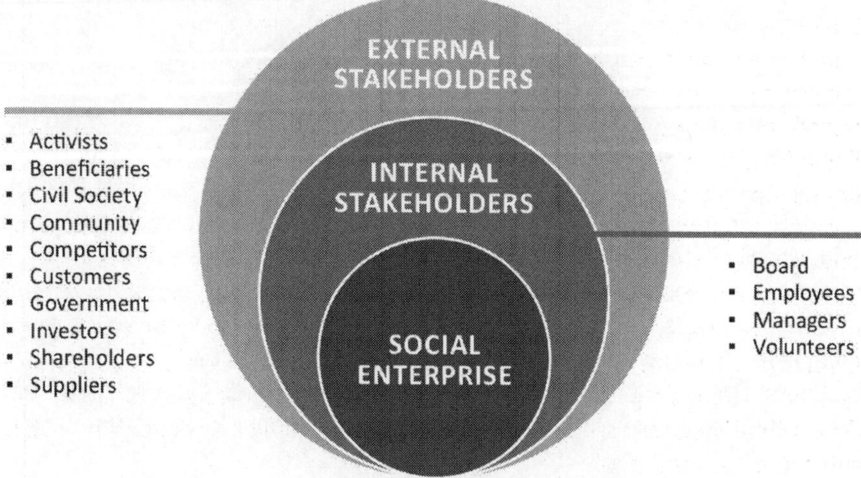

Fig.3: Stakeholder Mapping

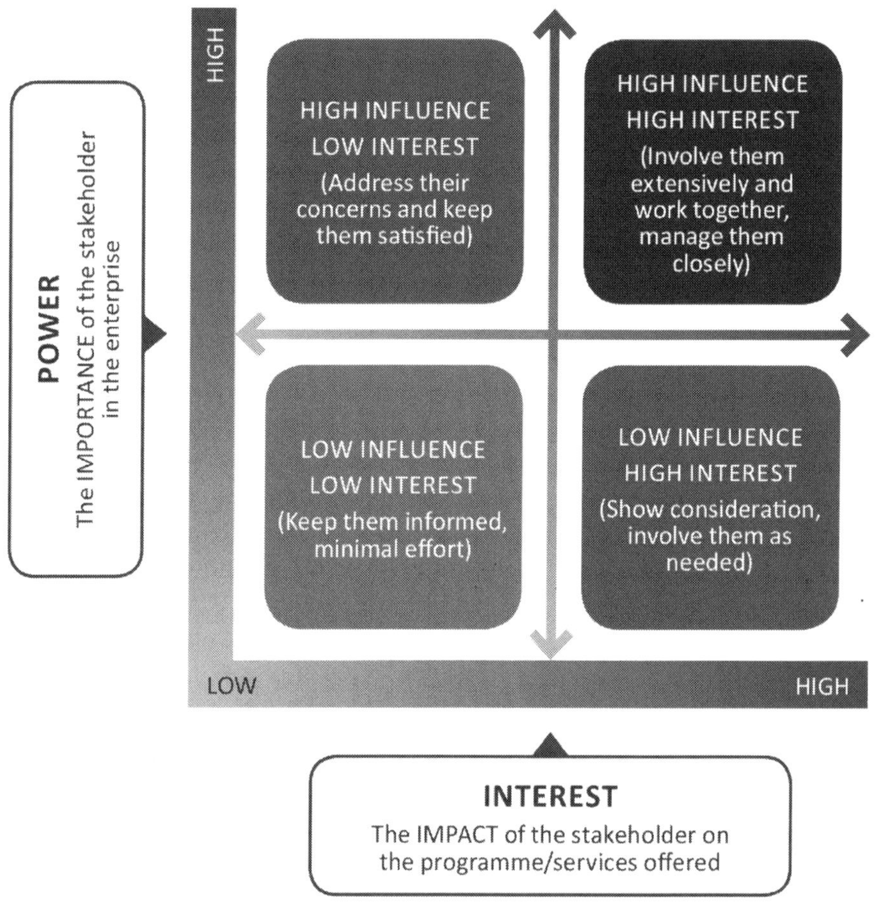

Fig.4: Stakeholder Power/Interest Matrix

Given the importance of stakeholders and their influence, it is essential that the enterprise has a rigorous governance policy on how stakeholders should be managed. *Stakeholder management* is concerned with the identification, analysis, planning, and implementation of all actions designed to engage with stakeholders. The King Code (King IV: 2016), referred to in Chapter 1 of this book, recommends that a stakeholder-inclusive approach be adopted by all enterprises, in which the needs, interests, and expectations of stakeholders are balanced with what is in the best interests of the enterprise in the long term. In addition, when it comes to governing stakeholder relationships, it is beneficial to have the following three documents in operation at your enterprise:

- **Policy document**
  - Sets out how stakeholder relationships must be approached and conducted. We recommend that this policy document should reference the role of the stakeholder committee and how it relates to the full Board of Directors that governs the social enterprise.
- **Stakeholder Management Plan,** which includes:
  - Methodologies for identifying stakeholders (individual and groups);
  - Identify material stakeholders based on the extent to which they affect, or are affected by, the activities, outputs, and outcomes of the enterprise;
  - Management of stakeholder risk;
  - Formal mechanism for engagement and communication with stakeholders, including the use of dispute resolution mechanisms and associated processes;
  - Measurement of the quality of material stakeholder relationships, and appropriate responses to the outcomes.
- **Stakeholder Management Report,** which includes:
  - An overview of the arrangements for governing and managing stakeholder relationships;
  - Key areas of focus during the reporting period;
  - Actions taken to monitor the effectiveness of stakeholder management and how the outcomes were addressed;
- **Future areas of focus.**

(The King IV Report; 2016: 71) Institute of Directors in Southern Africa

When it comes to reporting to stakeholders, enterprises need to ensure that they disclose relevant information, provide transparent and timely communications, and create consistent and comparable reports. Making sure that the relevant stakeholders get the right information at the right time is essential for them to make informed assessments of the enterprise's performance and its short, medium, and long-term prospects.

Stakeholders require relevant and meaningful information to make effective decisions. Whether it be decisions about future growth or actions to be taken in the face of impediments to achieve outcomes, stakeholders need an accurate picture of how the enterprise, or its programs, is progressing. Transparent reports provide a balanced account of the positive and negative aspects of an enterprise and its program implementation. These reports should include the indicators and reporting frameworks used to assess impact and the financial components. Consistent and detailed reporting over a period enables stakeholders to compare current results with previous results. Apart from comparing its own results, an enterprise's report should also allow for comparisons against industry norms, standards, and benchmarks.

Enterprises must also ensure that their stakeholders know where and how to access information that has been disclosed, especially anything that might negatively affect them. The King IV report on *reporting governance* recommends that the following information and reports be accessible to all stakeholders:

- Annual reports, financial statements, sustainability reports, social and ethics committee reports, or other online or printed information issued, must comply with legal requirements, and meet the legitimate and reasonable information needs of material stakeholders.
- Annual integrated report, which should include:
  - A standalone report which connects the more detailed information in other reports and addresses, at a high level, and in a complete and concise way, the matters that could significantly affect the enterprise's ability to create value; or
  - A distinguishable, prominent, and accessible part of another report, which also includes the annual financial statements, and other reports that must be issued in compliance with legal provisions.
- The following information should be published on the company's website, or on other platforms or through other media as is appropriate for access by stakeholders:
  - Corporate governance disclosures
  - Integrated reports
  - Annual financial statements and other external reports.

(The King IV Report; 2016: 48) Institute of Directors in Southern Africa

Impact management and measurement

In today's world of work, in order for an enterprise to claim that their activities are making a difference, they need to provide evidence or **'proof of impact'** to show exactly what and how much difference was made. Investors, funders, executives, boards, and communities want to know how their time, money, and efforts are being used to deliver the intended impacts they signed up for. To obtain this proof that the activities are effective, the enterprise must manage and measure – in detail – the entire change process, as well as the short and medium-term results.

The Development Co-operation Directorate (OECD-DAC) defines impact as any effects (positive, negative, or neutral) arising from an intervention. We tend to think of impact mostly in positive terms, otherwise why do an intervention at all? Social enterprises must be aware that sometimes, despite their best intentions, these interventions can have a negative impact on their customers, or even have no impact at all. Without impact management and measurement, they may be unaware of those impacts and thus miss the opportunity to apply timely and corrective measures. The opposite is also true. If their interventions are working well, then impact management and measurement can help the social enterprise reinforce these positives.

Two complementary types of proof are needed to determine impact: quantitative measurements and anecdotal evidence. This combination allows social enterprises to collect strong and supportive information that is manageable and easy to interpret. Quantitative measurement involves the use of numerical data such as performance measures and indicators to determine progress and change, or the lack thereof. Anecdotal evidence is the story behind the data collected. Taken together, these give a true reflection of the effect of the intervention.

Authors Corner: Sometimes the numbers do not reflect the entire picture. For example, an intervention, aimed at equipping 30 unemployed youth in work readiness skills training that would increase their chances of employment, experienced a high dropout rate during the training program. Research beforehand indicated the expressed need for training due to poor education and life skills preparation, their lack of financial resources to access training, and their inability to enter the job market without the necessary skills and paperwork. Research also indicated that they all needed transport and airtime/data to attend and access the training on and off-site. The youth all received a monthly stipend that would meet these needs and requirements. Despite this, the program experienced a dropout rate of 40%. If we merely use the quantitative data, it seems that the program was not that successful. Obtaining anecdotal evidence helped us to understand a bit more of the story behind the results. Factors contributing towards the dropout rate included an inability to manage the stipend and budget accordingly for the month's transport and airtime/data costs. Never having earned or worked with money beforehand was too much for some of the youth and they ended up spending it on non-program related requirements. Some of them, coming from extremely poor families, were pressured to hand over the money to their guardians in order to buy food for the family and thus could not get to training or participate in the online classes.

Lastly, some of the youth were unable to shake off the apathy that comes with impoverished backgrounds. While they liked the idea of gaining skills, the lack of a tangible employment-offer at the end of the training was enough to fall back on old ways of thinking that "nothing ever changes, so why do anything at all?"

In terms of its original objective, the program itself was not a failure. The anecdotal evidence allowed the enterprise to go back to the drawing board to work on the changes needed to better assist future participants. These included adding budgeting skills to the program, daily stipend payments, family education on what a job could do for the family in the long run, and recruiting more service providers on board to offer learnership opportunities to help the youth transition into workplaces.

The impact of any enterprise intervention can be felt at both community and program level. The impact of single enterprise-activities on participants is referred to as program-level impact. The impact that multiple actors, working together, have on a specific population such as a school or town is referred to as community-level impact. It is important to differentiate between the two when measuring impact, as their scope is quite different. Program level impact purely measures the performance of the social enterprise's specific activities (programs and services). On the other hand, measuring the community level impact on a specific population is a far more complex affair, as this must consider multiple actors such as key individuals, groups, non-profits, enterprises, and government.

Measuring Impact

Keyte & Ridout (2016) in their article on the 7 Steps to Effective Impact Measurement, refer to Impact Measurement as a systematic assessment of a program or project over a period of time. Done continuously, this assessment makes sure that events remain on track and, should there be any modifications or adaptations required, that these occur timeously. Impact Measurement allows us to understand how much change has occurred, and whether that change can be attributed to the intervention or enterprise activity. Some impacts are hard to measure or attribute to specific causes (e.g., a change in attitude towards gender violence). When things such as attitudes, feelings of well-being, and happiness etc. have to be measured, it is better to establish contributory relationships to show how actions fit into the larger strategy implemented by many partners, as opposed to causal attribution.

If social enterprises are to publish impact results confidently, their measurements must produce both longitudinal and comparative data. It is thus essential that they engage in regular planning and create structured evaluation frameworks. This is important, not only for guidance and governance purposes, but also to ensure that the enterprise grows and remains sustainable. Ultimately, an enterprise needs an ethical, clear and well-thought-out process to measure impact, detailing from start to finish, the What, How and Who they measured in order to get results, to showcase the extent to which planned goals and objectives have been met.

The following basic framework will help enterprises to measure their impact.

Create an impact measurement vision

The journey starts with the creation of a vision, which describes the enterprise's overall aim and purpose for measuring impact, as well as the values and ethics it will follow whilst measuring. Once the aim and purpose are clear, it becomes easier to determine the overall measurement approach and the internal and external expertise the enterprise should include to assist with the process. An internal expertise or resource is someone already involved in the measurement process, while an external expertise or resource could be an impact measurement consultant, researcher, or third-party verification organization, all of which could be employed specifically to support the enterprise with designated steps in the measurement process.

Prioritize which outputs (activities) require measuring

Albert Einstein once said that "not everything that counts can be counted and not everything that can be counted, counts". Unless you have unlimited resources, its best to prioritize measuring the most important elements first. Enterprises must soberly consider why they need the data - Do they require it for learning, growth, or fundraising? They must also determine the scope of their impact measurement - Should they focus on a particular target audience or the whole program?

Decide how to measure these outputs (activities)

There are four parts to deciding how to measure outputs. The first involves *developing and selecting the most fit-for-purpose indicators and metrics.* Used as a standard of measurement, these indicators and metrics will help identify and track the progress and extent of change resulting from the activities. Listed against each output, these indicators and metrics are specific pieces of information that serve as proof that something has taken place (e.g., one sustainable project that benefits 1700 people completed successfully and within budget). The emphasis is on the word specific; here more is better than less. Each indicator and metric should be fully explained so that there is more context and no chance of misinterpretation. To ensure quality, maintain a balanced combination of quantitative and qualitative indicators.

The next step in measuring outputs is to decide which methods will be used to collect data of the enterprise's indicators and metrics. Depending on available capacity, the enterprise may want to make use of existing data collection tools or develop its own custom-made metrics. Questionnaires or surveys are by far the most common data collection tools and are effective so long as care is taken to avoid bias. Bias is any tendency that prevents unprejudiced consideration of a question or response. Loaded or assumptive questions, double-barreled questions, double negatives, or poor answer scale options are all examples of bias questions. The Laureus Monitoring & Evaluation Toolkit, developed by the Laureus Sport For Good Foundation, is an excellent resource for finding reliable non-biased questions already in use.

The third step is to work out which sources of data collection will be most suitable. Data can be collected from an entire target group, or a representative proportion of this target group, known as a sample group. Although it is always better to use as many members of the target population as possible, cost and population size considerations make sampling the best option. Samples can be random, where everyone has an equal chance of being included, or non-random, where people are selected systematically.

Lastly, data collectors must be trained to deploy the data collection tools effectively, and to efficiently collect and manage data. This training should focus specifically on data quality, software, and security, so that they can confidently recognize high quality data versus poor quality data for the specific outputs being measured. The data collectors will also require training on selected software (i.e. Excel spreadsheets) that is used specifically to manage and analyze data.

Data security must be guaranteed via clear guidelines and policies. This will cover the confidential use and safekeeping of data, including data sharing with other parties. Once data security has been established, it must be communicated to all parties who have access to the data. All information used should comply with regulations such as the Protection of Personal Information (POPI) Act, as non-compliance can lead to ethical and legal challenges.

Analyze and interpret the collected data

The well-known quote by Jim Bergeson, President and CEO of the Bridgz Marketing Group, "Data will talk to you if you are willing to listen", rings true. "Listening" to the data requires that it be broken down and analyzed and then, based on the interpretations and conclusions drawn, this is used to make well- informed decisions.

If not explored in a meaningful way, data remains cold facts and figures. Data analysis is the process of organizing, inspecting, structuring, and transforming data, and then presenting it in a useful way so that it can be used to aid data interpretation. Data interpretation entails using this analyzed information to draw conclusions for informed decision-making. Key data-analysis tools include Microsoft Excel, Python and SQL. It is best to use both written and visual formats such as graphs and charts when presenting data. Ultimately, the data should tell the story of what happened while the activities were carried out by the enterprise. The report should also share the lessons learnt by the data gatherers.

Reporting on the results

The social enterprise's impact report should be readily available and accessible to stakeholders. These include its impact investors, finance directors, policymakers, NGO leaders, communications, marketing, and corporate social responsibility departments.

The report should show a clear correlation between the reported impact and the defined purpose and strategy of the intervention. It should clearly articulate the identified issue and the activities taken to meet the outcomes and the overall objective within a specified timeline, and provide solid evidence of how these medium-and long-term goals were met, as well as a description of evidence collection. Analyses of the collected data or evidence should be presented both visually and in written descriptions and interpretations. All positive and negative results must be included.

The most important section of the report is the sharing of the lessons learned and the plan for improvements. Careful documentation of the lessons learned, what they mean for the enterprise and its interventions, and the plans for improvement will raise the transparency and accountability stakes for the enterprise and its stakeholders. Defining the next action steps and assigning roles and responsibilities to these actions and timelines will garner further understanding and buy-in from stakeholders and will go a long way in ensuring that the proposed improvements or changes will happen.

Authors Corner: In March 2021 Nation Builder (a social impact initiative in South Africa) released a standardized Impact Management Reporting Guideline for the country's social impact sector. This Guideline was the culmination of an 18-month collaborative learning and co-creation journey alongside social investors and non-profit organizations (NPOs) in the Nation Builder community. One of the authors served on the National Steering committee on Impact Reporting. The committee comprised various implementing organizations and social investors (each represented in the Nation Builder Community in South Africa), and these members met on a regular basis to provide input, support, and guidance to create the Guideline.

The driving forces behind creating this Guideline include:

- To help non-profit organizations (NPOs) and social investors align better and measure the impact of their efforts and investments more effectively. The development of the Guideline serves as a bridge-builder, as it allows NPOs and investors to have a greater understanding of each other's environment, context, challenges, constraints, priorities, and mandates. This deep collaboration and the accompanying robust discussions have resulted in a shared understanding of what all parties are hoping to achieve; essentially, they want to ensure that everyone is aiming for the same end goal, and that each party brings something of value to the table.
- There is a lack of standardization of impact measurements to compare and determine which impact approaches accomplish the best results. This has made it difficult to develop effective strategies based on quantifiable data and, consequently, has hindered a national view of where support is needed most. The questions that need to be asked are: "*What does good impact measurement and reporting look like?*" "*What makes for good impact strategies?*"
- Future funding: At a time when funding has slowed and social needs have increased dramatically, it is all the more important for social investors and NPOs to be able to quantify their social impact and provide evidence or "proof of impact" of the difference they have made in the lives of their target group. Stakeholders want to know what is being done and how their time, money, and efforts are being used to bring about the intended impacts they signed up for. Good impact reporting should provide this proof so that stakeholders can make informed decisions.

The Impact Management Guideline can be downloaded from the Nation Builder website – www.proudnationbuilder.co.za.

Advantages of measuring social impact for an enterprise

Sustainability and growth: Without data collection, analysis, and interpretation, it would be difficult to grow an enterprise or make the necessary changes and improvements to ensure sustainability. Results from its impact measurement can be used to improve existing interventions and activities, or create new ones. Collecting and analyzing data allows enterprises to remain on top of their processes and performance. This places them in the best position to respond in a timely manner to any challenges that may arise.

Ethics and governance: Impact measurement compliments the practices of accountability and credibility. Providing stakeholders with honest, reliable, and accurate feedback on measurement processes and results goes a long way to developing trust. This affects future possibilities for growth and sustainability by attracting new funders or stakeholders. Aligning some of the enterprise's goals, activities, and impact measurement indicators to the relevant SDGs (Sustainable Development Goals) and ESG (Environmental and Social Governance) is beneficial as it signals to investors and stakeholders that the enterprise is professionally managed and less of a risk.

Informed decision-making: Knowledge is power. Having the right data at the right time can position an enterprise on a growth trajectory and this sets the bar for others to follow. Informed data decision-making can only happen if the enterprise follows a basic data cycle of collection, analysis, interpretation, decision making, reporting, and monitoring.

Collaboration: Sharing its findings with stakeholders provides the social enterprise with more opportunity to engage with them. The more these stakeholders engage, the more information the social enterprise obtains. This aids their planning and action of stakeholder engagement.

Cost efficiency: Cost-reduction opportunities in an enterprise are always there. The correct implementation of data analysis processes can alert the enterprise to opportunities for cost efficiency.

Marketing a social enterprise involves communicating the message of its product, mission, and social impact to the public. A social enterprise cannot generate sales solely on the strength of its compelling story; it must also deliver a demonstrated and valued product that gives credit and credence to its mission. If the enterprise is to be sustainable, it must leverage both its product and mission to build customer loyalty. It is both wise and critical for social enterprises to remember that a good mission and story cannot substitute for a shabby product or service. The latter will damage the social enterprise's reputation, and this will translate into fewer sales, less revenue, and a reduced social impact. To this end, the chapter began by introducing the reader to the elements and tactics associated with a virtuous marketing cycle.

The section on Impact Reporting has dealt primarily with the way social enterprises measure and report their social impact and incorporate these results into their marketing strategy. These metrics should be added to those which track their financial performance, thereby creating a dashboard which adheres to the principles of integrated reporting, and which can inform their management, Board, and internal and external stakeholders.

Chapter 7

RISK MANAGEMENT

Risk and Risk Management

The contemporary field of risk management is a useful lens through which to view the social enterprise's entire operation. Building risk management into its organizational culture is critical to the safety of its workforce, as well as to its sustainability. By the time the enterprise reaches maturity, and before it embarks on a new growth phase, it must ensure that it has completely institutionalized its risk management strategy.

Irrespective of whether they are incorporated as for-profits, non-profits or cooperatives, social enterprises must think about risk management before they present their first business plans and project proposals to potential funders. The authors of these plans are required to list their assumptions concerning all facets of the proposed project or business. They do so by asking questions such as *"Why do we think our enterprise will succeed?" "What will make it succeed?"* In addition to soliciting the ideas of others, the creators use their answers to imagine the consequences they may encounter should they not succeed, by asking themselves the following question: *"How will the enterprise respond to the stresses of an adverse situation?"*

The creators of the business plan engage in the enterprise's first risk assessment exercise by using planning tools such as the SWOT analysis to measure the enterprise's internal **S**trengths and **W**eaknesses, as well as the **O**pportunities and **T**hreats that lie outside its boundaries. They uncover weaknesses within its proposed structure and operations along with threats posed by competitors, regulators, and other stakeholders. Their deliberative response is to create plans that reduce or eliminate the impact of these weaknesses and threats on their enterprise. These plans become the foundation for their risk management strategy.

Risk analysis and mitigation is not a task to be assigned to a single person or department. Social enterprises must assemble a team of people to look at its risk management system in a systematic and rigorous manner. This chapter provides this team with a conceptual and institutional framework that can be adapted to their social enterprise and the unique challenges it faces. However, risk management does not begin with an initial risk assessment and end with the creation of a risk management strategy. A social enterprise that manages risk successfully will add a third step to these two. This stage sees the enterprise practicing the risk policy and related plans, making necessary modifications to these, and evaluating them regularly to ensure that emerging risks are being taken into account.

Irrespective of their form, social enterprises face a growing array of regulation in the form of practices and standards which are mandated by their local, state, and national government, or through ethical codes which have been created by their peers or interest groups. A 2014 Forbes article by Kasia Moreno cited a study of 400 US CEOs in which many reported spending 50% of their work time addressing risk and regulation. A study by Deloitte and Touche South Africa (2012) listed over 300 regulations which affected organizations in South Africa. Since many regulations are often intended to allow enterprises to manage their risk better and carry strict penalties for those who fail to do so, it makes sense for social enterprises to see what value they can leverage by mitigating or reducing their risks. Social enterprises should not hesitate to advocate for policy and regulatory reform when regulations inhibit or increase the cost of their operations, and minimize their social impact as a result.

What is Risk?

Risk refers to the degree of exposure that a social enterprise has to internal weaknesses and external threats. If these factors increase, the enterprise will suffer harm, realize lower profits, and may have to cease operating in its entirety.

Risk may also result from deliberate actions or from inaction. A social enterprise can fall into one of two risk categories. *Internal risks* arise when a weakness within the enterprise is amplified through the actions or inaction of internal stakeholders, especially its Board and employees. *External risks* arise when a threat from outside the enterprise's boundary is magnified by the actions of other organizations and players.

The Risk Management Cycle

The social enterprise incorporates a risk management cycle into its ongoing operations so that this becomes part of its operating rhythm. This cycle is captured in the enterprise's operating calendar and is brought further to life through the work of committees, written policies and practiced operating plans. The four sequential components of the risk management cycle are represented in the following graphic (Figure 1) with each of these components then being considered in greater detail.

Fig.1: The Risk Management Cycle

Risk Identification

The cycle begins with the identification of the internal and external risks to the enterprise's sustainability. Using the Systems Approach to understanding the enterprise allows its employees and Board to answer the question *"What are the risks that our social enterprise is exposed to?"* Another useful tool is the enterprise-specific risk assessment tool that is referenced in the next section.

Assessment of Probability and Impact

After all the risks have been listed and discussed, the risk committee and employees should rank them according to their occurrence probability (i.e. the likelihood that they will occur). Once this exercise has been completed, they continue their assessment by determining the impact each risk would have on the enterprise *if they were to happen.*

Risk Mitigation

Mitigation refers to the plans and actions the social enterprise takes to reduce the likelihood that each of the identified risks will be occur. While it is impossible to eliminate the risk, it is possible to take proactive steps to limit its impact on the social enterprise's operations. Therefore, the management and employees are responsible for including provisions to mitigate these identified risks in all their operational plans. Furthermore, they need to regularly review and update these plans. In doing so, they help to maintain the integrity of the enterprise's risk management cycle.

In addition to these plans, there are a further two sub-components of the enterprise's risk mitigation phase. The first is the customary and regulatory requirement that the enterprise protect its operations by purchasing a range of insurance policies (these will be discussed in a later section). The second sub-component is that the enterprises create an ethical organizational culture which applies the written codes and policies by practicing them daily, institutionalizing them through continuing workforce training events, and highlighting them whenever the enterprise celebrates its accomplishments.

Risk Monitoring

The final step in the risk management strategy is for the enterprise to monitor its risk factors, assessing how disciplined it has been in adhering to its risk management strategy as an integral part of its business operations, and whether it has created mitigation plans and updated them on a regular basis. The ultimate responsibility for monitoring the enterprise's risk rests with its Board of Directors. They are to appoint a Risk Committee to assist them, and engage independent experts, such as auditors and insurance underwriters, to provide it with periodic reviews. These reports will show how well the enterprise is mitigating the risks it faces.

Creating an Enterprise-specific Risk Analysis tool

The Six Capitals provide enterprises with a conceptual framework with which to create their risk policy and their risk mitigation and management plans. The sections below will uncover some of the risks a social enterprise can expect to encounter as it mobilizes and responds to each of the Six Capitals. By exploring how they mobilize their capitals, the enterprise's employees can create a tool that will identify the unique risks in each of these six sectors.

Risks to Natural Capital

Climate change poses significant risk to the natural capital that social enterprises depend upon, as phenomena such as pollution and droughts have a direct impact on the ability of social enterprises to produce and deliver their products. These risks threaten not only their facilities and operations, but also those of their suppliers and customers.

Risks to Human Capital

The individual and collective health of the social enterprise's workforce is critical for its competitive advantage, success, and sustainability. Illness and unsafe working conditions constitute a risk to the social enterprise, and the latter carries with them additional reputational and regulatory risks. If these are not eliminated, the social enterprise will face financial penalties from regulators and from litigation in court following workplace accidents. Managerial incompetence will result in the enterprise losing its talent at a greater rate than it can be replaced. Furthermore, poor management may cause a drop in employee morale, and this can lead the workforce to engage in industrial action or go-slows. Weak or over-active governance also constitutes a risk to the enterprise as it typically motivates talented top managers to leave the company. In addition, the power vacuum which this creates may result in the social enterprise becoming over-reliant on certain key staff members. Workplace deviance and ethical lapses by the Board of Directors and employees also constitute risks to the organization. Examples of workplace deviance include harassment and assault, theft of property, fraud, bribery and intentionally wasting company resources such as time and supplies.

In addition to these internal risks to the human capital of social enterprises, this capital is also threatened by the external environment. The largest external risk to its human capital come from the wider educational and health sectors and, in particular, the degree to which these have disadvantaged the communities from which the social enterprise draws its workforce. A poor education system puts the social enterprise at greater disadvantage because it will need to invest more to train its workforce with the skills that they need to be productive.

Risks to Financial Capital

Recessions pose a serious external financial risk to any social enterprise as due to the negative impact on customers, suppliers, and funders. Fluctuations in currency rates, as well as inflation and debt rates in the country where it operates and those with which it trades, are also forms of financial risk facing social enterprises. Financial mismanagement by the banks, key suppliers, and customers the enterprise trades with may result in a loss of money, a cash flow crunch, and lower profits. Weak or nonexistent internal financial controls at the social enterprise may create the opportunity for its employees to commit fraud. Threats or delays in procuring the inputs which it needs to create its products, as well as having too many completed products in its inventory also constitute risks to the social enterprise's financial capital. When taken together, these factors serve to weaken its financial position over the short and medium-term. If these risks are not identified early enough, their manifestation can result in the social enterprise going out of business.

Risks to Intellectual Capital

The theft of any intellectual property (patents and copyrights) belonging to the social enterprise, whether by its employees or competitors, constitutes a risk to its operations and viability. Social enterprises can attempt to mitigate this risk through contractual tools such as non-disclosure agreements wherein parties agree to keep the enterprise's intellectual property confidential. With the rise of the digital economy, information technology and related hardware is now an integral part of the way social enterprises collect, store, and retrieve information and data. Securing these technology sources and repositories from data loss and breaches is no longer just of concern to major economic and political players. All organizations, including social enterprises, must take active steps to protect themselves, their staff, and their customers from the cybercriminal malfeasance. These steps can include on-site network safeguards such as firewalls and multi-factor authentication protocols for business and employee devices.

A weak or poorly executed business strategy is detrimental to a social enterprise's operations as the failure to invest in product and customer research and/or new product development puts the social enterprise at risk. This failure increases its chances of becoming irrelevant through the loss of market share and brand value.

Sound governance, management and operational policies, processes and practices constitute a key part of the intellectual capital which social enterprises employ. The failure to create and follow them also constitutes a risk to the social enterprise. Management and the Board must remain vigilant during the creation and delivery of the product or service to avoid lapses in ethical judgment by individual employees or the social enterprise as a corporate whole.

Risks to Social and Relationship Capital

Ethical lapses which begin within the social enterprise and then extend to its external stakeholders, constitute a risk to its social reputation. Their reputation will also be threatened if the integrity of the product which the enterprise produces is compromised in some way. Customer and vendor dissatisfaction is a threat to the enterprise's social and relationship capital. This risk increases exponentially when their dissatisfaction leads them to take legal action against the enterprise. The loss of clients, either through natural attrition, or as the result of concerns about the enterprise's reputation, damages its social and relationship capital. Aggressive moves by existing and new competitors are an ever-present danger. Social enterprises must also consider the effects of political instability and polarization, the loss of support from local communities, and unexpected regulatory changes made by administrative and elected officials.

Risks to Manufacturing Capital

Damage to, or the destruction of, the physical location where a social enterprise bases its operations is a well-recognized risk. The damages and interruptions described in the previous paragraph may also include damage to critical equipment and machinery which the enterprise depends on daily to create and sell its product. This includes vehicles, computer hardware and networks, and specialized machinery such as commercial ovens and roasters.

In addition to these types of manufacturing capital, most social enterprises contend with the risk of failures to the larger power, communication, and water grid which they rely on. A related risk arises from their dependence on the transportation networks which delivers inputs to them and then carries their finished products to their customers. Rolling electricity blackouts, compromised water systems and damaged bridges are some examples of these threats.

Finally, social enterprises must continually review and update the different technologies they use in their operation. Technological obsolescence is thus a risk to their manufacturing capital.

Risk Management Practices

Once social enterprises have identified the unique risks they are likely to encounter, they should outline steps to mitigate those risks in their risk management plan. The choice of actions that they follow can fall into passive strategies (such as purchasing insurance) and proactive ones, which result in them creating, practicing, and evaluating internal policies and procedures.

Passive Strategies

Social enterprises will encounter the terms "insurance" and "assurance" as they educate themselves about risk management. The standard types of insurance policies purchased by social enterprises include general, property and liability insurance, worker's compensation, director and officer liability, and business interruption policies. These types of insurance policies are reactive in nature and are purchased to cover the enterprises for a specified period. Their purpose is to help reimburse them for losses incurred during a defined hazard (such as a workplace accident) where payments are made to cover the medical expenses sustained by the injured employee.

Assurance is a forward-looking risk management tactic. The organization uses a third-party professional to assess the accuracy of the financial information released by their proposed or existing business partners. Assurance gives them the confidence to make an informed decision on whether to enter into contracts or continue to do business with these partners. While small to medium-sized social enterprises are unlikely to use assurance services until they experience business expansion, they should always work on the assumption that third party assurance companies are assessing them on behalf of larger corporations and even governmental entities.

Proactive Strategies

Because risk management is tied to the social enterprise's decisions and organizational culture, it makes sense for the enterprise to build the risk approach on their ethical foundation. Ethics provide decision makers with a structure in which they make decisions, and which bring those values to life.

Social enterprises should maintain two good practices: Firstly, the creation and adoption of a code of ethics which becomes an integral part of their regular business operations. Secondly, make these codes known to all their employees through a specific presentation during the onboarding process, and again during the subsequent, regular training events.

Creating a code of ethics often begins by looking at those that have been created for the industry sector in which the social enterprise operates. Trade associations, such as the World Fair Trade Organization, are a reliable source of industry codes. While it is tempting for social enterprises to merely adopt a code that they have downloaded, it is much wiser to go a step further and use this code to craft one which is unique to the enterprise's market and purpose. By doing so, the Board and management of the social enterprise will have created a key part of their internal and external marketing materials. These materials, along with the code, helps the enterprise to generate the training materials it uses when orienting new employees. But these training materials and ethical codes also serve another purpose. They allow the enterprise to practice hypothetical decision-making scenarios where values and ethics play a central role. Understanding how an enterprise will handle controversy helps to build its resilience.

The risk mitigation phase provides social enterprises with the opportunity to have their operational plans, policies and procedures include activities which minimize their exposure to the risks they have identified. These staffled activities can include review meetings and the completion of checklists which address protocol and equipment. Boards should ensure that their governing policies explicitly state the risk parameters within which management is expected to operate. Boards must also begin the process of succession planning by outlining the process and emergency steps the social enterprise will follow, should it need to replace its principal Board and management members at short notice.

The individuals who are entrusted with managing the social enterprise are also responsible for creating similar succession plans for other key personnel. Part of this exercise should include a regular workforce analysis to identify when the social enterprise is likely to experience an attrition in its workforce. An example of this is projected retirements, which will be of particular concern should an enterprise rely heavily on the older generation for its workforce.

Another example of a risk mitigation plan is the presence of a workplace safety policy. This policy addresses one of the first risks to an enterprise's human capital identified earlier in this chapter. Workplace safety policies are reinforced by procedures which outline the steps the enterprise and all its employees will take to keep their workplace safe and to minimize accidents.

Other common risk mitigation plans include plans to deal with the negative impacts which natural and human-made disasters may have on the social enterprise. For example, social enterprises working in coastal communities, areas which are increasingly prone to hurricanes and cyclones, have created standard plans to close their operations as these storms approach and then re-open them once they have passed. These plans include protocols to handle communications with internal and external stakeholders, as well as how the enterprise will respond to the different scenarios that it has identified and planned for.

Social enterprises can also adopt a best practice from the emerging field of integrated reporting, an accounting approach whose adoption continues to be encouraged by the International Integrated Reporting Council. Integrated reporting allows social enterprises and their auditors to employ the concept of the Six Capitals and show how they are creating value in a sustainable manner. What this means is that one section of the integrated annual report addresses the unique risks the social enterprise faces, as well as the efforts it is taking to mitigate these risks. Integrated reporting allows social enterprises to follow this best practice by sharing key points from their Risk Committee's report to the Board of Directors in the enterprise's annual report. For example, in their 2008 annual report, the former Blue Financial Solutions in South Africa listed HIV/AIDS, fraud, crime, and unethical competition as the external risks facing this micro-finance company. It also mentioned the initiatives the company were employing to mitigate these risks.

Risk Management Infrastructure

A social enterprise's risk management strategy and system begins with its governance body and extends to its senior management who are responsible for implementing measures to mitigate that risk. The best practices in corporate governance include the requirement that all social enterprises follow a board-approved risk policy. The King IV Code lists risk management as one of the seventeen principles that the Boards of Directors should adhere to. Risk management is the preview of two board committees; these are the Finance and Audit Committee, and the Risk Committee. Per regulatory requirements and best practices, it is accepted that all social enterprises provide their shareholders and other stakeholders with timely and accurate financial statements and independent audits. As part of the independent audit, auditors review the internal financial controls the enterprise has put in place to protect its assets, including those which it has sourced from outside parties. While the shareholder model has always required public corporations to monitor their financial risk, the idea of what constitutes business risk has grown to include financial and non-financial factors. This has brought risk management more in line with the stakeholder model. It is for this reason that Risk Committees have emerged as a separate board committee.

The Board Committee on Risk Management

A Risk Committee can only be created after the bylaws have been adopted during the legal incorporation of the social enterprise. Depending on when last an enterprise reviewed its bylaws, it may be necessary for established social enterprises to revisit their bylaws to see whether the section on committees should be modified to include a Risk Committee.

As part of its approved risk policy, the Board of Directors must establish a Risk Committee, appoint Board members to serve on it, and charge it with the responsibility for regularly reviewing this policy to ensure that the enterprise, at a minimum, complies with the necessary regulations which govern it. The policy creates the risk management function by requiring management to create, communicate, implement, and evaluate risk management across the enterprise. The policy also stipulates that the Board is to receive periodic reports about the enterprise's risk exposure and mitigation plans.

The Risk Committee is supported by key management staff from the social enterprise. It is recommended that the Board Development Committee include *experience of risk management* as a qualification on the Board matrix it uses to identify and recruit new board members. Another best practice is to incorporate the topic of risk management trends and issues into the continuing education opportunities and training the social enterprise offers to both its board members and employees. Another rule of thumb is that the Risk Committee meets four times a year. This frequency allows the Committee to fulfill its charge to update the full Board on developments in the enterprise's risk environment, and to assure them that the enterprise is sensitive to, and is mitigating, the risks it is encountering. However, this tempo does not allow the Board to interfere with management's responsibility for creating operational risk mitigation plans and for leading the enterprise's daily operations.

Risk Committees are also tasked with evaluating the social enterprise's risk management policies, charging staff with the responsibility to identify key risks, developing strategies to address them, and providing board oversight for the enterprise's risk management function. It is a good idea for the committee to develop and communicate its annual work calendar to the Board and the employees. This calendar will include a schedule for reviewing the enterprise's risk management plan and reviewing the audits that are conducted by independent consultants or vendors. The calendar will also schedule regular discussions with key employees about the current and anticipated risks to the social enterprise. When reporting to the full Board of Directors, the Risk Committee uses the enterprise's unique risk analysis tool which reflects the

Six Capitals as its framework. The social enterprise also uses this tool and the committee reports when it prepares the risk management section of the enterprise's annual report.

Part of the internal control function is to ensure that each of the social enterprise's operational committees are responsible for including risk management in their particular program areas. For example, a social enterprise which sells or rents housing will have a Loan Committee that reviews and underwrites resident or homeowner applications. Creating, enforcing, and evaluating those underwriting requirements and ensuring that they meet all statutory requirements would be part of this Loan Committee's responsibilities. Senior management must take responsibility for monitoring the progress of this committee's risk management task, and provide periodic updates to the Risk Committee and Board on the organization's current degree of compliancy in this area. Employees, as the resident experts on emerging market and regulatory trends, would also be responsible for recommending updates to the enterprise's risk management policy where it pertains to this area of operations. In this way, the enterprise is safeguarded and can take advantage of any opportunities that might emerge.

Depending on the industry sector and the scale and complexity of its operations, a maturing social enterprise may need to eventually create the position of Compliance Officer or Internal Auditor. This person will be tasked with ensuring that the enterprise is operating within its approved risk management policies, that it is implementing its strategies, and that it is compliant with all pertinent government regulations.

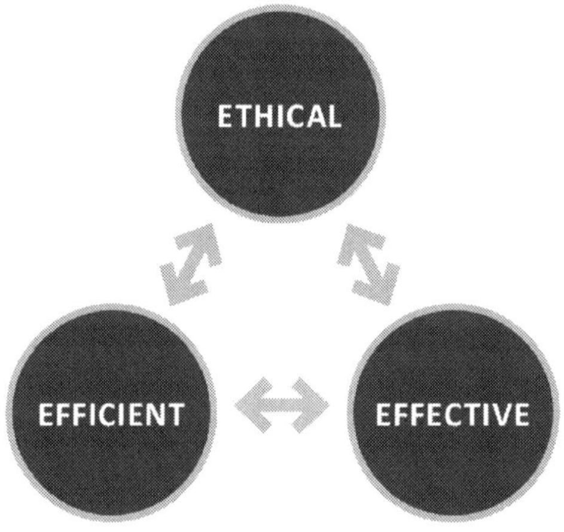

Fig.2: E3

In conclusion, the increasing scale of social problems they seek to address, along with the rising expectations of their stakeholders, require that social enterprises mainstream their risk management approach. This is necessary so that they can continue to deliver positive social impact whilst replenishing and growing their sources of capital. To do so, social enterprises must become E3.

It is not enough for social enterprises to pursue the correct goals and strategy whilst employing their resources to create the most value and impact; they must also operate in an ethical way. An ethical mindset grows from the enterprise's commitment to address a social issue, along with its mature and confident tolerance of the risks that it must plan for, and will encounter. All of this must be done while making a positive impact on the community in which it serves.

Social Enterprises must go beyond a passive approach to risk management. Viewing risk management as a planning tool will allow them to build the necessary confidence and tolerance and to grow as a sustainable enterprise that delivers the desired social impact in a profitable way.

Chapter 8

MANAGING OPERATIONS AT SOCIAL ENTERPRISES

Operations Management involves the value-added process that takes place within the social enterprise. More precisely, it is concerned with how effectively and efficiently the social enterprise mobilizes inputs from its available sources of financial, intellectual, human, and manufacturing capital, and transforms them into a product that is valued, cost-effective, and positive to society and the environment. Operations Management is launched when the social enterprise asks the question *"What product will we create that will add value to our customer?"* It encourages social enterprises to answer those "What" and "How" questions they must ask if these enterprises are to grow their market share:

- *What physical and social product are we creating and delivering to our customer or client? How are we creating and delivering this product?*
- *How can we improve the way we create and deliver this product?*
- *How do we learn from one another, and from our customers and other stakeholders?*

Operations begin once the social enterprise has created its organizational structure. This structure refers to the horizontal and vertical connections between the different work units that constitute the social enterprise. It includes the organizational chart, work unit descriptions, and individual job descriptions, along with their tasks and assignments. Organizational structure also includes how the intellectual and technical processes combine to produce the product or service.

By unpacking the term "Operations Management" we arrive at two important insights into what this practice entails. The word *Operations* refers to a transformative process which combines inputs in unique ways to create outputs in the form of a valued product and waste. The sweet spot in operations management is to have the customer pay for as much of the indirect costs associated with the product as possible.

Management in this context refers to the creation of tactical plans, scheduling work tasks so that the transformation takes place, purposefully leading people in a participatory way to accomplish those tasks, and then measuring the outputs to see if they have met the objectives laid out in the plan. Key insights and problems which are identified at this stage are then introduced back into the planning phase of the ongoing management cycle. It is important to remember that social enterprises are focused on twin output goals, namely profitability and social impact. For example, an urban farm that embodies the principles of social enterprise and draws its workforce from a marginalized group (e.g., a homeless population), may have as its tactical goals the increase of crop harvest and to reduce absenteeism amongst this workforce. The farm has a good crop coming in and wants to mitigate spoilage by having enough of its workforce available at harvest time. It will also want to ensure that as many of its workers as possible remain employed, since this will make it more likely that they will remain in decent housing. Thus its tactical plan goals should include steps to ensure that both of these goals are met.

Fig.1: Managing Operations

By structuring their operations effectively and managing them efficiently, social enterprises are well positioned to develop their competitive advantage. It has been our experience that sustainable social enterprises have fewer managerial levels, use cross-functional teams, and grant a large degree of autonomy to their teams and their leaders. These managers and teams are knitted together by the enterprise's strong mission and values statement. They also create policy documents which provide these teams with the necessary boundaries within which to operate.

Social enterprises must have an empowerment contract in place if they are to grow responsibly and be sustainable.

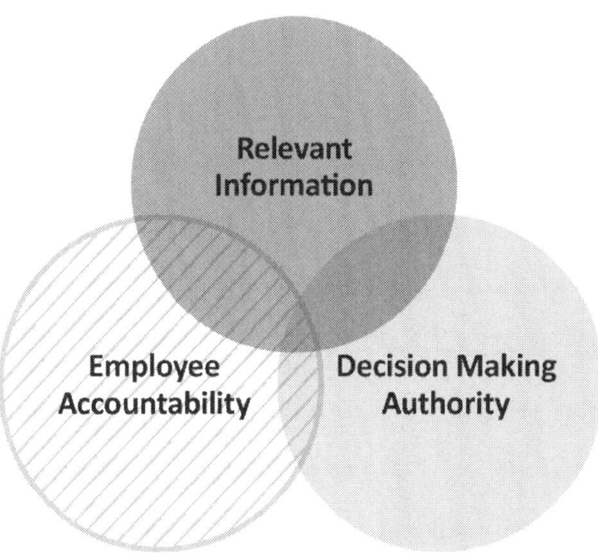

Fig.2: Three Components to an Empowerment Contract

As depicted in Figure 2 above, there are three components to this contract:

- Relevant information about the enterprise's operations and finances must be shared amongst the teams.
- Decision-making authority must be appropriately distributed throughout the enterprise with a bias towards devolving more to those teams who work with customers and stakeholders.
- Accountable employees are to accept the twin responsibility of being literate about the enterprise's operations and being responsible to their team and enterprise for their individual actions.

Innovation Cycles

Using the life cycle process from the S-curve allows social enterprises to determine whether they are in a period of incremental or episodic change (See Chapter 10). Some authors refer to these two types of change as 'disruptive and sustainable innovation' (Williams, 2019). Episodic or disruptive change is characterized by the introduction of new technologies and business operations. During this phase, the social enterprise develops and experiments with different prototypes before selecting one that transforms its operations and allows it to capture market share. This phase of the organization closely resembles the startup phase in the Sigmoid Curve model (see Chapter 2).

A period of incremental change follows this startup phase, and it assumes that the social enterprise has survived and that its product is valued by the market, with sales fueling business growth. Incremental change sees the enterprise focus on bringing this product to market more quickly, perhaps with a few more improvements, and producing it more cheaply. This practice is referred to as compression. The social enterprise facilitates compression by mapping its manufacturing process and costing its inputs to see if these can be either substituted by cheaper ones, or if the existing inputs can be sourced more cheaply.

This period of incremental change will inevitably be followed by another period of disruptive change. Social enterprises can navigate these changes by balancing the steady production of a valued product with the R&D of the next generation of its product. Rather than assigning new product development to a team that is already involved with producing a winning product, the social enterprise instead creates a new team and unit to work on the new prototype.

Concerns with Quality and Waste

The theory and practice of Operations Management goes on to examine how enterprises create quality (value) and reduce or eliminate waste. This section will explore these two concepts in greater detail.

Quality

Quality can be defined as those elements of the product that are valued by the customer because it meets their needs. They value the product highly enough to pay for it. A general quality cycle draws on the four management principles of planning, organizing, leading, and controlling. By organizing and empowering teams to create quality policies and products, social enterprises can improve their engagement with employees and customers. They incorporate customer feedback into their product, as well as into the way they organize the production cycle. Social enterprises use employee participation and team engagement to direct their teams. They also put the necessary quality controls in place to ensure that the product is indeed the one that the customer values and pays for. These quality controls also allow the enterprise to identify and control waste.

Waste

In the Operations Management context, waste is defined as any production activity that utilizes resources, but that does not add any value for the customer. Since the customer does not pay for this activity, it therefore creates no value for the social enterprise. Another way must be found to subsidize this activity as it increases operating costs and adds to the enterprise's risk of failure. Waste originates when there is a lack of harmony between the internal systems that comprise the enterprise and the capital it draws from its intellectual, human, manufacturing, natural and financial sources.

Lean production understands waste as taking three forms: uneven workflows, overburdened staff and equipment, and worthless activities and products.

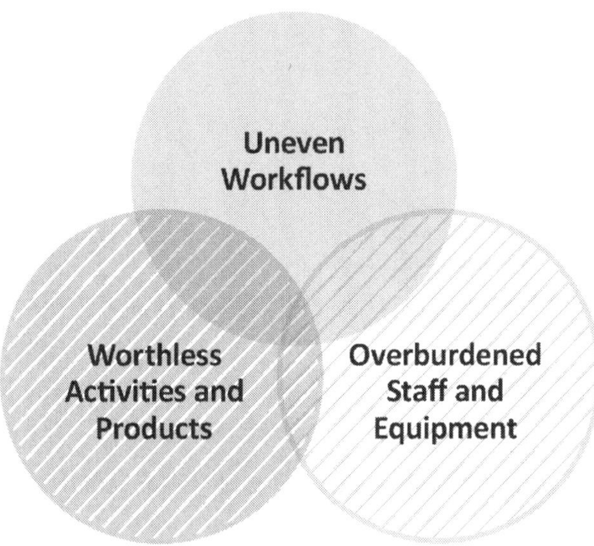

Fig.3: Operations Management: Waste

Uneven workflows manifest themselves in the form of frequent periods of intense activity followed by ones in which nothing appears to be happening. These manifestations may occur during the normal workday or seasonally, and result in some parts of the social enterprise being under-utilized. Common causes of uneven workflows include the lack of standard policies and procedures, as well as poor planning.

If certain parts of the social enterprise are being under-utilized, then it is possible that other parts are being over-used on a continual basis. This leads to the second form of waste which is *overburdened staff and equipment*. This type of waste manifests itself in the form of burnt-out personnel who resign from the enterprise, equipment failures, and accidents.

Worthless activities and products include the following:

- The social enterprise *overproduces* its core goods and services because it fails to obtain accurate information on what is transpiring in its customer's world.
- This leads to too much *inventory* on hand, something that consumes space and is unproductive because it does not generate cash flow. The converse is also true. A shortage of inventory can result in the next form of waste.

- *Waiting* is the time the social enterprise's employees and equipment are idle because they lack the necessary information and inputs with which to create their product.
- *Unnecessary transport* occurs when inputs and completed products need to be moved on a regular basis because they are "in the way" of other items.
- *Unnecessary processing* takes places when too much effort is put into a product. These added features are not ones that the customer particularly values or needs. Unnecessary processing therefore constitutes a diseconomy of scale.
- *Unnecessary human motions* lower productivity because they force employees to take extra steps to complete tasks and to produce the product (e.g., materials and tools being out of reach, or simply the failure to recruit enough employees so that the enterprise can meet orders and generate a profit).
- *Defective* products consume time required to repair or replace. They increase customer dissatisfaction, which could result in the enterprise losing its market share.

It is important to note that waste in the context of Operations Management refers to the inefficient methods of product creation. It does not refer to the physical and natural waste products that are created during the production process.

Conceptual methodologies for contemporary Operations Management

Social enterprises approach their Operations Management by means of two conceptual methodologies; these are termed Systems Thinking and Lean Production. When used together, these methodologies allow enterprises to leverage their Six Capitals to create their valued product. Those who occupy the senior leadership and management positions at the social enterprise are responsible for understanding these conceptual frameworks and are also responsible for using these insights to create an organizational culture which gives expression to them. Furthermore, senior management must ensure that all employees are trained in the terms associated with these frameworks, as well as the tools that they have given rise to.

Systems Thinking

In Chapter 2 we discussed the benefit of using Systems Thinking to map the social enterprise's internal and external components and stakeholders. Improving their understanding of this interaction will help the enterprise to create its unique and valued product. We were reminded that enterprises, when understood as a system, consist of inter-related sub-systems with feedback loops that can reinforce or maintain, and that they enjoy a permeable boundary with their external environment. Reinforcing or accelerating feedback loops are either virtuous or destructive to the enterprise. Maintenance or balancing loops serve as brakes that prevent the enterprise from burnout.

Senior leadership is responsible for putting the social enterprise "on the board" as a complete system. The phrase "on the board" means that these leaders draw and display a visual map which shows how the enterprise operates. Staff can view and comment on this map. This allows senior management, their team leaders, and teams to anticipate and plan for changes. Team members also come to understand how their individual team decisions will impact the enterprise's ability to operate efficiently. This wide-lens view is critical because it reduces the chance of individual teams making sub-optimal decisions which, while they make sense and improve conditions and results in one area, have a zero or detrimental impact elsewhere in the enterprise.

From a systems perspective, the goal of Operations Management is to ensure organizational efficiency by carefully balancing harmony with competition. Since social enterprises are concerned with delivering a valued product which simultaneously addresses a critical social problem, a systems perspective is helpful as it allows leadership to oscillate between working with the big picture and improving the quality of their product. This quality improvement may be operationalized by embracing the concept of the Theory of Constraint.

In 1984, Eli Goldratt introduced the business management world to the Theory of Constraint when he published his business novel entitled *The Goal*. The story begins when a senior manager is charged with turning around a failing manufacturing plant in his hometown. After his initial efforts fail, a chance encounter with his former high school teacher leads him and his management team to view and then resolve the plant's underperformance by means of the Theory of Constraint. This insight allows the manager and his team to identify and remove bottlenecks in the plant's manufacturing process, thereby allowing the plant to become profitable once again.

The Theory of Constraints is a useful tool for senior and middle management in social enterprises. It begins by asking those leaders to clarify their organization's mission (*Why are we in this business*?) so that they can use this clarity as a yardstick against which they can measure their stated improvement goal. The improvement goal is the problem they have been tasked to address. Once they have clarified this, the next step is to look at all their internal processes to identify those that are preventing (constraining) them from reaching peak performance. Constraints may assume a physical form such as old equipment or inventory inefficiencies. They may also arise from the enterprise's human resources, such as a large pool of untrained and younger workers.

Once those constraints have been identified and prioritized, the enterprise can go ahead and address them. It is important that senior management is entrusted with employing this systems-wide lens, because they have the decision-making authority to address systemic constraints. Removing constraints may require the enterprise to change its procurement and human resource policies. It may need to invest in new equipment and technology. It may require changes to the way in which the enterprise manages its inventory flow. Responsibility for these decisions falls outside the parameters within which the enterprise's work and product development teams operate. The intellectual discipline of the Theory of Constraint can be applied anywhere in the organization, and remains a powerful enterprise-wide approach because it creates an enabling environment within which the entire enterprise can work.

Senior leadership ensures that the balanced scorecard the enterprise employs reflects their progress in removing constraints. Traditionally, balanced scorecards have measured a business or organization's progress in the four areas of finances, customers, business process and, learning and growth. We recommend that a social enterprise use the Six Capitals when creating their version of the balanced scorecard.

The balanced scorecard template featured in Table 1 is for a fictitious social enterprise that provides affordable homeownership opportunities.

TYPE OF CAPITAL	OBJECTIVE	METRIC
Natural Capital	Increase energy efficiency at all operational centers by 20%	# of KwH consumed Units of Water consumed Lbs of materials recycled
Financial Capital	Reduce material and housing inventory by 20%	# of units under construction # of units sold # of days that materials are stored. # of days to construct a house
Human Capital	Reduce employee turnover by 10%	# of employees on 1/1/20XX # of employees at 12/31/20XX
Manufacturing Capital	Increase equipment productivity by 20%	# of days equipment is in use # of days that equipment is undergoing maintenance # of new equipment purchased during year
Intellectual Capital	Create 1 new housing product	# of prototypes created # of prototypes tested # of prototypes sold
Social Capital	Increase pool of qualified homebuyers by 50%	# of applications received per month. # of applicants completing underwriting requirements per month. # of homebuyers qualified by 12/31/20XX

Table 1: Balanced Scorecard for Glenwood Housing Inc.

Lean Production

Lean production (or contemporary Scientific Management) has emerged from the post-Second World War economic competition between the United States and Japan. The principles and practice of Lean manufacturing entered the popular lexicon with the publication of *The Machine That Changed the World* by Womack, Jones, and Roos in 1991. In this book, the authors described a revolutionary manufacturing process which the Toyota Motor Corporation used to manufacture its vehicles. This revelation was followed by concepts and practices such as Six Sigma, Kaizen and 5S being added to the Operations Management toolbox. Since then, these concepts have entered other sectors of the economy including software engineering. In 2011, Eric Ries reflected on his experiences of applying Lean manufacturing in the software startup sphere when he wrote "The Lean Startup". Ries was invited to share his insights with General Electric, who subsequently used them to create their FastWorks methodology.

SCRUM (Systematic Customer Resolution Unraveling Meeting) was first practiced by software and manufacturing companies. It is a Lean method that grew out of the Agile approach to daily management. We introduced you to the Agile approach to teams in Chapter 5. This approach is of particular use when designing customized services for niche clients, as it follows the same process of speeding up the development cycle by engaging a cross functional team internally, and then quickly engaging customers. The principles behind SCRUM are ones of customized product development and are linked to the idea of building small batches of items.

Some of the key principles which underpin Lean Production:

- A belief that everyone in the enterprise can and wants to learn, improve, and succeed, and that everyone has the potential to do so. Social enterprises intrinsically believe this and gravitate towards hiring individuals and groups who are marginalized.
- Use a whole systems approach to identify and solve opportunities and problems.
- Continually apply the Action-Reflection method to organizational learning.
- Success results from the synthesis of entrepreneurial vision and the solution of a customer's problem.
- Empowered teams drive innovation.
- Innovation is fundamentally about learning through experimentation.
- Learning consists of hypotheses that are substantiated by data.
- These hypotheses can be measured, improved upon, and managed.
- Failure is an accepted part of the learning process.
- Long-term planning by top-level management is obsolete.

These principles have given rise to the following practices:

- Learning is iterative. This means that the production team quickly receives feedback on the prototype they have created. They incorporate these lessons into the subsequent versions of the prototype product.
- The production process begins with the question *"What do we want to learn as we create or improve our product*?" This is followed by *"What and how will we measure what we have learnt?"* The production team then builds a prototype and tests it by selling it to a customer who likes to be known as an early adopter. The production team accompanies the customer as they use the product so that problems can be solved as they arise. The collected information is given to the rest of the production team who, in turn, use it to further refine the product.
- The enterprise creates cross functional teams whose members are drawn from those departments responsible for manufacturing, marketing, and selling the product.
- The enterprise is less hierarchical, with fewer levels of management. This not only keeps its indirect costs down, but also reduces the number of steps in the approval process.
- It is the customer's reality that counts! The team has to suspend their assumptions about what will work best for the customer. Instead, they engage the customer in the early stages of the build cycle and retain that engagement. Social enterprises connect with the customers who will purchase their social product, as well as those stakeholders who will benefit from the positive social impact that the enterprise is creating.
- Teams identify their customers by focusing on a few who are known as "early adopters". These customers are willing to pay for an incomplete prototype that will meet their minimum requirements in exchange for being known to have been amongst the first to have tested and adopted the product. These customers have confidence in their ability, and that of the social enterprise's team, to solve any problems that might arise with the product.
- The enterprise and its teams establish milestones early in the learning process. These milestones coincide with the metrics which are created through innovation accounting. They also mark key decision-making points, usually associated with determining whether to proceed with the product as is, whether to improve it or, whether it needs to be abandoned. In the last scenario, the team uses what it has learnt from this failure to build a new prototype product.
- The enterprise creates innovation metrics to track its performance in areas such as customer sales and the cost of the inputs going into the

product. Enterprises and their teams can seek inspiration for these metrics from the efficiency ratios they use to track performance, as introduced in Chapter 4. The team establishes its baseline for each metric and then collects data to track their progress. When the numbers stall, it is time for the team to pivot to either a new iteration of the product, or to return to the drawing board and create a new one.

- Enterprises provide teams with dedicated budgets and the necessary autonomy to make their own spending decisions.
- The enterprise generates small batches of products at any time. This practice speeds up the team's learning cycle and is more likely to result in a quality, customized product. It reduces waste, because teams incorporate Lean Practices such as 5S and Kaizen into their daily operations.
- Teams learn from their mistakes and the feedback that they receive. They have the necessary autonomy to modify the product or pivot to a new one should that be necessary.
- The enterprise recognizes the innovations that teams have made and reward them accordingly.
- Enterprises customize the concept and language of Lean to fit their unique circumstances, thereby promoting its adoption by all their employees.

Sustainable social enterprises must incorporate and follow Lean principles in all facets of their operation if they are to survive and generate positive social impact. Lean has the potential to revolutionize the way their employees approach their work and community obligations. Empowered work teams allow for meaningful individual development and participation, and this promotes a sense of economic identity and belonging. Social enterprises must apply the discipline of Lean not only to the product which they create for profit, but also to the methodology they use to create their social impact.

Improving Operations Management to sustain growth

The practice of 5S

5S is a tool that reduces clutter and operational inefficiency by cleaning the workspace and then maintaining it in that state. By doing so, the social enterprise improves morale, maintains workplace safety, sets the stage for site visits from customers and supporters, and creates a mindset of positive productivity. The 5S concept begins with 5 action verbs which inform the following diagram:

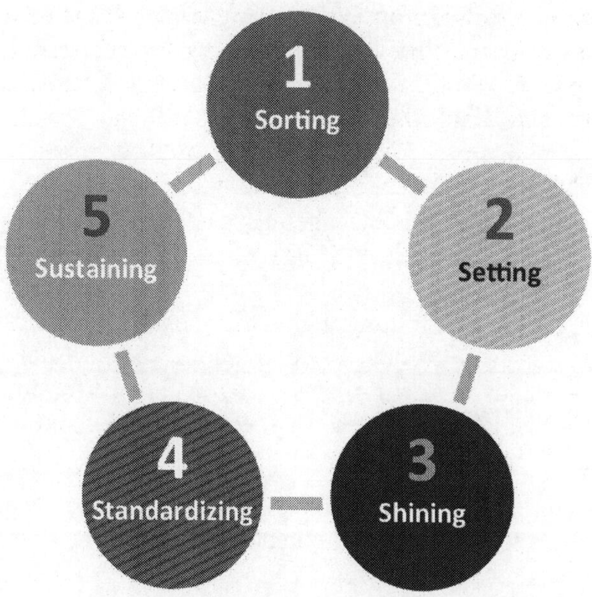

Fig.4: 5S concept

Sorting involves organizing all the contents into three piles. The first pile contains essential items which must be kept in the workspace. The second pile contains necessary items which are periodically used, and which can be stored elsewhere and retrieved when they are needed. The third pile contains broken items or ones which are no longer used. In other words, they are junk items which can be discarded or recycled.

Setting is the phase when the contents of these three piles are transported to, and arranged in, these three spaces. This phase also involves creating an inventory system to track their movements and their use, and when they will need to be replaced.

Shining refers to the physical cleaning of the workspace and, if necessary, its renovation and painting so that it is transformed into a welcome and safe space for the employees who work there.

Standardizing involves creating and implementing regular schedules to clean the space, sort through the accumulated items, and reset them in their respective three spaces.

Sustaining occurs when management creates a system of accountability and rewards which promote the preceding 4S's of sorting, setting, shining, and standardizing.

The 5S concept should be applied in every corner of the social enterprise. It is a powerful way to introduce employees to the concept of empowerment and it becomes a building block of participatory practices such as Open Book Management and Lean manufacturing.

Using Flowcharts to map the Value Stream

The origins of flow charts in management can be traced to the era of Scientific Management and the work of Henry Gantt in the early 20th Century. He designed and popularized the Gantt Chart which maps out the sequential steps a team or business follows within their sphere of responsibility, to bring a service or physical product to completion. These visual representations represent the standard process that is followed. They differ from project management tools which are created for specific projects, and which reflect the specific time frame that has been set aside for the project.

All levels of the social enterprise must create a visual display of every activity performed by a team and its individual members. Once it has been created, this map serves several purposes:

- It is an educational tool that can be used when orienting new employees.
- It reminds every staff member what their role is and how their actions help to create value.
- It minimizes the likelihood of sub-optimal decisions.
- It stimulates discussion about how to make the enterprise's operations more efficient by seeing what steps are unnecessary (non-value-adding), and thus these can be eliminated or combined to generate savings to the enterprise. These savings then help the social enterprise to replenish its capitals.
- It serves as the springboard for improving both products and the process whereby they are created.

Flowcharts, or Value Stream maps, may be depicted as a visual picture or as a chart, with sequential steps organized on the Y-axis and the time of each recorded on the X-axis. These charts and maps contain the following information:

- Sequential steps
- The start and end points of the process
- Time allocated for each step
- Inputs required at each step
- Outputs from each step
- Directional arrows to reflect sequence and feedback
- Responsible parties
- Decision points, including production number and quality checks

Square	Circle	Triangle	Diamond	Arrow
■	●	▲	◆	→
MEANING: **Start/End of Process**	MEANING: **Decision-making Point**	MEANING: **Process**	MEANING: **Input or Output**	MEANING: **Direction**

Table 2: Basic Flowchart symbols

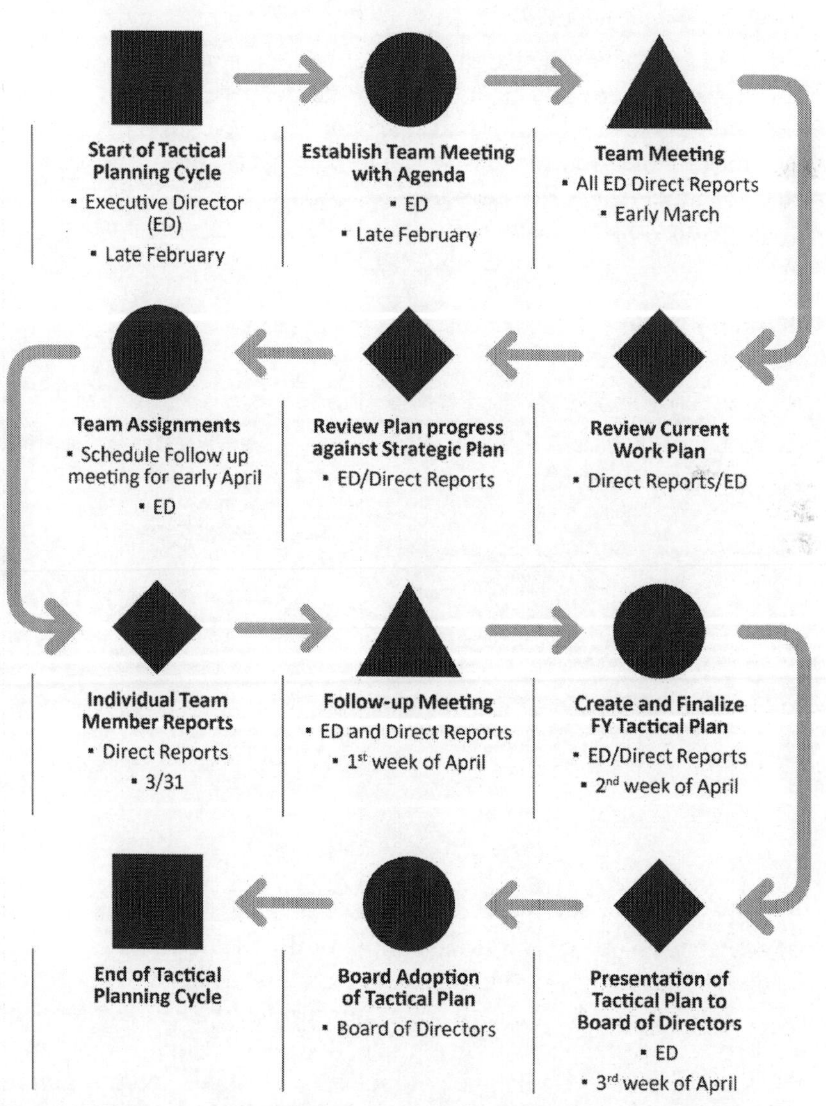

Fig.5: Sample Flowchart for a senior management annual tactical planning process

Having a Sunset Policy that provides for transitions

In *Managing in Turbulent Times*, Peter Drucker (1985) calls on organizations to create abandonment policies. Such policies provide social enterprises with the intellectual justification to regularly review their products and processes to see whether they are still necessary, and whether they are still creating value. If they are redundant, they must be ended so that the enterprise can instead focus on the current and new products which deliver the desired results. According to Drucker, an abandonment policy answers two questions:

- *Should we abandon this product or process?*
- *How should we abandon this product or process?*

The first question takes the hard and objective look at all products and processes through the lens of their economic costs and benefits to the enterprise. The second question recognizes that abandonment also carries psychological implications for the social enterprise and its employees. It is therefore crucial that the abandonment policy also includes steps to address identity and role concerns by drawing on the work done in the field of transition management. We will return to this topic in Chapter 10.

Bringing it together

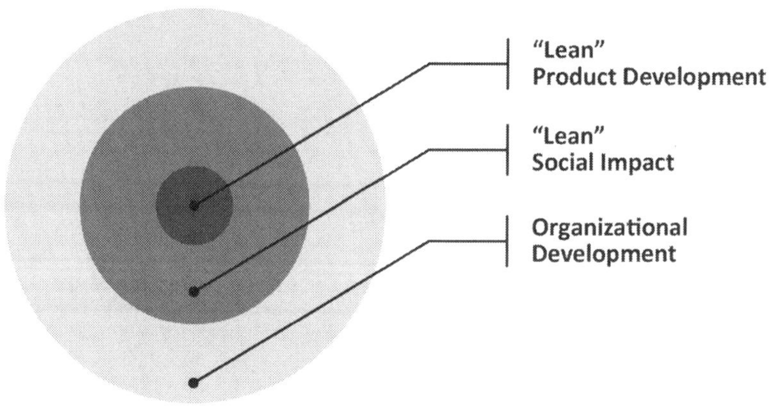

Fig.6: Bringing it together

Operations Management enjoys a mobius-like relationship with organizational development. Since the sustainability of the social enterprise depends on its teams constantly working to ensure a quality and improving product, it stands to reason that workplace teams need to be trained in, and operate, the principles and practices of Lean production. This central activity is represented by the core of the diagram in Figure 6, which also portrays product development and improvement as being the primary responsibility of teams in the social enterprise. Product development is critical to the social enterprise's ongoing financial viability.

Since a social enterprise intentionally creates social impact through its valued product and service, it must consider how the enterprise will add positive social value to the customers and communities that it serves. Rather than viewing social impact as a passive externality, the social enterprise needs to apply the same level of rigor and motivation to this as they do when they are creating products. Senior managers must make this second ring on the diagram explicit and shepherd the enterprise through it.

The third and outermost ring on the diagram depicts the responsibility of senior management and leadership. Not only must they create and change the organizational structure, safeguard its purpose, and establish practices to protect all its Six Capitals, but they must also manage these changes and transitions in ways which allow the organization to survive, and which honor its internal stakeholders. This is the realm of organizational development.

In conclusion, contemporary Operations Management can be thought of as scientific management with a human face. It is inspired by the belief that empowered employees have the knowledge and expertise to drive improvements, especially when this is tied to the benefits of more efficient operations. Once the enterprise reaches a growth phase when it can scale up its operations and impact, then it should apply the principles and practices that govern responsible growth. These form the basis of Chapter 9.

Chapter 9

WISE GROWTH TO ENSURE SUSTAINABILITY AND IMPACT

The Paradox of The Growth Imperative

The growth imperative is built into our economic and cultural systems and individuals are judged on the material resources and social capital they have access to. Businesses and non-profits are evaluated on the health of their income statements and balance sheets, with an additional requirement that non-profits demonstrate their value through their program outcomes. Communities and countries are also ranked on factors such as their employment and poverty rates and the performance of their Gross Domestic Product (GDP).

Growth provides a benchmark with which to measure success and relative deprivation. It also creates conflict which generates the moral imperative for innovation, especially when it comes to addressing the social inequalities, humanitarian crises and environmental costs which flow from that growth. These conditions give rise to the need for social enterprises to serve as peace builders because they introduce the discipline and creativity of business entrepreneurship when addressing social issues. The continued existence of these issues is the reason why social enterprises must focus on growth and expansion.

The paradox of growth is that it is a balancing act between short-term gain and long-term prosperity. The two are not always in sync with each other. The imperative of economic growth demands that for-profit businesses focus on short-term gains, which are expressed in their quarterly earnings reports. It is this part of the market, which is represented by investors and traders, that drives the growth imperative. This places enormous pressure on the business leaders and managers to deliver consistent returns. The pressure that this imperative generates, along with the loss of their individual and corporate moral compasses, often lies at the root of many corporate scandals. There are also individual and social health costs associated with the growth imperative, including the stress associated with overwork, burnout and trying to earn enough to meet household expenses.

Since many social enterprises trace their roots to, or draw their managers and boards from the for-profit sector, it should come as no surprise that social enterprises themselves have to respond to the growth imperative. How they go about doing so is the basis for this chapter.

The Good Angel Dilemma

In addition to the peril of the economic growth imperative that social enterprises share with their traditional for-profit counterparts, they are also tempted to be the Good Angel. We are introduced to the Good Angel through the Hasidic tradition in Judaism. In this story, an angel is deeply grieved by the cycle of death and destruction amongst people on earth. The angel intercedes with God and is granted permission to remove these conditions. Over the course of the year, utopia begins to emerge. Prosperity arrives in the form of bountiful crops and harvests. Death and decay are no more, and the angel is pleased and returns to God. But the angel soon hears voices of anguish rising from the earth. The bread, which they have baked from the wheat they have harvested, is unpalatable. The angel learns from God that death and decay is necessary for renewal and life.

In the Christian tradition, the Gospels tell that Jesus spends 40 days in the wilderness. During that period, he is visited by Satan who subjects Jesus to three temptations. These temptations speak to the illusions of power, immediate gratification, and social acclaim.

Both stories hold uncomfortable truths for those who establish and lead social enterprises, since they shine light on the growth imperative, albeit from other angles.

Journeying up the S-Curve

The context for the remainder of this chapter is the growth phase on the Sigmoid Curve as represented in Figure 1:

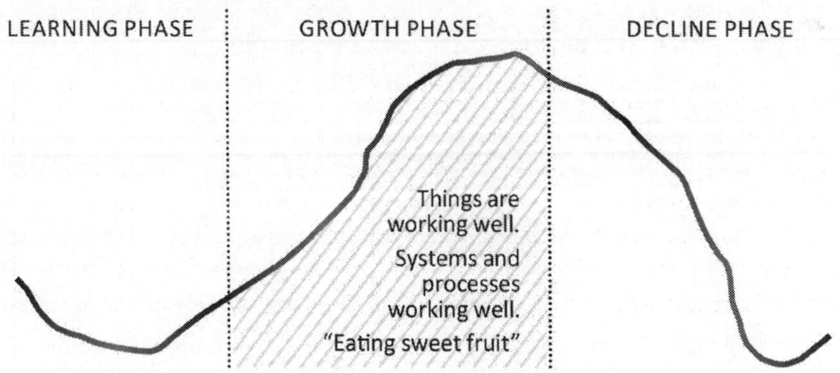

Fig.1: Journeying up the S-Curve

At this point, the social enterprise has matured. It has progressed past its initial start-up phase and is now realizing greater stability and profitability.

Its systems and personnel are comfortably in place, and it is experiencing predictable growth. But its leaders and managers understand this period will not last indefinitely and that they need to take advantage of this period to expand the enterprise so that it continues to be sustainable. The S-Curve is a powerful tool which guides the social enterprise to understand that change will be required at some point, and it provides clues as to when that should happen. This dynamic is captured in Figure 2:

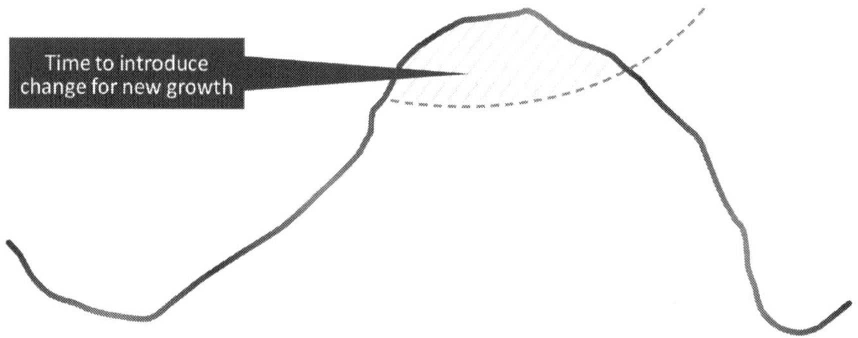

Fig.2: Time for change and growth

Social enterprises can grow their operations and expand their impact in the following ways:

- They can refine and expand their current product and business line by looking for an order from a big client that will catapult them into that higher level of production, revenue, and profitability.
- They can replicate their existing model and products in other geographic markets.
- Through internal innovation, they can add a new business line or product to their existing one.
- They can purchase an under-performing, yet promising business opportunity. However, social enterprises must be prepared for the possibility that they may have to close unproductive business lines down in future.
- They can disrupt the market by questioning the conventional assumptions they and their peers have been making about the market. They can use these new insights to create a radically new product or service. An example of this is the introduction of micro-credit or digital literacy training.

In Chapter 5, we introduced the reader to Sihle Tshabalala, CEO of the non-profit company Quirky 30. Sihle and his team have established offices (mobile and fixed) in Cape Town townships to train unemployed youth, vulnerable groups, and ex-offenders – all of whom are at risk of prolonged unemployment, crime, and poverty – in high-value technology skills. Students are taught a variety of coding languages and digital skills to enable them to build web sites and mobile applications, and to work as coders in established businesses. Training also includes learning some soft skills such as job readiness training, CV writing and interview skills, presentation and communication skills, design thinking and project management. The shortage of coders in Cape Town, which is South Africa's tech capital, makes this training program a viable growth path and option for Quirky 30.

Challenging Growth Scenarios

There are two additional scenarios which might trigger the growth and change the inflection point shown in Figure 2. These are the need to downsize a social enterprise, and to scale up production to meet the demand of a single, powerful customer. These two scenarios will now be explored in greater detail.

Scenario 1: Downsizing a Social Enterprise

Just like their traditional for-profit counterparts, social enterprises are not immune to the siren call to grow by adding additional business lines. The common scenario is where another enterprise closes its doors and thus leaves important social needs unfulfilled. It also leaves behind assets for the remaining enterprises to assume or purchase at little to no cost. Entrepreneurial-minded enterprise leaders assume those assets and programs, but often lack the necessary skills and resources to make them sustainable. These "new" programs absorb more of the social enterprise's tangible and intangible resources. The emotional and resource investment already made in this new venture makes it hard for the enterprise to complete an honest cost-benefit analysis. The decision to end or re-imagine the new venture is therefore delayed. This generates conflict within the organization. The social enterprise's core business then suffers, resulting in a sub-par product or service.

When presented with the opportunity to acquire or start a new business line, a social enterprise should remember that it is the responsibility of the Board of Directors and the Executive leadership team to commission a thorough and objective assessment of the new venture using their growth plan (this is described later in the chapter). The team then generates recommendations and presents these to the Board for their discussion and final decision.

The decision to close an unproductive business line is never easy. People and equipment will be lost. The social enterprise's financial statements will show a loss in revenue and assets, while its reputation may suffer over the short-term. All this weighs heavily on the shoulders of the Executive leader and Board of Directors. There is no way to avoid this decision. Nevertheless, it is important that the executive leader and Board prepare staff and stakeholders for this eventuality through regular communication and by using the insights provided from transition management.

Scenario 2: Taking advantage of large orders to scale-up

If social enterprises can run the risk of operating too many business lines, then the reverse is also true. Their over-reliance on a single product or service can make them over-dependent on a particular resource or customer. When addressing this dilemma, social enterprise leaders must also remain sensitive to the fact that fulfilling this large order will come at the expense of other customers. This may increase their enterprise's vulnerability over the long-term.

Dealing effectively with this situation requires a healthy organization with mature leadership. If an enterprise decides to accept large orders, then it requires that "all hands be on deck". This order provides the social enterprise leader with the opportunity of learning more about their large customer's needs, timelines, and priorities. The executive leader needs to be in regular contact with his or her counterpart at the large company to ensure that they have a good understanding of each other's needs and constraints. The rest of the executive team and employees at the social enterprise should focus on ensuring that their operating capacity and model are working as efficiently as possible. The marketing and sales teams must seek out new customers. Communication, information, and updates need to flow regularly between the social enterprise's operations and their executive leader when they are out in the field interacting with the client.

Growth begins with conversations about the Big Questions

The reference made earlier in this chapter to the Good Angel reminds us that there is a spiritual dimension to a social enterprise. Bringing faith and spirituality into any discussion about business is fraught with tension, given the negative experiences that so many people have had with restrictive religious practices. Nevertheless, many people who establish and/or work in social enterprises do so from a faith perspective and find their work there to be spiritually nourishing. Answering the "Big Questions" (listed below) draws from people's spiritual reserves and the insights that they glean from working in this space individually, and also at an enterprise level.

- *What lasting impact do we want to have on those whom we serve?*
- *What does "good" look and feel like?* (Note that we have used the word

"good" instead of success. We have done so for a specific reason. In the Creation story in both the Bible and the Torah, God speaks the word "good" or "Tov" at the end of each workday, as a pronouncement on the constructive work done that day).

- *How will we promote growth?*
- *How will we assess our growth opportunities?*
- *What do we need to put in place so that we can grow?*
- *How will we structure ourselves so that we remain true to our core mission and values?*
- *How will we retain our human-scale while expanding?*
- *How much is enough?*

These conversations need to happen throughout the enterprise, not only in board room, or at the coffee shop on the corner, or at an annual retreat. It's never too early to begin discussing these deep matters. Too many times, social enterprises either miss opportunities or seize the wrong ones because they have not had these conversations before developing their growth plan. Instead, they hide behind the convenient excuse that now is not the time to do so, that they are too busy, and that they will have them when a future time allows for it. Responses such as these are nothing more than kicking the proverbial can down the road. The role of wise board members – or in their absence, a coach – is to encourage the social enterprise to persist in these conversations.

The rationale behind a written Growth Plan

All discussions that a social enterprise undertakes about growth must be captured in a written growth strategy document or Growth Plan. A Growth Plan facilitates critical analysis and deliberate, intentional decision-making. It also reduces the likelihood that the enterprise will make an impulsive decision which it will come to regret.

The Growth Plan should include:

- The social enterprise's answers to the Big Questions.
- The criteria whereby they will assess opportunities for growth.
- Minimum readiness standards.
- The results of the preliminary SWOT analysis.
- Plans to address the readiness gap which has been found to exist between their current capacity and the minimum readiness standards.

The final document is considered for approval and periodic review by the social enterprise's governance and senior management. The final test to which the Board subjects any proposal for growth and expansion is *how well it scores against the criteria laid out in the plan.* While the executive leadership and employees of any social enterprise should be tasked with proposing ways in which the enterprise can grow its impact, the process to decide whether to embark on a particular growth initiative should be a deliberate one. The final decision (to proceed or not) rests with the enterprise's governance body which must approve any major transactions associated with the expansion project. Finally, those who serve as directors should also use this plan to scout out potential growth opportunities that the enterprise can take advantage of at this point, or in the future.

Growth Plans are structured in such a way that they address the following key points and involve the following steps:

Fig.3: Growth Plans

Criteria for assessing opportunities for growth

Once the social enterprise has formulated its answers to the Big Questions, the next step is to use those answers to create a set of criteria. Developing this allows the social enterprise to assess every growth opportunity it encounters so that it does not drift from its core mission and business model. Furthermore, well-crafted mission criteria prevent an enterprise from squandering valuable and limited natural, human, financial, intellectual, operating, and social capital on impractical expansion opportunities. Having these criteria in place will allow enterprises to be flexible so that they can quickly respond when their external environment changes. But this also allows the enterprise to remain rooted and true to its founding principles and values.

What might these measures look like? Social enterprises should consult their program, financial and risk management dashboards when they develop these criteria. By way of example, a social enterprise that employs physically handicapped persons (whose limitations have excluded them from working in the economic mainstream), may answer the question about lasting impact as being one that sees their employees being fully accepted and able to participate in their community. These individuals find value in the work that they are employed to do, and the community recognizes their value by purchasing the product which these individuals help to create at the social enterprise. So, a growth opportunity that allows the social enterprise to expand into a new market where it can then employ a fixed number of individuals with disabilities who are currently unemployed would count as an opportunity worth considering. This would need to be balanced by the results of a market study, which tests whether the local community will purchase products made by the social enterprise. Other financial benchmarks will also need to be considered.

It is the responsibility of the social enterprise's Board of Directors to define these mission criteria after engaging with the organization's stakeholders. These criteria should be the subject of the Board's periodic review process, enjoy a place on its calendar, and be assigned as a responsibility to the Board's Risk Management Committee.

We agree with Lynch and Walls' (2009) rationale that social impact is the only justification for the growth of a social enterprise. Therefore, a social enterprise must subject any opportunity for growth to the test of whether this will allow it to generate greater social impact, thereby reducing the extent of the social problem it is targeting for redress. The related question that should be asked is whether this opportunity will merely create more work for the organization, resulting in staff burnout and the inefficient deployment of the organization's resources. Finally, any growth must add to the enterprise's bottom line and increase its financial resilience, without devaluing its social mission.

Establishing minimum readiness standards

The social enterprise creates these standards when they answer the following question. "*What do we need to have in place before we can expand?*" Once again, social enterprises should rely on the framework of the Six Capitals when they establish these standards.

Human capital standards

Since growth places additional burdens on a social enterprise's existing employees, leaders and managers, the Board and its Executive leader will need to carefully monitor these employees' energy and commitment. The excitement generated by the growth is guaranteed to increase leaders' adrenaline surges – but that energy is limited as there are other professional and social demands on their time. Growth may also require that they need to invest in developing new skills or undergo retraining in ones that they already possess. Stephen Covey (1990) reminded leaders and managers to regularly "sharpen their saws".

Social enterprises therefore should ask what additional and new skills expansion will be required from all levels of their workforce, and assess the level of workforce motivation before they embark on an expansion project. Askinosie's (2017) description of a participatory business vocation at Askinosie Chocolate indicates that this is a useful tool for creating a workplace environment where all employees are motivated to fully engage in the enterprise's growth opportunity.

A healthy workplace culture is a prerequisite for successful growth because sustained growth will place greater demands not only on current employees, but also on the human resource systems which surround them. It is crucial that the enterprise does not lose its existing workforce through burnout and turnover. Growth will probably result in new staff being added to the social enterprise; however, it is critical that they be onboarded in such a way that they assimilate the esprit de corps that has caused the social enterprise to become successful. It is also important that they be welcomed as equal members of the team. Therefore, other minimum standards for this human capital category include a robust onboarding protocol, and a healthy workplace culture.

Financial capital standards

The social enterprise must establish the level of capital reserves it needs to have on hand before it considers opportunities for growth and expansion. Furthermore, it must regularly assess whether its current sources of capital (investors, banks, or donors) would be interested in funding its future expansion. As much as is possible, enterprises should have these sources lined up so that they can quickly employ their allotted reserves and outside funds to take advantage of any opportunities for growth and expansion.

Intellectual capital standards

The enterprise must determine whether its existing governance and management systems are sufficient to accommodate its ongoing work as well as the demands of expansion and growth. The enterprise must establish whether its production processes (along with any intellectual property that it has developed and harnessed) are secure and that they are being utilized to their highest potential.

Social capital standards

These standards refer to the necessary goodwill that the social enterprise has in place from both its internal and external stakeholders. As mentioned already, the social capital criteria for internal stakeholders, include a healthy organizational culture and robust training and onboarding practices. Criteria for external stakeholders include whether they will enthusiastically embrace expansion, or whether they will consider it to be a form of mission creep which leads them to withdraw their support. By regularly investing in the relationships they have with their external stakeholders and by acknowledging the concerns and input of this group, social enterprises can build up the trust and support that they will require from these stakeholders when they embark on their future expansion projects.

Manufacturing capital standards

Based on their unique industry and product, social enterprises need to establish what minimum physical space and equipment must be secured and operational before they embark on expansion. The capacity of their manufacturing capital must be such that it can comfortably support existing operations whilst the basis for expansion is laid.

Natural capital

The creation of minimum standards for their natural capital is one of the more challenging tasks a social enterprise must deal with. They should ask themselves, "*Do our current operations allow social enterprises to meet our obligation to be good stewards of the natural capital that we employ?" "Have we met those obligations through our current operations?"* Social enterprises can use these questions when calculating their readiness to embark on an expansion project.

Assemble a New Initiatives team

The literature on innovation, change management, and Lean Production all point to the importance of establishing a team whose sole responsibility is to seek, assess and recommend growth opportunities and expansion projects to businesses. This team should consist of people that the enterprise can spare from its daily operations, or freelancers who can be contracted in. The size of such a team needs to be in proportion to the size and scale of the social enterprise. This group should be cross-functional, which means that it reflects the different components of its operational model. Individuals who serve on the team should bring good insights into its internal operations, as well as the evolving interests and concerns of its external stakeholders.

Some terms of reference that can be assigned to a New Initiatives team include:

- Helping to create, review and update the Growth Plan.
- Developing new products.
- Assessing possible products.

Conduct a SWOT analysis

Employing a SWOT (Strengths, Weaknesses, Opportunities, Threats) analysis will allow the social enterprise to create a snapshot of its current capabilities and deficiencies, and supplement these with an assessment of what is happening in its external environment. Strengths and weaknesses identify the enterprise's current reality, especially when it comes to its existing capacity. These strengths and weaknesses allow it to identify the gaps it will need to close, so as to meet the minimum readiness standards created in the previous step (see *Assemble a New Initiatives team*).

Identifying opportunities and threats allows the social enterprise to begin shifting its focus to see possible opportunities for future growth and expansion. Doing so encourages the enterprise to consider new solutions to the current social issues the social enterprise wants to impact through their work.

Threats refer to competitors and forces which can inhibit the enterprise's growth. The solution is to conduct a market study. This study must determine whether the market can sustain more of the same product, and whether it will accept the new one that the enterprise plans to produce. The enterprise must ascertain not only whether the need exists, but also what price point the market is willing to pay for the goods or service. It is critical to source this information early in the process so that the social enterprise does not waste its limited resources on an opportunity which ends up providing little or no opportunity for growth.

Create and monitor the Growth Plan

The final step in creating a Growth Plan is to record all the findings. This written plan should end with short-term plans and their accompanying schedules, so that the social enterprise can reach the minimum readiness standards it has established.

Is there a right growth? Two books share different perspectives on what constitutes "right" growth for a social enterprise. Lynch and Walls, the authors of *Mission Inc. (*2009), express the opinion that social enterprises are obligated to grow so that they can increase their social impact. They argue that all growth opportunities need to be carefully considered and that these must not only be financially viable but must expand the enterprise's social impact. Lynch and Walls share the agony they endured when they had to downsize business lines that were unprofitable. In their experience, growth emerges when social enterprises apply the discipline of Lean Production to their operations. This discipline allows them to expand or scale-up the size and impact of their operations.

In *Meaningful Work*, Askinosie (2017) puts forward an opposing argument which he terms "reverse scale". He argues against scaling-up an operation by noting that there are significant downsides to doing so. For one, it often comes at the loss of human connection and humility, and carries with it the need for bureaucracy. Scaling up and a fixation on growth can potentially lead to that growth being driven by mergers and the emergence of monopolies, rather than the creation of new enterprises. Instead Askinosie asks social enterprises to remain at their most efficient human size. If applied widely, then local communities and their economies would consist of many highly performing, small- and medium-sized enterprises and organizations. The question of how to scale up (increase) the social impact that each of these enterprises generates will be the focus of the last part of this chapter.

Towards a "Right" Organizational Structure

Thus far, this chapter has focused largely on the criteria and steps a social enterprise must take when positioning itself for growth and when it is considering potential growth opportunities. The literature and social enterprise practitioners agree that social enterprises should not grow too quickly. There is also agreement that this growth should not come at the expense of their unique "soul" and that it should honor the principles of the human scale, financial sustainability, and the development of ongoing, valued relationships between stakeholders. However, scholars and social enterprise practitioners are to remain mindful that these enterprises must increase their positive social impact. The depth and breadth of social problems facing their communities and the globe will not allow social enterprises to be complacent and remain where they are.

The next logical step in developing the criteria for, and contents of the growth strategy and the desired social impact that it generates, is for them to consider which type of operating organizational structure will best suit this growth. We argue that, as social enterprises grow and expand their area of operations, they should seriously consider using federalism as their organizing principle.

Askinosie's (2017) use of the term "human scale" leads us back to E.F. Schumacher's 1973 bestseller entitled *Small is Beautiful – Economics as if People Mattered*. In his chapter on large-scale organizations, Schumacher writes that an organization alternates between periods of centralization and decentralization. Fueled in part by the growth imperative, this tension is generated by the paradoxical relationship of freedom and order. People and organizations desire the freedom to be unique and entrepreneurial, yet neither individuals nor organizations can tolerate much disorder. Therefore, with this freedom, they simultaneously desire order along with the structure and discipline that it brings. This same tension is also found within social enterprises.

Schumacher, and later Charles Handy (1989), recommend that enterprises address this tension by using federalism as their organizing principle. Federalism allows for local autonomy, innovation, and nimbleness whilst building interdependent relationships between these units so that they can exploit economies of scale. By carefully managing this tension, enterprises can remain at human scale while delivering greater economic, environmental, and social impact. This organizational arrangement also allows enterprises to quickly consider growth opportunities when they present themselves.

Businesses were inspired to begin using federalism as an organizing principle when "empowerment" re-emerged as a popular management concept in the 1980s. But we argue that a genuine commitment to federalism as an organizing principle begins with the understanding that a social contract exists at the heart of a social enterprise. This contract binds all the stakeholders together, and it is informed by the Six Capitals. At its core, the social contract comes about when people agree to collaborate on a project. They understand that they will need to surrender some of their freedom if they are to realize a beneficial outcome that meets their interests. They also understand that it is their partnership that provides them with a more efficient means to achieve that outcome. This is a negotiated agreement, often implicit, but it does need to be made explicit so that it can be remembered, refined, and revisited. The Six Capitals provide social enterprises with a framework to envisage what their social contract will look like. It stretches them to consider their impact on the natural environment, as well as their community.

By employing federalism, an expanding social enterprise appreciates that there are two basic organizational units that serve as its building blocks. These are the *Local Unit* which exists at the community level (e.g., it could take the form of the factory where the product is produced, the physical or virtual shop front where the product is sold, or the physical space where the service is dispensed). Local Units look like one another and largely produce the same product or service. But they are responsive to, and reflect, the community where they are located.

The second building block is the *Center*, or the heart where the social enterprise's DNA is stored, and this re-circulates energy, finances, and ideas throughout the social enterprise. The Center reflects the common interests of the local units, and it exists solely to serve, represent, and advocate for the Local Units.

These two building blocks are bound together by a contract. This contract is negotiated between the Local Units and the Center, with the powers and responsibility of the latter emerging from the consent of the Local Units.

The rights and responsibilities of the Local Unit

The Local Units have line authority. This authority is rooted in the principle of subsidiarity. Drawn from the Papal Encyclical *Quadragesimo Anno,* which was issued by Pope Pius XI in 1931, this principle can be summarized as follows: "A higher order body should not take onto itself responsibilities which properly belong to a lower order body". Freedom and responsibility rests with the Local Unit of an organization. The Local Units decide what powers they are willing to give to the Center. The bulk of the work which the social enterprise performs takes place through these Local Units.

Local Units are responsible for producing and delivering the social enterprise's product. They must have the authority and ability to customize the enterprise's product to meet their customers' needs. Local Units should be ever mindful of the fact that they are constrained by the requirement to meet these needs in a way which is profitable, so that they can continue to deliver meaningful social impact. The Local Units of a social enterprise are also responsible for delivering that social impact in their service area. As autonomous work units, they are responsible for driving innovation and for modeling the enterprise's values through a caring customer service. They are accountable to their stakeholders and their peer units for the way in which they mobilize the Six Capitals. The contract therefore gives them freedom (through the decision-making authority vested in them) to employ the Six Capitals at the local level. It also provides discipline by holding them accountable for delivering positive social and environmental results, as well as profitable returns on financial investment.

Local Units, having their own identity, respect the idea of human scale and therefore are more likely to attract and motivate members and employees. This translates into increased productivity and social impact.

The rights and responsibilities of the Center

The Center has staff authority. This serves to protect the Local Units, as the Center's role is limited to setting direction, monitoring impact, encouraging innovation and service, and modeling restraint. Through negotiation, the Center establishes a set of minimum standards that the Local Units agree to adhere to; this ensures that the integrity of the social enterprise's product and brand is maintained. These standards are kept to a minimum so as not to suppress local innovation, since the final test of each Local Unit is for it to be profitable. A solid Center is characterized by patient restraint and boundary management. Those employed at the Center can be viewed as its rangers and shepherds. They share their expertise with the Local Units at the invitation of those units. The Center only intervenes in a Local Unit if it is mismanaged or repeatedly under-performs.

The Center's role is also to "hold space" where the Local Units can gather and strategize. It does so by providing training and serves as a Knowledge Center where units can learn together. The Center is tasked with connecting Local Units to the whole through a common language and shared experiences. The Center is also tasked by the units to be forward-looking, to search out new opportunities, to warn the Local Units of external threats, and to identify and secure sources of financing. Again, all of this is with the blessing and request of the Local Units.

Dealing with the tension between the Local Units and Center

One of the tensions that is built into federalism is determining when the responsibility to act lies with the Local Units or when it lies with the Center. Tension comes to the fore when either side fails to respond to a problem or concern. This tension can create an organizational power vacuum if the Center is either too timid to act, or it over-reacts, thereby overstepping the boundaries of the authority given to it by the Local Units.

Federated organizations address this tension in two ways. The first way is through proactive planning and established principles to deal with growth opportunities when they emerge. The second way is that the Center collects and publishes impact statistics it has collected from the Local Units.

Local Units not only need to have strong managers and leaders, but these must also recognize that they need one another and the Center. Fortunately, there is a solution to this. By combining the key, common services that all units need and redistributing them across the federated organization, the Local Units are regularly reminded of the benefits they receive from the larger organization.

Some final cross ties

Federated organizations allow founding and affiliated organizations to scale up their impact by growing their core business product and service across geographical and product areas. In addition to the practical principles of subsidiarity and interdependence, a federated social enterprise knits the Local Units together with the following cross ties. A federated social enterprise binds the Local Units together by promoting a common operating language and common standards. It uses rituals and rewards to acknowledge outstanding performance; this drives innovation and thereby reduces the likelihood that Local Units will underperform. The enterprise ensures that its management, governance, and monitoring functions are separated and distributed across the organization and its stakeholders. It develops and reinforces a common mission statement to remind all members of the Local Units and Center that they are simultaneously "citizens" of their Local Unit and the larger social enterprise. A successful and growing social enterprise that is structured as a federated organization will depend on trust, shared values, and a common language and purpose.

Example of a Federated Social Enterprise

Habitat for Humanity of Georgia

Habitat for Humanity was founded in 1976 in Americus, Georgia, in the south-eastern United States. It has grown to include roughly 1600 affiliates in communities across the United States as well as national programs in nearly 90 countries across the globe. Some affiliates and country programs proved to be unsustainable and were closed; since 2005, this geographical footprint has decreased to around 1,300 affiliates in the United States and to 70 countries in 2020.

Habitat for Humanity's co-founder, the late Millard Fuller, can be likened to a modern-day Johnny Appleseed. After the founding of Habitat for Humanity, Fuller traveled across the United States and internationally to popularize the idea of eliminating substandard housing by building local partnerships between households in need and more affluent members of their communities. These partnerships resulted in the construction and sale of well-built and affordable home ownership units to these households, thereby enabling them to meet their shelter needs. This also increased the likelihood that they would break the cycle of poverty in which they found themselves. This model and Theory of Change has proven to be successful and enduring.

Habitat for Humanity serves as a good example of an unintended federated organization. Yet its members and founders understood it to be more of a franchise model, and this mentality continues to shape the organization's ongoing internal deliberations about how best to structure and finance the relationship between the community-based affiliates and the international parent organization.

However, a better example of how the federated model has evolved within the Habitat for Humanity family comes from their State Support Organizations. One such organization is Habitat for Humanity of Georgia. One of the authors served as the President of its founding Board of Directors. This organization was therefore not created by the parent organization. Nor was it imposed on affiliates. Habitat for Humanity of Georgia was chartered, not to duplicate their members' activities, but to focus on the following areas, namely: advocacy, resource mobilization (especially finance), training and capacity building, and disaster preparedness and response. Georgia affiliates recognized that they could increase their impact in their individual communities and across the state if they collaborated in these areas. All Habitat for Humanity affiliates in Georgia are members of Habitat for Humanity of Georgia. The organization's Board of Directors are required to have experience serving with a Habitat for Humanity affiliate, they must be passionate about the organization's mission, and must bring professional skills to allow the Board to meet its oversight and advocacy duties. The Board of Directors recruit and manage its Executive Director. Habitat for Humanity of Georgia has also created an Affiliate Advisory Council comprising a representative sample of its affiliate members. One of its Board members attends the quarterly meetings of this Council so that they can share affiliate concerns and priorities with the Board of Directors (Willoughby: 2021).

Chapter 10

LEADERSHIP AND MANAGEMENT

"The only constant in life is change" – Heraclitus

Change has been a constant theme of this book with social enterprises experiencing change on two levels/dimensions. On the one hand, they desire to bring about positive change to an existing social condition such as homelessness or the economic marginalization of a particular group of individuals. On the other, their enterprise model is disciplined by changes in the market in the form of fluctuating customer preferences, and the unpredictable actions of competitors and suppliers, to mention but two. Remaining aware of what is happening on both planes places an additional burden on those who lead social enterprises, one that is not automatically shared by their counterparts in a traditional, for-profit business.

It is ultimately the responsibility of the enterprise's leadership to manage organizational change effectively. This includes changes in their workforce, product, and services, as well as helping their management teams and employees to understand and navigate the psychological transitions that accompany organizational change. Failure to plan for, communicate or address the tangible and psychological issues stemming from organizational change can result in what Covey (2006) terms "low-trust environments". These environments are characterized by internal strife and low morale which rob social enterprises of their focus and strength to remain sustainable and to grow. Building enduring, high-trust environments is an important leadership skill that every leadership and management team wants to have in place when weathering organizational change. We will cover the importance of this further on in the chapter.

What is organizational change?

Change is integral to the concept of the S-Curve which alerts social enterprises to the fact that all products and organizations have a finite life span and that their sustainability requires proactive supervision of that change. This change, referred to as organizational change, is best described as an enterprise's transition from its current state to a desired future state. This adjustment can be incremental, episodic, or radical. The concept and practice of Growth Plans (see Chapter 9) speaks to incremental and radical change. The following section on change management will be of particular value to social enterprises who are undergoing episodic change.

Incremental or Developmental change is first-order, proactive change which is initiated by the social enterprise itself. This change focuses on improving and enhancing current operations through the application of Lean principles (see Chapter 8). Examples of this type of change can be found in Operations (improving processes), L&D (learning and upskilling) and in HR (campaigns to promote positive change in employees' attitudes and behaviors, or to boost morale, creativity, and engagement). The concept of growth plans provides insight into this process.

Episodic or Transitional change seeks to achieve a necessary state which is different from the current one. These changes are imposed on the social enterprise by its external environment and require that it adapt if it is to survive and remain relevant. Referred to as second order change or "shifting gears", this necessitates fundamentally different actions. Existing processes are replaced with new ones, which could include the introduction of new services. The enterprise can serve new geographic markets and customers or adopt new technologies. Restructuring and/or growth could also see the social enterprise increasing or having to downsize its operations and, with that, its workforce.

Radical or Transformational change is the result of internal and external pressures combining to force fundamental change to a social enterprise. This type of change often occurs in long-standing social enterprises. It is not uncommon for a social enterprise to outgrow its original purpose. The need which it sought to address has been resolved or it has morphed into something completely different. An example of this is the paradigm shift that occurred with the de-stigmatization of mental health.

A radical change in strategy is called for when a social enterprise's strategy, culture, vision, mission, structure, and processes change to such an extent that the enterprise no longer resembles its original shape. In addition, the creation of a new vision, along with the establishment of new systems to support this vision and strategy is also needed. An example of radical change is when social enterprises engage in policy advocacy as well as continuing to create and sell their original products.

Managing organizational change

Whether organizational change happens for planned or unplanned reasons, it is vital that the leadership of a social enterprise be prepared to manage the change. They must understand the nature of organizational change and the reason for it. They also need to be adept at managing the psychological transitions that accompany organizational change. Managing organizational change is concerned with scope, speed, and communication. The scope of management is proportional to the intended impact: the greater the impact, the greater the need for effective change and transition management.

Problems often occur in an organizational change management process when employees feel overpowered by the speed at which the changes occur, especially when they feel that they have not had adequate support and time to adapt and assimilate them. Employee resistance to the change process, and at times sabotage, is not uncommon in such instances. This is compounded if employees are excluded from the change process, or if insufficient communication or reasons have been provided about the need for the change and how it will unfold.

It is important for leaders to balance the speed with which organizational change must be made with the time that the enterprise's employees need to make the transition to the new reality. This adaption and assimilation process is eased when the change is communicated clearly, when employees are allowed space to grieve and accept the change, and when they are actively engaged throughout the change process. Helping employees understand the reason for the change, involving them in some of the decision-making, monitoring the impact of the change on the enterprise and all its employees, and then communicating this back to them, goes a long way to building trust. This trust, together with treating employees as valuable resources by applying all the HR principles in Chapter 5, will help enterprise leaders to go far in managing organizational change.

The activity of managing organizational change is commonly referred to as change management. This refers to the careful, pro-active planning and implementation of all the sequential activities that must occur to make this change process a reality. Change management is successful when the enterprise reaches its desired future state with minimal disruption to its operations and a low psychological cost to its employees.

The change management process should be headed up by the enterprise's leaders because they must help their managers and teams understand the need for the change and help them to implement it. The leaders should create a change management plan that guides this process. Social enterprise leaders would be wise to base this plan and their actions on several conscious leadership principles.

In times of uncertainty, instability and change, all eyes tend to be on those who lead the social enterprise. These founders and leaders, to quote John Maxwell (1995), *"know the way, go the way and show the way."* Leaders must be transparent, communicate well, be visible, and tell the truth throughout the change management process, as this is the only way they will get managers and employees to buy into the change. The dividends that they will realize from doing so include increased product value, improved service execution, accelerated enterprise growth, enhanced team innovation, and improved employee engagement, collaboration, and loyalty.

For reasons of confidentiality, not all employees will be privy to some of the discussions that senior management have about the change process. However, they do need to know why the change is necessary, what it will entail, how it will impact them, and where they can turn to for support. This kind of transparency is aided by ensuring that communication lines remain open between leaders, management, and employees throughout the change process. These lines, which include regular meetings such as town halls, team meetings and one-on-one meetings, allow employees to participate in the change process by sharing their feedback, concerns, and ideas. Sometimes transformation does not always go according to plan. Employees may experience some negative effects during the initial period of change and will need to adapt accordingly. While leaders need to remain optimistic in public, they also need to acknowledge and honestly address any potential challenges or issues. Sugarcoating the issue will rarely ease employees' concerns and fears. Instead, this behavior undermines the trust they have in their leaders.

Those leading the social enterprise must consciously engage their management teams when creating the change management plan. In the case of a smaller enterprise, a specific person can be appointed to serve as a change agent, or the enterprise can engage a consultant to facilitate the process. This plan sets out the detailed steps required to adopt the upcoming change and will smooth the change process for both employees and the enterprise. In larger social enterprises, the HR department plays an essential part in creating this change management plan and they are involved throughout the subsequent process.

The change management plan begins by making the case for change. This includes naming the problems that the social enterprise is facing with its current model of operations, and thus its reasons for change. These reasons then need to be formulated into a detailed description of the proposed change, complete with goals, outcomes, activities, anticipated areas of impact and timelines. This description sets the scene for where the enterprise is heading, and what it will look like once the change is implemented.

The plan then needs to address who will be involved in the change process and in what capacity. It should outline what new roles, responsibilities and skills employees will be expected to take on once the new changes are in place. This can often evoke negative reactions in employees, so the plan must clearly communicate why the change is necessary, what training and support will be provided to help them master the new changes, and how this training and support will be provided. The plan must also clearly convey the benefits of the changes and how it will impact employees' futures at the enterprise.

A detailed communications plan must form part of the change management plan. It identifies all the stakeholders who will be impacted by the change, outlines what form of communication will be used to engage with them, along with the frequency with which these communications will be made. Common types of communications include the use of emails, reports, individual and group presentations.

The change management plan includes a budget which details the costs associated with the entire change management process. The plan concludes with a readiness assessment that leaders can use to determine when the enterprise could best start its change management process.

It is important that the enterprise's leaders and managers regularly monitor all aspects of the enterprise to ensure that the change process is on schedule. Potential problems must be red-flagged, and any issues must be addressed as they arise.

Authors Corner: A final word of advice on change management. While it is natural to want to implement change with speed, our experience has been that change works best in strategic, well planned increments, with enough time given to allow all those involved and impacted by the change process to adjust to the new way of doing things.

Transition management

Human transition within change is often over-looked during the leaders' pursuit of a successful change. The idea of transitions and their management was developed by William Bridges, who began studying this phenomenon in the early 1970s. In *Managing Transitions – Making the Most of Change* (1991), Bridges applies his theory of transitions to organizations undergoing change. His central thesis is that organizational change is concerned with what is observable and external to individuals in organizations. Change involves new roles, titles, brands, logos, and organizational charts. It is imposed on managers and employees. Bridges argues that change management only succeeds when it takes transitions into account. Transitions refer to the psychological processes that take place within the individuals who are experiencing that organizational change. A range of conflicting emotions are unleashed by change, and leaders and managers need to understand and manage this with empathy if the social enterprise is to successfully navigate the next part of the S-Curve. Bridges' insights apply to individuals, groups, and organized settings such as social enterprises.

Bridges (1991) views transition as consisting of three stages. The first stage, which he refers to as "Letting Go, begins when employees are informed of the change. Feelings of bewilderment and anger often give way to depression and a lack of motivation. Managers should be sensitive to what people stand to lose with this change and what they will carry forward from this current period. Interventions such as celebrations – and structured opportunities where staff can acknowledge their losses – are critical. Managers and leaders also need to show how this period lays the basis for future growth.

Bridges terms the middle stage as being “The Neutral Zone”. People notice that changes are being made. Equipment is dismantled, some people leave the enterprise, and new structures come into operation. Anxiety and a lack of certainty and clarity reduce employees’ motivation levels. If this phase is not managed well, then factions can develop on the work teams and key staff may begin to leave the enterprise. Confidence in the enterprise’s leaders reaches a low point and productivity drops. Strategies to avert this include creating cross-functional teams which allow people to work on new products that fit into the enterprise’s growth and expansion plans. These work teams should be complimented and given opportunities to gather informally to build relational bonds. Managers need to emphasize the key lesson from the S-Curve, namely that this is an ongoing process or voyage. It is essential that managers build new boundaries around these teams to protect their identity as they begin to implement and live out this change.

The final or third stage, known as “New Beginnings”, sees the second S-Curve take off with the emergence of a new “normal”. However, this normality can also bring feelings of anxiety before people finally accept the changes that have been made and immerse themselves in their new role. Managers need to reinforce the themes of why the change was necessary, celebrate the journey that has been made and the small wins that continue to emerge. They should also use rewards to reinforce the change and transition that people have made.

Leadership and management in the social enterprise

Leadership is regarded as the ability to motivate people to take action to achieve a common goal – whether this is to meet a need, provide a service, or solve a problem. A leader motivates, inspires, and provides directives on what needs to be done. Leaders forge the path ahead for the enterprise by modeling its values and behaving as servant-leaders. Managers, who also possess some of the leadership qualities necessary for this role, scrutinize the directives from the leaders to plan and organize their teams’ work so that these instructions are implemented in the best possible way. Using a bike analogy, leaders steer the handlebars while managers turn the pedals. Both are on the same bike heading in the same direction, they are just operating at different levels.

Much is expected and required from those who lead social enterprises. Founders and subsequent leaders contribute “sweat equity” in the form of their own capital, time, and energy to sustain the enterprise, especially during its start up. However, there comes a point in time when this “sweat equity” is no longer sustainable because those leaders have nothing more to give. Walls and Lynch (2009) refer to this as "blood equity". Unsustainable "sweat equity" occurs when leaders burn out or lose their vision and passion for the purpose of the social enterprise. This can often cause an existential threat to the enterprise's sustainability, especially if there is no succession plan for its founder and key staff. Building up resilient new leadership is one of the most important tasks that social enterprise leaders can engage in, because it will ensure that the enterprise continues to grow and flourish. Succession is the focus of the remainder of this chapter.

Since leadership is such a key factor in social enterprise success, the next section will consider what qualities make a good leader, as well as the associated roles and requirements needed to fulfill such a leadership role.

The eight qualities of a social enterprise leader

Social enterprise leaders are:

Passionate Visionaries: As big picture thinkers who are dissatisfied with the status quo, these leaders are keenly aware of where they want to go and what they need to do to get there. They can articulate and communicate this vision to others, and motivate these people to join them on the journey. Excellent leaders can translate their vision into a strategic plan, complete with goals and activities with which to achieve it. They are responsible for balancing their enterprise's social vision and values with the reality of making hard choices about its commercial activities and products.

Innovative: Leaders continuously seek opportunities to learn new skills and generate new ideas, not only for themselves but also for the social enterprise and its stakeholders. They also recognize that some of the best ideas for innovation come from collaborative experiences and team engagement. They actively create innovation opportunities for the enterprise's internal stakeholders.

Decisive when executing: Indecision wastes time, opportunities, and resources, and it negatively affects the way employees view their leaders. Decisive leaders instill confidence in their employees and stakeholders but, at the same time, they are not afraid to make the tough and unpopular decisions to serve the enterprise's best interests. Decisive leaders step up in times of crises and prove themselves to be dependable, confident, and clear-sighted, no matter how tough the situation might be.

Trustworthy: Leaders who act ethically and with integrity will always have a following. Characteristics of trustworthy leaders include consistent authenticity, compassion, competence, reliability, and accountability. When faced with difficult decisions, they will not compromise on values and issues that are important to them, nor will they fail to uphold standards of excellence. This takes courage and self-confidence, and trustworthy leaders exhibit both traits.

Committed: True commitment to the social enterprise's cause equals conviction. In his book *The Heart of Success* (2002), Parsons describes several laws or principles of success. One of these is a steadfast belief that the job you do has value and that it makes a difference. When leaders act on this belief, together with their vision and conviction, they demonstrate their commitment to the cause and create powerful "buy-in" from employees and stakeholders alike.

Competent: Good leaders strive for excellence in all they do and are fit-for purpose, in that they are adequately equipped with the right skills, knowledge and experience to accomplish the task of leading the enterprise to achieve its overall objectives. By continuously engaging in self-awareness, self-development and other learning opportunities and experiences, they keep an open mind to new ideas, retain flexibility, and stay ahead of the learning pack. Good leaders are humble enough to acknowledge when they are at fault or when they are in need of training and coaching. They view failure as an opportunity for future growth.

Empathetic: Without passion and empathy, leaders in a social enterprise will struggle to make a positive impact in their work environment; thus, they must practice empathy, as well as communication skills, if they wish to build good relationships with employees and stakeholders. This, in turn, increases the loyalty that these stakeholders feel towards the leader, and thus to the social enterprise. Strong emotional connections and trust give a leader special access to, and influence over, their environment. This enables them to achieve greater impact, whether that is in getting their vision across, building stronger support systems, effecting change, or in nurturing new leaders.

Empowering: Tom Peters said, "Leaders don't create followers, they create more leaders." Good leaders will develop and empower others to reach their full potential. Leaders know that individuals cannot achieve great success on their own and that they need the help of others along the way. As such, they build productive management teams by mentoring and motivating them to help take on the load that comes with creating a sustainable enterprise. Social enterprise leaders know that this sustainability rests on developing new leadership talent, or the "enterprise builders of tomorrow".

Brown speaks of a "strong-back, soft-front" leader in *Braving the Wilderness* (2017), which perhaps best summarizes all these leadership characteristics. Strong-back leaders set, maintain, and respect boundaries. By being clear with people about what constitutes acceptable behavior, they walk their talk and are not afraid to be disliked or to disappoint people if the reasons for doing so hold fair and will help grow the enterprise. Strong-back leaders step up to the plate and take responsibility for what they are responsible for and to, never afraid to offer meaningful apologies or own what they need to.

They are trustworthy, act with integrity and do not engage in people-pleasing behavior. Strong-back leaders do not play the blame or shame game, but instead practice generosity by sharing resources, praise, trust, and accolades when these are due. By choosing courage over comfort, they can show vulnerability by asking for, and accepting, help when needed. They do not function in helper or fixer roles.

In conjunction with a strong-back, the soft-front part of the leader refers to their ability to face criticism, change or pushback. They stay soft and open rather than going on the attack, or becoming defensive, or shutting down. This is a special kind of bravery and, if embraced, can lead to growth and development of not only the leader, but also the entire enterprise.

It is our experience that leaders of social enterprises will not exhibit all eight of these qualities. This is normal and is not to be interpreted as weakness. We encourage leaders to assess how well they epitomize each of these areas and, where there is room for improvement, that they be open to develop those particular characteristics further.

Tasks of a social enterprise leader

- The social enterprise leader must *provide effective leadership* by not only setting the enterprise's vision and direction, but also by creating the right conditions and resources needed to propel it towards that vision. Managers help to translate this vision into tangible and incremental actions steps for the rest of the enterprise to follow. Social enterprise leaders balance their simultaneous roles of being visionary with that of strategic leader. The two roles should complement each other to ensure that the enterprise stays true to its social purpose and remains viable.
- Social enterprise leaders must have the ability to *plan and develop long-term strategies* that add value and growth opportunities to the enterprise. Enterprise sustainability and growth is a team effort, and all leaders and managers at every level of the enterprise must buy into the vision and strategy. They need to know what is expected of them as they implement it. Since strategic plans will invariably need adjustments, leaders and their managers need to remain flexible, responsive, and adaptable to these changes. At times they may even need to seek them out.
- A key determinant of an enterprise's culture is its leadership. Leaders who exhibit all the qualities mentioned in the previous section are bound to let most of these qualities trickle down and permeate throughout the enterprise to good effect, *creating a high-performing workplace culture.* The mission of every social enterprise is to deliver valued products and create social impact, and it makes sense that leaders of the social enterprise would want to do good and impact their own managers and

employees by creating a safe and inspiring place for them to work in. In high-performing workplace cultures, the right working conditions and physical resources are made available for all employees and their managers to carry out their tasks and functions. Employees feel supported in their job functions and receive ample coaching, on-the-job training, and other learning opportunities. They also participate in regular performance reviews and are offered constructive feedback, praise, and guidance. Mistakes are tolerated and encouraged as a way of learning. There is also evidence of a strong learning culture and talent development paths, including opportunities for promotion. Employee contributions are recognized and rewarded, and people share credit abundantly. There is a high degree of accountability, and transparency is a practiced value. Perhaps the best indicator of a high-performing workplace culture is that information is shared openly, and employees can talk frankly and confront real issues without fear of reprisal. There is real communication, real collaboration and continuous contacts between the leader, the managers and the employees involving discussions and decision-making on matters that affect everyone in the enterprise. A high-performing workplace culture cannot be missed – you will recognize it by the enterprise's momentum, and you will feel its palpable vitality and energy when you engage with its leaders, managers, employees, and external stakeholders.

- *Financial planning and budgeting* require good management and management skills. Most of these responsibilities tends to rest on shoulders of the leader of the social enterprise and the senior management team. However, managers at all levels of the enterprise need to be made aware of, and empowered, to plan their budgets and make spending decisions for their specific projects or programs. This allows them to gain valuable insights for further along their career path.
- *Risk-taking* cannot be avoided if the leader of a social enterprise wants to seize opportunities for enterprise growth or change. When assessing and taking risks, leaders and managers are reminded to do so within the context of the enterprise's risk management plan (see Chapter 7).
- *Problem-solving* will always form part of any leadership team's functions. Effective leaders deal with problems head-on and constantly look for creative and innovative ways to deal with them, either through the introduction of new strategies, products, technology, and people, or through work processes.
- Social enterprises should work with other enterprises to bring about intended social change or impact. This requires that their leaders engage in *building and maintaining partnerships* to develop mutually beneficial "win-win" relationships with these enterprises. However, while building these alliances and negotiating their agreements and working

relationships, leaders must remain true to the values and ethics of their own social enterprise.

- *Succession planning* entails planning for emergencies and raising up the next generation of leaders, and this is probably one of the most important functions a social enterprise leader will perform. The rationale for succession planning incorporates the replacement of key people due to retirement, serious illness or death, voluntary separations, and term-limited positions in the enterprise, such as those of board members and officers. The failure to plan for succession constitutes a strategic failure. Leaders in social enterprises appreciate that the success and sustainability of their enterprise rests on building outstanding management teams and future leaders. By developing leadership capability in their enterprise, the leadership can expect to get the best from their employees, which in turn impacts on the enterprise and all those who benefit from it. Maxwell (1997) states that leaders are not born, but rather developed. By developing future leaders through training, coaching, mentoring, experiential and participative learning, existing leaders multiply their influence and secure a future for their enterprise and its employees. Wiseman (2010) speaks of the "multiplier effect", in that any manager's goal should always be to multiply the skills, talent, productivity and performance of the employees beneath them. These managers can only produce the multiplier effect if they themselves have experienced it from good leaders above them. This cascading of leadership development from the top down becomes the true test of leadership success – a leader who develops other leaders who in turn, develop other leaders and so on.
- A leader must hire the best people for their social enterprise, and then bring out the best in these people by *delegating authority and responsibility* to them while remaining in touch with them. It requires much of the leader to get this balance right between delegation and staying in touch. If leaders have difficulty in letting go, then the leadership potential and growth in their reports will be stifled. Leaders must be able to discern when they need to step in, such as when the enterprise faces critical issues or key threats, and when they need to step back and leave less critical issues for their managers to deal with. Increasing levels of participatory leadership across all levels of management is one way of executing delegation. When leaders delegate, part of that delegation involves placing trust in their manager's ability to execute the assigned tasks in a way that reflects best on the enterprise. A leader can check on these trust investments by regularly assessing and auditing the enterprise's management capability at an individual and organizational level and taking steps to improve on it where necessary. They can do this through surveys, skip-level conversations, and regular one-on-one meetings.

Preventing leadership burn-out: Keeping social enterprise leaders and managers healthy and resilient for the long haul

The previous paragraphs should bring home just how important the leaders and managers are to the success of any social enterprise. A weighty responsibility rests on them to keep the enterprise going in the right direction, to ensure a prosperous future for its internal and external stakeholders. Furthermore, these leaders and managers operate in a fast-paced, ruthless, and competitive world which often leaves them feeling that they are on a hamster wheel from which they cannot escape. They experience continued busyness during long workdays and weeks. They are expected to do more with fewer resources. These conditions place them on the very real road to workplace burnout. Their health and well-being are undermined and eventually exhaustion sets in. If there is no chance for rest or recovery here, then burnout will follow.

The term *burnout* was first coined by psychologist Herbert Freudenberger in the 1970s. He regarded burnout as severe physical, mental, and emotional exhaustion caused by exposure to high and prolonged levels of stress. This stress exposure can be work, trauma, political or even safety related, and it renders those affected by it unable to cope with their normal, every-day responsibilities. Nowadays, workplace burnout is officially recognized as a medical diagnosis by the World Health Organization with its own ICD-10 code. This stress condition demands that every enterprise pays it the attention it deserves.

Causes of burnout, particularly among leaders and managers

Our studies and experience have shown the most common causes of burnout among leaders and managers to include the following.

Personality: The classic Type A personality, which is characterized by control, perfectionism, multitasking, competitiveness, ambition, and a high work and goal focus, can drive a leader or manager towards burnout if not carefully managed. However, the opposite is also true. Individuals who are predisposed to depression, low energy, low self-esteem, inflexibility, passive, and defensive behavior, are just as prone to burnout as the Type A personality.

Workplace culture and structure: If the enterprise's culture and structure does not afford its leaders or managers opportunities for a certain level of autonomy or high engagement in decision-making, this can also contribute towards their burnout. If they are mismatched to a particular job because they do not have the necessary skill set, or if they derive little job satisfaction from the work, then they will experience daily stress. If not addressed, this can lead to burnout. A culture and structure devoid of adequate monetary or recognition rewards, unfair remuneration, cheating and favoritism, and where disrespect and unethical work practices prevail (and are even rewarded), also contributes to burnout amongst an enterprise's leaders and managers.

Excessive work demands: Leaders and managers tend to be dynamic, go-getter people who are prone to burn the "candle at both ends". If they work a schedule that does not balance work with sufficient rest and recovery time, then they will eventually run out of steam. An inability to delegate some their workload, or not having anyone to delegate tasks to, along with tendencies to micro-manage, will contribute to burnout. Sometimes, the nature of their work will call for what is termed work-sprints. This means that it will be "all systems go" for a certain period until a particular product is launched, or a project completed. However, if this work sprint become the new normal, then the pace will be unsustainable, and the danger of burnout will increase.

Pushback or resistance: It is exhausting when a leader, who has the vision and drive to implement something that would benefit the enterprise, is met with pushback or resistance. This pushback, resistance or "hand-tying" could come from either the Board of Directors, or from the leaders' direct reports, or from employees who resist change by decreasing their productivity and increasing their absenteeism etc.

Workplace conflict: Conflict situations are naturally draining and work life accounts for most of our daily hours. Ongoing or unresolved workplace conflict places strain on working relationships and drains energy from leaders and managers. Prolonged exposure to interpersonal conflict at the enterprise can result in leaders and managers experiencing burnout.

Limited job resources: It is extremely frustrating when leaders and managers have insufficient resources with which to accomplish the task at hand.

Mental health capacity: While a certain amount of worst-case scenario thinking is necessary for social enterprises to grow and thrive, too much of this can paralyze their leaders and managers. When they find themselves worrying, overthinking, or experiencing negative thinking, then they need to take stock and refocus on the positives. Too much worrying and negative thinking is an unnecessary energy drain that taxes the mind and body.

Life: Personal crises such as the death of a loved one, divorce, illness, or a personal family situation that suddenly requires a lot more time and care can render leaders and managers incapacitated or taxed beyond what they can deal with. A sign of good leadership is when those who find themselves in this situation recognize it and step away for a period so that they can recover.

Signs and symptoms

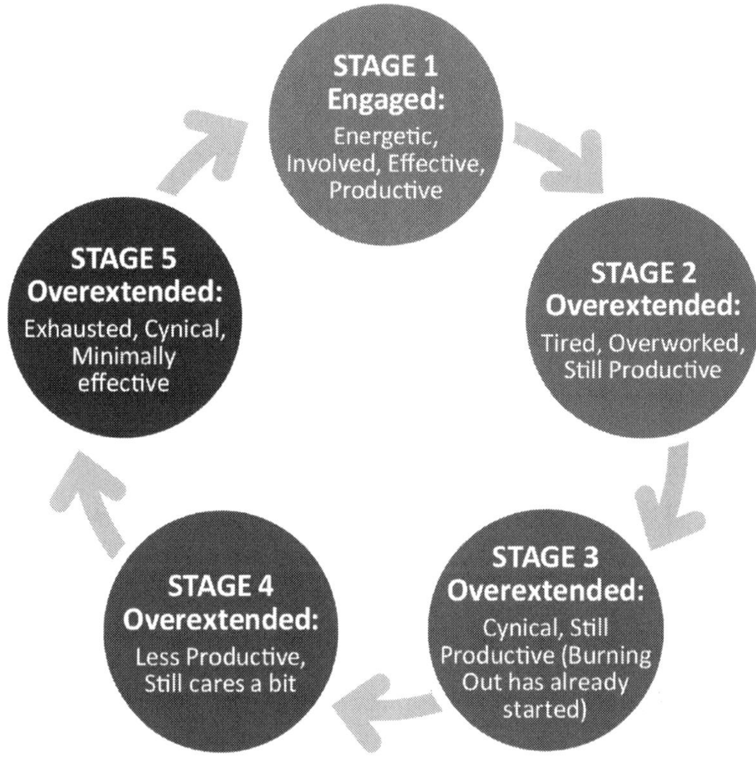

Fig.1: The Five Burnout Profiles (Sciencedirect.com 2016)

A great deal of research has gone into pinpointing five profiles or stages of burnout. Stage 1 (Engaged) and Stage 5 (Burnout) are endpoint profiles. A leader in Stage 1 does not have to be concerned about burnout. However, a leader who has reached Stage 5 needs medical and psychological treatment. Stages 2 (Overextended), 3 (Disengaged) and 4 (Ineffective) are transitional stages and leaders who find themselves in one of them should be concerned. If no interventions are made or help sought, then the individual is well on their way to Stage 5.

FEELINGS	BEHAVIOUR
Cynicism and excessive use of sarcasm.	Increased illness, and the risk of incurring serious health problems (e.g. cardiovascular disease, diabetes, depression).
Low to zero energy – bone tired. Physical and emotional exhaustion.	Dread getting out of bed each morning and motivating to go to work.
Depersonalization.	Reoccurring headaches or heart palpitations (panic or anxiety attacks).
Discouragement.	Insomnia – the inability to fall or stay asleep due to the worries and anxieties about work that prevent you from being able to switch off.
Pessimistic or negative outlook towards life.	Low efficacy or ineffectiveness at work - missing work goals and deadlines, loss of productivity, poor performance.
Hopelessness and helplessness.	Fantasize about leaving your job, especially one that you used to find fulfilling.
Feeling persecuted.	Lose perspective and ability to work smart – it takes hours to do something that would take half the time previously.
Sense of failure and self-doubt.	Job dissatisfaction or loss interest and enthusiasm in work activities you used to enjoy.
Trapped and defeated.	Mood swings that are hard to control or losing your temper in the workplace on a regular if not daily basis.
Detachment, feeling alone in the world.	Despite being exhausted, you are unable to switch off and relax or to find the time to recharge and rejuvenate.
Loss of motivation - feels like you have nothing left to give and nothing seems remarkably interesting or inspiring to you anymore.	Habitual complaining, being over-critical and impatient towards colleagues and the enterprise itself.
Decreased satisfaction and sense of accomplishment.	Tendency to self-isolate and hide from the world – not answering phone calls, emails etc.
Irritability.	You stop caring, period.

Table 1: Burnout Signs and Symptoms

Managing burnout

By the time a leader or manager becomes aware of symptoms of burnout, the burnout level is probably already acute. The good news is that burnout can be prevented and that, if it has already occurred, there are realistic steps to be taken towards recovery. However, depending on the gravity of the burnout, reversing the damage can take a few weeks, months, or sometimes even years. Preventing burnout starts with managers and leaders being aware of the signs and symptoms of burnout, especially in terms of its onset and progression. Then they need to ensure that they have regular check-ins with themselves and trusted senior management members so that they can act to "nip burnout in the bud". Other actions we recommend are listed in the rest of this chapter. It is important to take note that all the proactive steps and actions listed in this chapter can become a skill set that is passed on from leader to leader across the customary life cycle of any social enterprise. In addition, as these skills are transferred to leaders' households and communities, they allow employees to succeed outside of their working environment.

Proactive steps leaders and managers can take to prevent personal burnout

Disconnecting or regularly unplugging from electronic devices: Long before the start of COVID-19, remote working or work-from-home was becoming the norm for leaders and managers, with the added expectation that they were to be available or online 24/7. This constantly exposes leaders and managers to stressors that hinder their ability to rest, recharge and refocus. Whether it be taking one evening off a week, or perhaps only having designated times to respond to voicemails and check in on emails during weekends, it essential for leaders or managers to disconnect. This will help them to conserve energy and prevent burnout and, as a by-product, they model self-care and boundary-setting for the rest of the management team, and these people also learn excellent and necessary work habits.

Practicing regular self-care: Good self-care is not just about eating healthily and exercising regularly. It is means engaging in a variety of activities that can help leaders to rebalance themselves. Examples of these types of self-care might include regular time outdoors, a spiritual practice, a gratitude journal, reading a good book, or even cooking. Setting aside time for self-care benefits the leaders and also benefits others around them because the leader is functioning at their best level. While long vacations may be the answer to help reduce stress and burnout, daily self-care is just as important. We can all incorporate many little things into our day that [when added together] will brighten up our mood considerably.

Leaning on support systems: There is a real tendency for those who are experiencing burnout to self-isolate and withdraw from other people, resist socializing, or even avoid social gatherings altogether. This, however, is the time when they do need people who can speak truth and wisdom into their lives and help them to see the "wood for the trees". One of the ways to overcome burnout is for leaders to build positive social support in both their personal and professional lives, either by organizing get-togethers with friends and family, hanging out socially with work colleagues, or just spending some quality time with people who care about them. This all goes a long way to helping leaders to think about something else other than work and to be reminded that there is life and fun to be had outside of work.

Dealing with denial and pride: There is still far too much stigma attached to burnout, anxiety and even depression and many leaders and managers feel uncomfortable talking about it. Denial and pride can accelerate burnout, because rather than admit that they are not coping or handling things as well as they should, fear and pride will prevent leaders and managers from asking for that help. The antidote is humility. By starting the dialogue early on about the kind of help and assistance that they need, leaders can help prevent the crash.

Managing time and energy: The most valuable assets leaders and mangers have is their own time and energy. They should ensure that they allocate this in the best and most efficient way, and become more discerning about the work they take on. Knowing when and how to delegate or outsource certain tasks or even streamline certain processes is a learned skill. While it may not always be possible to cut all work demands, the leader should adjust their workdays to allow time for doing certain aspects of their job that they really enjoy - particularly something that restores that "it's all worth it" feeling.

Retaining perspective: The weight of leadership which arises from the stress over finances, enterprise growth and sustainability, personnel issues, and crises, is an ever-present, tremendous responsibility that many leaders and managers find impossible to ignore. Even when they are taking a day off, or are on vacation, this weight never really leaves a dedicated leader or manager. Despite this, life still goes on and leaders and managers need to constantly rebalance and adjust their perspectives so that they do not get sucked into a negative, overwhelming vortex of stress. They should constantly check that their energy levels and thought processes are not being hijacked by the weight of leadership; if so, they need to take action to adopt a more productive mindset.

Proactive steps leaders and managers can implement in their teams to prevent burnout

Burnout is often seen as mostly an organizational problem, and thus organizational change is necessary to any plan that fights burnout. Leaders and managers can implement a few of the following steps to ensure that they are managing their employees correctly to help prevent burnout.

Adopt a people-first approach: A 2019 survey conducted by Gallup on preventing and dealing with employee burnout in the workplace revealed that when managers listened to an employee's work-related problems, those employees were 62% less likely to be burned out. Leaders and managers cannot underestimate the value of making sure that have regular one-on-one time with their employees. Prioritizing people ahead of the "forever-there" job tasks will make for a much more engaged and productive workforce, which translates into less people issues to deal with. Leaders need to be a human first and a manager second.

Encourage your teams to disconnect and unplug: Leaders and managers set the pace and culture of the workplace, and if they operate in an "always-on" mode, then employees will follow suit. There are some workplace cultures where employees try and outstay each other, not wanting to be the first to go home as that is indication of not working hard enough or shirking responsibility. It would also not be uncommon in these cultures to find that leaders, managers, and employees do not use all their available leave. They fear that their absence from work will be perceived as a lack of commitment, or they are concerned that their work will pile up during their absence. A recent study showed that 55% of Americans did not use all their vacation time, with Forbes declaring the US a "no vacation nation". To overcome this trend, responsible social enterprises should mandate that all employees take their leave as part of their employee health and well-being protocols. However, leaders and managers remain the best communicators of the value of disconnecting. They need to ensure that they live out this value by doing it themselves.

Create a culture of collaboration: As mentioned in the previous paragraph, one of the reasons employees fail to take leave is that they are afraid to return to a large pile of work. If they are the key leads, then they may also be concerned that their absence will result in all work coming to a halt. This fear can be remedied by creating a strong culture of collaboration, where key projects and task are openly discussed, delegated, and shared so that the project continues when a team member is absent. Placing all the responsibility for a project on a single person or small team is setting them up for burnout. Leaders and managers are responsible for establishing and championing this kind of culture in the workplace.

Show up as authentic and honest: Many people wear daily masks, coming to work presenting an "I'm fine" façade, outwardly looking and acting like they have it all together. However, eventually things do start to crash. HR statistics of presenteeism and absenteeism show just how prevalent the "I'm fine" mask-wearing façade is. Leaders and managers have an important task to show up honest, authentic, and vulnerable if they want to prevent burnout in their enterprise. They need to model vulnerability. They need to communicate that it is safe for employees to share when they are not functioning at their best or are struggling with some tasks. This safe space allows employees to speak up and ask for help before it is too late. Leaders and managers should also value authenticity in their workforce. Employees perform at their best when they can be truly authentic, bringing their own nuances and quirks to how they perform their role. In some workplaces, management has a stereotypical idea of how employees should behave and perform their tasks. Unfortunately, when employees are expected to fit themselves into a narrow set of expectations, based on management's assumptions of how they should behave and perform, then burnout tends to be high. Leaders and managers must celebrate the richness that authenticity and diversity bring to the enterprise.

Allow for sufficient autonomy and flexibility: When leaders and managers allow employees to have more of a say in how they carry out their work, or involve them in decisions that affect their work and workplace experience, then the leaders can help keep burnout at bay. In Chapter 8, we introduced you to the practices of individual and team empowerment. When practiced, these levels of autonomy and flexibility increase employee engagement because they feel trusted, respected, and valued. All these go a long way in the fight against burnout.

Promote workplace community and engagement: Burnout's polar opposite is engagement. Any enterprise wanting to keep its employees safe from burnout must work on promoting workplace engagement. Workplace engagement is the quality of social interaction in the workplace. Good engagement is characterized by a collaborative workplace culture with high levels of teamwork, openness, and trust. Employees respect one another and offer praise where it is due. Competitiveness gives way to high levels of support to ensure that the job gets done for the prosperity of all. Employees enjoy each other's company, both on- and off-site. By contrast, low engagement is characterized by employees tending to keep to themselves. There is a lack of respect and support from managers and colleagues, and an unwillingness to take on tasks or get involved in team efforts. All this leads to increased workplace ineffectiveness and a general feeling of being unfulfilled in their jobs. There are several tools that leaders and managers can employ to help increase workplace community and engagement. CREW (Civility, Respect and Engagement in the Workplace) is one such tool that involves the training of all employees on aspects of civility. This includes helping employees become aware of how they interact with each other and how these interactions affect the quality of their relationships, and subsequent work. What is learnt at work then transfers to their home lives. These interventions help them to break bad social habits, and establish new, healthier ones. The intention behind CREW is to eliminate all the time and energy wasted on dealing with employee's interpersonal conflicts in the workplace by building a more civil and socially adept workforce.

Reward beyond the financial: While financial rewards certainly bring much joy to employees, recognition for a job well done or for creating a positive impact in the workforce is a powerful tool that leaders, managers and other employees can employ to combat burnout.

Walk the talk with enterprise values: When leaders and managers "walk the talk," and behave consistently in line with the enterprise's values, then employees' experience of the workplace tends to be less stressful.

Set the tone of fairness: When it comes to remuneration, promotions, rewards, workplace decisions or workplace treatment, leaders and managers must strive to set a tone of fairness and support and treat all employees justly. Employees who perceive leaders and managers as fair-minded are less likely to experience stress leading to burnout.

Authors Corner: Burnout doesn't go away on its own. On the contrary, if left untreated, it can lead to serious physical and psychological illnesses. It needs to be taken seriously and treated with the right medication and psychological help. While it can be overcome, the healing process takes time and cannot be rushed. It is not uncommon for people who have suffered burnout to be extremely oversensitive and hyper-alert to stress and anxiety. After any trauma, the body and the sub-consciousness remembers what happened, and develops mechanisms to protect itself to prevent another burnout. Sometimes this effect lessens after years, but sometimes it never disappears. With the help of a psychologist and life coach, the person who's experienced the burnout should work on restoring balance back into their lives and allow ample time for rest and restoration. Decisions will also need to be made around whether a new job description and working environment is required or how the old one can be restructured for better functioning. One thing is certain though, after a burnout, very few people emerge from it the same as before. Change is a necessity because going back to the old way of doing things will not suffice. If this is you, take heart. Through increasing self-awareness and understanding of your limits, you can go on to create a much more balanced, productive, and sustainable new normal.

CONCLUSION

"Seek ye first the political kingdom and all else shall be added unto you." – Kwame Nkrumah, President of Ghana (1960–1966) and Chair of the Organization for African Unity (1965–1966).

"I am not a die-hard capitalist. I do not view capitalism as a credo. Much more important to me are freedom, compassion for the poor, respect for the social contract, and equal opportunity. But for the moment, to achieve these goals, capitalism is the only game in town. It is the only system we know that provides us with the tools required to create massive surplus value." – Hernando de Soto Polar.

Sustainable social enterprises are driven by the urgent need to address the social and environmental challenges which face communities around the world. This places them squarely at the nexus of the political and economic spheres. They are an overlooked yet critical tool that must be used to allow communities and nation-states to meet the 17 Sustainable Development Goals that were agreed to by the United Nations in 2015.

The quotes from Kwame Nkrumah and Hernando DeSoto Polar point to the promise and challenges which face social enterprises. If these organizations are to flourish, they need a political order which protects their legal rights as corporate entities, and which also respects and protects the basic human rights of those they employ and serve. These legal protections lie at the base of DeSoto Polar's quote and his life's work. The reality though is that the political status quo may be indifferent or even hostile to social enterprises. Political interests may be threatened by their existence and seek to close them down through legal maneuvers and outright economic sabotage, as was the experience of Koinonia Partners (See Chapter 1).

Social enterprises may be subject to capture by special interest groups. The economic kingdom has not automatically followed the political kingdom. This means that the extension of political rights to ensure a democratic system of government has not automatically led all citizens to enjoy economic opportunity and the benefits of their community and nation's subsequent economic growth. This state of affairs is especially apparent when the political kingdom is captured by special interests, when it fails to respect human rights, including economic ones, and when it fails to build and respect an independent legal and judicial system. Furthermore, political institutions do not have a good track record of creating viable economic units. However, economic growth and community life cannot emerge without the stability, the rule of law, and the strategic investments that flow from political order.

Social enterprises exist to make local markets function more effectively and fairly. They aspire to correct some of the imbalances and inequalities that flow from the "bigger-is-better" growth model by seeking to exploit the (missed) opportunities this model creates. Social enterprises provide an example for an integrated model of community and economic behavior. In doing so, they point towards a non-violent alternative to sectarian and populist power politics. Social enterprises make possible DeSoto Polar's aspiration that all people enjoy freedom, that the poor are respected and are afforded genuine opportunities to own and participate in local economic activity, and that the social contract (essential for a resilient and sustainable community) is realized. But market economies require discipline, hard work and innovation. We have repeatedly stressed that sustainable social enterprises must generate a profit or surplus if they are to deliver social impact. They cannot be indefinitely subsidized by outside parties such as philanthropies and government. For this reason, this book has focused on how a social enterprise can mobilize their Six Capitals and create a competitive advantage.

The following sections will highlight the key points covered in this book. It is our hope that, as you implement these points in your own workplaces, you will become peace builders in the communities in which you serve.

For those of you in the religious, philanthropic, business and government sectors, we've made some suggestions regarding how you might practically support social enterprises.

We leave you all with an idealistic image of what it would be like for a local community to be served by a social enterprise that is not only achieving its goals of running a successful business but also achieving the highest possible social impact. This image, we hope, will encourage social enterprises to answer the question "*What does **good** look like*?"

How then shall we go about our work?

These are some of the key lessons and recommendations we have for founders, leaders, and managers of social enterprises.

- Social enterprises need to operate from a secure intellectual framework. The concepts and tools associated with Systems Thinking, Theory of Change, and the S-Curve empower leaders and teams to build enduring enterprises and programs.
- The concepts of the Triple Bottom Line and the Six Capitals provide social enterprises with a powerful framework with which to plan, create, and market their product and impact. Social enterprises already understand

that they are in the business of the double bottom line and consequently they confront the requirement to be financially and organizationally sustainable by providing a valued product whilst simultaneously meeting a social need. The text reinforces this important trend but shows that, just like the traditional business and government sectors, social enterprises must be sensitive to how they use, replenish, and account for the natural resources on which they depend.

- Many social enterprises draw their inspiration from faith traditions. Given how important their faith is for so many of their leaders and teams, social enterprises have reason to be open to, and embrace, those faith traditions. In addition, they should draw inspiration from the universal wisdom these faith traditions bring to the communities where they operate. They can draw inspiration from countless social entrepreneurs who have applied their faith to address social injustice.
- Those who establish, lead, and manage social enterprises must carefully choose a legal form that places them in the best possible position to sustainably address the social need they face. Business laws in the United States and South Africa permit social enterprises to use hybrid legal forms; this includes using subsidiaries and cooperatives to attract capital and forge partnerships. We encourage social enterprises to explore all the options and to not immediately limit themselves to taking the non-profit route.
- Sustainable social enterprises incorporate and practice good, aligned governance and management. This is the one area of the enterprise that they can control, and the manner in which they do so sets the tone for organizational culture and sustainability. The themes of good governance and management are reinforced by the provisions of the King IV Code. These guidelines keep the enterprise's leaders focused on its future by alerting them to the external threats and opportunities it faces, and allowing them to meaningfully engage with their stakeholders. They allow for the monitoring of its managers who are empowered to address the enterprise's immediate, daily operations and policies.
- Social enterprises must practice good financial management if they are to deliver impact and remain sustainable. Their financial statements should be transparent. This means that the information must be presented in ways that their stakeholders understand and can act on. Since employees are key financial stakeholders, it is important that they receive financial literacy training to empower them to participate in the enterprise's budgeting process and financial management. This will enable them to understand how their actions and decisions will impact the enterprise's profitability and how this will affect their personal financial and ownership interests.

- If social enterprises create organizational cultures which value their people, then employees will be inspired to view their work as more than a paycheck. They need to be motivated by the knowledge that the product that they are producing is improving their community; that it is tackling a specific social problem that is holding it back. The organizational culture of a sustainable social enterprise is one that invites people to become involved with it, where they can experience growth and fun, and where their work allows them to be of service to others.
- Social enterprises nurture the practice of participatory planning by engaging internal stakeholders in planning sessions during the startup and growth phases. These plans address both the product the enterprise delivers, as well as the social impact it seeks to have. Social enterprises also create and implement a range of plans to cover key operational areas including strategy, risk, and succession.
- Given their focus on tackling social and economic problems, social enterprises must create and implement human resource policies and practices that build employees' self-worth and dignity, along with their capacity for making responsible decisions that will grow the social enterprise.
- Consumers and communities hold social enterprises to higher standards than they do most traditional businesses. The only way that they can earn the trust of the internal and external stakeholders is through ethical marketing, stakeholder engagement, and integrated impact reporting. This approach and its related tools help the social enterprise to create its marketing strategy.
- The concept and practice of risk management facilitates planning and training and aids in identifying vulnerable areas that require internal operating policies and insurance cover. It provides the social enterprise with insights on how best to manage their risk, so that it remains relevant and sustainable.
- Successful social enterprises use teams to drive their operations. They train and empower them to apply the principles of lean production to all facets of the enterprise's operations.
- Ownership matters! You have been introduced to the practice of open book management and participatory budgeting. But for the internal stakeholder, ownership in a social enterprise needs to be more than just participation; it must be manifested as a financial ownership stake. Cooperative forms of ownership and ESOPs are some of the ways in which local communities and employees can become truly vested in the success of the enterprise. Since social enterprises are locally owned, Chapter 4 suggests some approaches they can follow which invites that local investment and related ownership.

- Finally, the wisdom chapters (see Chapters 9 and 10) introduced you to the need for enlightened leadership and tempering growth with ethical and human scale considerations. These chapters provided the big questions that all social enterprises should ask, both of the organization and of their own lives, along with illustrations of how the organizing methodology of federalism allows social enterprises to grow responsibly. Finally, we emphasized that social enterprises must invest in their leaders and managers, not only in the form of continued training but also in their mental and physical wellbeing.

Social Enterprises as Peace Builders

Deep-rooted social conflicts prove hard to resolve because the parties to them hold a zero-sum mindset. This means that any gain by the other side "the enemy" comes at a loss to the party that I belong to. The old apartheid-era saying that "the cake is only so big" summarizes this sentiment. In her 2019 TED Talk, Heather McGhee shows how zero-sum thinking continues to frustrate efforts to meaningfully address the legacy of racism in the United States. It traps individuals into a no-win situation where they fight over the size of the pieces that they need to share. Wiser questions such as "who says that cake has to be this big" and "how can we make the cake larger so that we can get larger and equitable shares" changes the lens through which this conflict is being viewed. These questions shift these conflicts from being binary, zero-sum ones to variable-sum ones which invite creative solutions.

Peacebuilding requires that active steps are taken to address the social and economic causes which underpin persistent social conflict in communities and nations. These conflicts are rooted in historical events of the communities and states where social enterprises operate. The enterprises are thus a powerful tool which can be used to address unresolved tension points in their communities. Social enterprises exist to create variable-sum outcomes. They are therefore at the forefront of quiet efforts to ensure that these old tensions are no longer employed by populist politicians and elites to promote their narrow interests and ambitions. The rule of law, along with constitutional checks and balances, is critical as this ensures that gains made by social enterprises, along with their assets, are protected from capture by state or sectarian interest groups. In addition, strong internal governance also serves as a check on these tendencies.

Fulfilling its peacebuilding mandate requires some additional skills from those who lead and manage social enterprises. These include:

- A sensitivity to community history which is balanced by forward-looking hope.

- An ability to show how the purpose and history of the social enterprise addresses the root causes of past community and social conflicts, and how it promotes variable-sum rather than zero-sum outcomes.
- Negotiation and facilitation skills that allow social enterprises to have conversations, especially when events and tragedies occur which trigger old concerns, stereotypes, and hatred.
- Communication and motivation skills that ensure sensitivity when working with marginalized groups, so that they are meaningfully included in the social enterprise's workforce.
- Business skills of management and marketing to ensure that the social enterprise remains sustainable and that its projects are financially viable. These skills can and must be shared with the community in which the enterprise operates.
- A service mindset believes the social enterprise should actively build and broker peace in its community. Part of the social enterprise's work and purpose is to serve as an active peace builder and occasional peacemaker, and yet this comes at a cost. Neil Alcock, the founder of a social enterprise in the Msinga District of KwaZulu-Natal, embodied the ethic of service and cost. He was assassinated in 1983 whilst mediating between warring factions whose violent conflict threatened the communities in which his enterprise was located. His example returns us to the core tenet of Ubuntu and reminds us that the "social" in social enterprise obligates enterprises and their leaders to actively promote peace. When they do so, they fulfill their social duty and their self-interests, allowing themselves and their community to survive, prosper and deliver social change.
- The ability to add peacebuilding to the international codes of conduct that govern fair and direct trade.

How then shall we support social enterprises?

It is not only the founders, leaders, managers, and employees who have a keen interest in making sure their social enterprise remains viable and endures; its external stakeholders also want it to succeed. Here are some suggestions and recommendations for stakeholders who have the resources to create an environment in which social enterprises can succeed.

- Philanthropic funders should expand the products that they offer to include social enterprises. They can create grant-to-loan programs to support the startup and growth phases at social enterprises. They should also create and/or advocate for development bonds that social enterprises can apply for and get, to help expand their capacity, products, and service areas.

- Faith-based institutions can create similar opportunities by drawing from their endowments to create revolving loan funds.
- All levels of government can support social enterprises by enforcing the rule of law and by creating a level playing field which allows social enterprises to compete and grow alongside established businesses. Government must extend the investment and tax incentives (already offered to traditional corporations) to local and social enterprises with the purpose of building resilient local economies.
- Large corporations can view social enterprises as vendors who can provide them with products and services they need.
- There is also a role for a social enterprise's international partners. They should be concerned when the basic human rights of that enterprise's employees and stakeholders are threatened. They should also be concerned when government policies threaten the economic viability of the enterprises they trade with.

What can our communities look like?

Diverse local economies consist of a myriad of small and medium-sized social enterprises, traditional businesses, non-profits, civic organizations, and government agencies. Sustainable social enterprises, which embody the principles and practices of community economic development, help their communities to become more resilient by adding to their economic and social diversity. Sustainable social enterprises allow for higher degrees of local ownership and their presence sees communities experience reductions in the number and size of social issues that face the community, the rate of persistent and structural unemployment, and reduced social inequality. When taken together, these conditions lead to greater peace in the community with fewer incidents of violence and crime. Those members of the community who have traditionally experienced economic and social exclusion are now included in the community, and are valued for the contributions that they make. All members of the community have the necessary skills to make them more resilient and capable of addressing both ongoing community problems and future challenges. The natural environment is restored, and this promotes individual and social wellbeing. It remains our fervent belief that social enterprises are important tools to help communities become more resilient so that they can realize and sustain this vision.

Appendix A

MANAGING CONFLICT AND BUILDING PEACE WITHIN SOCIAL ENTERPRISES

Conflict management refers to the process by which disputes are resolved fairly through creative thinking, negotiation, or mediation to reach a durable agreement which meets the interests of all the involved parties.

As important players in the peace building space, we charge the leaders and managers of social enterprises to take on the additional responsibility of modeling conflict management and peace building within their own enterprises so that its behavior and practices ripple into their surrounding communities and inspire their stakeholders to do so as well.

Organizational conflict is inevitable and necessary. Conflict that is poorly managed, or even avoided, is negative and harmful. Workplace conflicts that are not dealt with timeously will lead to lower employee morale, productivity and co-operation, and higher rates of absenteeism. It can also lead to a higher rate of workforce turnover, lower stakeholder confidence in the enterprise and, negatively impact its desired financial and program impact. However, if the social enterprise manages workplace conflict in a productive way, then not only does this contribute to a healthy work environment, but it will also improve the product that it delivers as well as its sustainability and impact. Conflict management practitioners advocate that leaders and managers should not avoid conflict, nor let it fester or get out of hand. Instead, they should learn how to manage and resolve it in an effective manner. This is key to managing the enterprises' diverse array of internal and external stakeholders.

The Conflict Iceberg

The Conflict Iceberg below provides us with a nuanced overview of the different sources of organizational conflict.

These sources of conflict are also found in social enterprises. Scholars of conflict and conflict management have categorized conflict as either being latent or manifest. Latent conflict lies below the surface. Some of the participants in a personal or organizational conflict may not even be aware of its existence. Latent conflicts include conflicts over roles and decision-making power, as well as different opinions on what values the enterprise should hold and what strategy it should embark on. These sources of latent conflicts

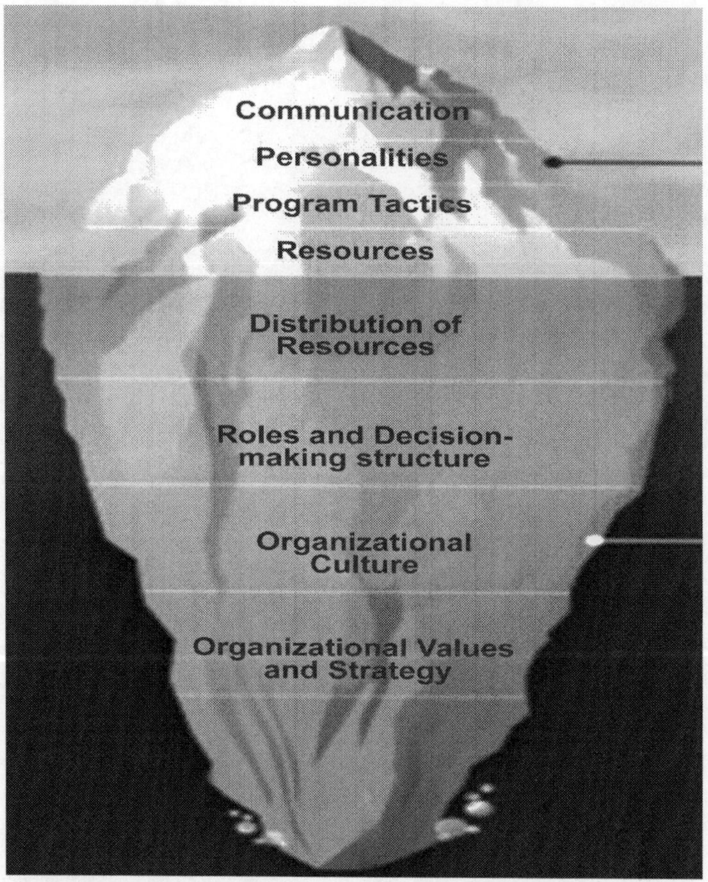

are powerful, as they arise from the enterprises' organizational culture. Their power and influence will not only determine what conflicts emerge, but how they will be managed. Managing and resolving these conflicts is the prerogative of the enterprises' management and governance body, working with external trainers and mediators when necessary. Latent conflicts are challenging in that they require a longer-time frame to be resolved and do not easily lend themselves to negotiation and mediation. Instead, their resolution often requires more facilitated interventions, such as interactive team-building and problem-solving workshops. However, parties will still need to apply the principles and practices of negotiation and conflict de-escalation so that these deeper dialogues can be effective and efficient. In the Conflict Iceberg image provided, the sources of latent organizational conflict are those that are below the surface of the sea.

On the other hand, manifest conflict is represented by that portion of the iceberg which is visible, and which is found above the sea's surface. It is much easier to identify manifested conflicts because they are visible, not only to the direct parties, but also to the people around them. These conflicts include the enterprise's individual employees and teams holding different assumptions and priorities, as well as the ways in which they handle interpersonal conflict. They also extend to disputes over the organization's resources. These conflicts are best managed through direct negotiation, third party mediation (assisted negotiation) or arbitration, where a manager makes a binding decision to settle the conflict.

The table below summarizes the sources of organizational conflict and the types of interventions that the enterprise can follow to manage them in a productive way. Effective conflict management begins with the parties who are directly impacted by the conflict (employees) resolving it themselves. However, if they are unable to do so, they then need to ask their managers to assist them to reach a durable agreement. While conflict management always begins with the enterprises' management, there are times when it is more proper for the social enterprise to engage external trainers, mediators, and coaches to help them to manage conflict.

Strategies to deal with Organizational Conflicts

If the Conflict is About…	**Then Possible Responses include…**	**Class of Intervenor**
Communication	Improving Communication Skills Negotiation training Interactive Team Building	Management External trainers
Relationships and Personalities	Training/Coaching Reviewing organizational structure Allowing for grieving and transitions Interactive Team Building	Management External trainers, mediators, and coaches.
Distribution of Resources	Policies and Procedures Negotiating Tactical Plans	Management Coaches
Roles	Governance and Management systems and coaching	External trainers and coaches Management

Organizational Goals, Strategy and Values	Facilitated dialogues. Periodic review of Vision and Mission Statements Interactive Team Building	External trainers and coaches

Social enterprises are created to address some of the underlying social and economic causes of the persistent conflict that their communities experience. The impact which they deliver will help to remove some of these root causes. Since conflict is inevitable, it will never be eliminated. Instead, it will be managed by thoughtful and skilled managers and leaders who intentionally create a culture, skills-base and effective processes to manage conflict productively. This starts within the social enterprise. This is the unspoken role that it is called to perform and model.

Both the authors are conflict management practitioners and engage in peace building-conflict management in their private practices. They can be contacted via their respective Linkedin pages or by visiting tessendorfconsulting.com.

BIBLIOGRAPHY

A

ACLED. 2019. *Armed Conflict Location & Event Data Project (ACLED) Codebook.*

Adair, J. 1996. *Effective Motivation*. London: Pan Books

Adams, F. and Hansen, G. 2nd ed. 1992: *Putting Democracy to Work: A Practical Guide for Starting and Managing Worker-owned businesses*. San Francisco: Berrett-Koehler Publishers. Eugene: Hulogosi Communications.

Anstey, M. 1993. *Practical Peace-making: A Mediator's Handbook.* Kenwyn: Juta and Co. Ltd.

Armstrong, M. 2014. *A Handbook of Human Resource Management.* London: Kogan Page Limited.

Avery, D. 2017. *The Resilient Farmer – Weathering the challenges of life and the land.* New Zealand: Penguin Random House.

B

Barnette, H. 1992. *Clarence Jordan: Turning Dreams into Deeds.* Macon: Smith and Helwys.

Bateman, S and Zeithaml, C. 1990. *Management: Function and Strategy*. Illinois: Irwin Professional Publishing (Division of McGraw - Hill).

Bertha Center for Social Innovation and Entrepreneurship. 2016. *A Guide to Legal Forms for Social Enterprises in South Africa.* Cape Town: University of Cape Town Graduate School of Business.

Beukes, P. 1989. *The Holistic Smuts – A study in personality.* Cape Town: Human and Rousseau.

Bhasin, M. 2017. Integrated Reporting: The Future of Corporate Reporting. *International Journal of Management and Social Sciences Research (IJMSSR)* 6:17-31.

Bhengu, M. 1996. *Ubuntu: The Essence of democracy*. Cape Town: Novalis Press.

BizNews Interview with Sarah Frazee. February 11th 2021. Meat Naturally: The environmentally friendly small business generating livelihoods for 2,500 communal farmers in SA. https://www.biznews.com/news/2021/02/11/meat-naturally.

Boon, M. 1996. *The African Way: The power of interactive leadership*. Cape Town: Zebra Press/Struik Book Distributors.

Bradshaw, G.J. 2008. *Conflict Management for South African Students – Theory and Application*. Cape Town: New Voices Publishing.

Brennan, L.L. 2011. *Operations Management.* New York: McGraw-Hill.

Bridges, W. 1991. *Managing Transitions – Making the Most of Change.* Reading: Perseus Books.

Brown, B. 2017. *Braving the Wilderness*. London: Ebury Publishing.

Burstiner, I. 1989. *The Small Business Handbook.* https://www.inc.com/encyclopedia/human-resource-management.html

C

CGC, 2019. *Business with Purpose and The Rise of the Fourth Sector in Ibero-America*, Madrid: Center for the Governance of Change, IE University.

Cambridge Dictionary. 4th ed. 2013. Cambridge: Cambridge University Press.

Case, J. 1995. *Open Book Management – The Coming Business Revolution*. New York: Harper Business.

Church Law Center. 2019. *When Should a Nonprofit Be Organized as a Trust?* https://www.churchlawcenter.com/2019/02/

Collins Dictionaries. 13th ed. 2018. Collins English Dictionary. Glasgow: HarperCollins.

Compton, B and Galaway, B. 1989. *Social Work Processes*. Belmont: Wadsworth Publishing Company.

Cooperman, J. 2017. How a criminal defense lawyer became a world-class chocolatier. *St. Louis Magazine*. https://www.stlmag.com/news/economy-innovation/shawn-askinosie/

Cortese, A. 2011. *Locavesting – The Revolution in Local Investing and how to profit from it.* New Jersey: John Wiley & Sons Inc.

Covey, S. 1990. *The Seven Habits of Highly Effective People: Restoring the character ethic.* Boston: Free Press.

Covey, S. 2006. *The Speed of Trust.* New York: Free Press.

Coy, P. 2020. Is it all about the Money? *Bloomberg Businessweek.* December 28th, 2020.

D

Dave Grace and Associates. 2014. *Measuring the Size and Scope of the Cooperative Economy: Results of the 2014 Global Census on Co-operatives.* https://www.un.org/esa/socdev/documents/2014/coopsegm/grace.pdf.

Deloitte and Touche. 2012. *Ensuring Regulatory Compliance – Integrating Risk Advisory and Assurance*. https://www2.deloitte.com/content/dam/Deloitte/za/Documents/risk/ZA_RA_EnsuringRegulatoryCompliance_IntegratingRiskAdvisoryAssurance_2015.pdf

Development Co-operation Directorate (OECD-DAC). 2021. *United Nations Climate Change*. https://unfccc.int/

Drucker, P.F. 1954 (re-issued 2006). *The Practice of Management*. New York: Harper & Brothers.

Drucker, P.F. 1985. *Managing in Turbulent Times.* New York: Harper Collins.

E

ecoDa/PWC. 2018. Video message from Prof. Mervyn King on Corporate Governance. Delivered at ecoDa/PwC joint conference *Long-term sustainability: Can Corporate Governance bring magic solutions?* 20 March 2018. Brussels. https://www.youtube.com/watch?v=WNAgbcvXnZM.

Elkington, J. 2018. 25 Years Ago I coined the Phrase "Triple Bottom Line." Here's Why It's Time to Rethink It. Boston, *Harvard Business Review*. June 25, 2018. https://hbr.org/2018/06/25-years-ago-i-coined-the-phrase-triple-bottom-line-heres-why-im-giving-up-on-it

Enrich, D. 2020. *Dark Towers – Deutsche Bank, Donald Trump and the Epic Trail of Destruction*. New York: Custom House.

Erasmus, J. 2014. *Sample Risk Committee Charter.* Johannesburg: Deloitte & Touche.

F

Forbes, E. 2015. *10 things to know about South African Non-Profit Companies.* Cape Town: Norton Rose

Freeman, E. 1984. *Strategic management: A stakeholder approach*. Boston: Pitman.

Fulbright. https://www.financialinstitutionslegalsnapshot.com/2015/09/10-things-to-know-about-south-african-non-profit-companies/

G

Gallup. 2019. https://www.gallup.com/workplace/313160/preventing-and-dealing-with-employee-burnout.

Georgia Center for Nonprofits. 2010. *Social Enterprise in Georgia.* https://www.gcn.org/sites/default/files/ctools/Social%20Enterprise%20in%20Georgia%20(2010).pdf

Germain, C and Gitterman, A. 1980. *The life model of social work practice.* New York: Columbia University Press.

Gleeson-White, J. 2020. *Six Capitals: Capitalism, Climate Change and the Accounting Revolution that can save the planet.* Melbourne: Allen & Unwin.

GlobeNewsWire. 2018. *VINCI and Ares create Liva, a company specializing in worksite logistics.* https://www.globenewswire.com/news-release/2018/06/18/1525549/0/en/VINCI-VINCI-and-Ares-create-Liva-a-company-specialising-in-worksite-logistics.html. [18 June 2018]

Greenwood, M. 2007. Stakeholder engagement: Beyond the myth of corporate social responsibility. *Journal of Business ethics*. 74:315–327 [July 24 2007] www.researchgate.net

Gubman, L. 1996. The Gauntlet is Down. *Journal of Business Strategy*. Vol. 17.1996, 6, p. 33-35.

H

Handy, C. 1989. *Beyond Certainty – The Changing World of Organizations*. London: Arrow Business Books.

Harris, P. 2005. *Managing the Knowledge Culture*. Amherst: Human Resource Development Press.

Hawken, P., Lovins, A., and Lovins, L.H. 1999. *Natural Capitalism – Creating the Next Industrial Revolution.* Boston: Little, Brown and Company.

Hodgson, G.M. (2006). What are institutions? *Journal of Economic Issues* 2006 vol. 40(1) :2-4.

Holland, H. 2019. *Gap between rich and poor growing, fueling global anger: Oxfam*. www.reuters.com. January 20, 2019.

Horoszowski, M. 2019, *Managing the Managers: Nine Tips to Help Social Enterprises Build Outstanding Management Teams*. https://nextbillion.net/tips-for-social-enterprise-management/

Howard, J. 2018. https://www.withoutprejudice.co.za/free/article/5255/view [February 2017].

https://b-labafrica.net/b-lab-south-africa

https://paymenow.app/employees.html

https://www.news24.com/news24/SouthAfrica/News/ex-con-opening-windows-of-opportunity-to-make-tech-hubs-out-of-sa-townships-20180712

Human Rights Watch. 2020. *South Africa: Widespread Xenophobic Violence – Implement National Action Plan; Hold Attackers Responsible.* https://www.hrw.org/news/2020/09/17/south-africa-widespread-xenophobic-violence

I

International Cooperative Alliance. 2021. *What are Cooperatives?* https://www.ica.coop/en/cooperatives/history-cooperative-movement

International Integrated Reporting Council. 2013. *Capitals – Background Paper for <IR>*. https://integratedreporting.org/wp-content/uploads/2013/03/IR-Background-Paper-Capitals.pdf

J

Johnson, J. 2018. Global Human Capital Trends Report. *Deloitte Business Quarterly*. 2018.

K

Keyte, T. & Ridout, H. 2016. *7 Steps to Effective Impact Measurement*. https://docplayer.net/100634731-Sim-guides-7-steps-to-effective-impact-measurement-keyte-ridout-infocus-enterprises-ltd.html

Khoza, R. 2012. *Attuned Leadership – African Humanism as Compass*. Rosebank: Penguin Publishers.

Kline, N. 1999. *Time to Think.* Great Britain: Octopus Books.

L

Lee, J. 2021. *4 Tips to Secure the Hybrid Workforce in 2021.* https://blog.zoom.us/4-tips-to-secure-the-hybrid-workforce-in-2021/

Leiter, M. 2016. *Latent burnout profiles: A new approach to understanding the burnout experience.* Science Direct Volume 3, issue 4, December 2016.

Leybourn, E. *Introduction to Scrum Student Guide* https://theagiledirector.com/images/IntroductiontoScrum-coursenotes.pdf

Lipman, V. 2018. *Why America Has Become 'The No-Vacation Nation'.* https://www.forbes.com/sites/victorlipman/2018/05/21/

Louw, H. 2021. https://www.diemersfontein.co.za/diemersfontein-shareholding-creates-better-future-for-staff-and-school/ platforms / https://wine.co.za/page/page.aspx?PAGEID=1645

Lynch, K. and Walls, Jr., J. 2009. *Mission, Inc. – the practitioner's guide to social enterprise.* San Francisco. Berrett-Koehler Publishers, Inc.

Lytle, T. 2015. *How to resolve workplace conflicts*. https://www.shrm.org/hr-today/news/hr-magazine/pages/070815-conflic

M

Mähöne, J. 2020. Integrated Reporting and Sustainable Corporate Governance from a European Perspective. *Accounting, Economics, and Law: A Convivium.* Volume 10: Issue 2.

Mail & Guardian. 1997. https://mg.co.za/article/1997-05-16-esopsfact-or-fable/

Maxwell, J. 1995. *Developing the Leaders around you.* New York. HarperCollins.

Maxwell, J. 1997. *Becoming a person of Influence.* New York. HarperCollins.

McGhee, H. 2019. *Racism has a cost for everyone.* https://www.ted.com/talks/heather_c_mcghee_racism_has_a_cost_for_everyone/up-next/

Mella, P. 2009. *The Holonic Revolution Holons, Holarchies and Holonic Networks. The Ghost in the Production Machine.* Pavia: Pavia University Press.

Merriam-Webster. 2021. Joint Venture. https://www.merriam-webster.com/legal/joint%20venture Springfield. G. & C. Merriam Company.

Mitchell, R Agle, B and Wood, D. 1997. Toward a theory of stakeholder identification and salience: Defining the principle of who and what really counts. The Academy of Management Review, Vol. 22, No. 4 (Oct., 1997), pp. 853-886.https://Journals.aom.org.

Mondragon Corporation. 2021. https://www.mondragon-corporation.com/en/about-us/

Monkeyland. 2021. https://www.monkeyland.co.za/Monkeyland-land-sale_article_op_view_id_3052

Monson-Rosen, M. 2019. *Companies with Purpose: The L3C Option in the US.* Mission Box Global. https://www.missionbox.com/article/401/companies-with-purpose-the-l3c-option-in-the-us

Moravec, J. 2016. https://www.educationfutures.com/blog/post/approaches-for-enabling-invisible-learning/

Moreno, K. 2014. *Regulatory Environment Has More Impact on Business Than the Economy, Say U.S. CEOs.* Forbes. https://www.forbes.com/sites/forbesinsights/2014/08/12/regulatory-environment-has-more-impact-on-business-than-the-economy-say-u-s-ceos/?sh=3bd66eaa684d

Moros, J. 2016. The Integrated Reporting: A presentation of the current state of art and aspects of integrated reporting that need further development. *Intangible Capital.* Volume. 12, 1: 336-356 http://www.redalyc.org/articulo.oa?id=54943657015.

N

Nation Builder. 2021. *Impact Management Reporting Guideline.* www.proudnationbuilder.co.za

National Center for Employee Ownership. 2020. *Employee Ownership by the Numbers.* https://www.nceo.org/articles/employee-ownership-by-the-numbers#1

Nkrumah, K. 1957. *Ghana: The Autobiography of Kwame Nkrumah.* Edinburgh: Thomas Nelson & Sons.

Novogratz, J. 2009. *The Blue Sweater – Bridging the Gap between Rich and Poor in an Interconnected World.* New York: Rodale.

P

Parsons, R. 2002. *The Heart of Success. Making it in business without losing in life.* London: Hodder & Stoughton.

Petersen, T. 2018. *Sihle's Story.* https://www.news24.com/news24/SouthAfrica/News/ex-con-opening-windows-of-opportunity-to-make-tech-hubs-out-of-sa-townships-20180712

Pilera, J. 2020. Democratizing the Fourth Sector: B Corps and Beneficiary Participation. *South Carolina Law Review.* 83:1-58.

Pitman, L. 2018. *History of Cooperatives in the United States: An Overview.* Center for Cooperatives. Madison: University of Wisconsin-Madison.

Pope Francis. 2018. *Business as a Noble Vocation.* https://www.catholicculture.org

Q

Polar, Hernando DeSoto. 2000. *The Mystery of Capital: Why Capitalism Triumphs in the West and Fails Everywhere Else.* London: Bantam Press.

R

Ries, E. 2017. *The Startup Way: How Modern Companies Use Entrepreneurial*

Management to Transform Culture and Drive Long-Term Growth. New York: Currency.

Roberts, G. Seldon, G and Roberts, C. 1993. *Human resource management.* Washington DC: Small Business Administration. Office of Business Development.

Russel, I. 2019. *The Other End of the Telescope. How to increase the metabolic rate and success of your business?* Gauteng: Tracey McDonald Publishers.

S

Sampson, A. 1999. *Mandela – The Authorized Biography.* New York: Vintage Books.

Saunders, H.H. 2001. Prenegotiation and Circum-negotiation: Arenas of the Multilevel Peace Process. *Managing Global Peace.* Washington, D.C.: U.S. Institute of Peace. pp. 419-432.

Schuetz, K. 2020. *Beyond Governance: A Better Way Forward for Boards, Executives, and Their Organizations*. Newport News: Morgan James Publishing.

Schumacher, E.F. 1973. *Small is Beautiful – Economics as if People Mattered.* New York: Harper and Row.

Senge, P. 1990. *The Fifth Discipline.* Boston: Doubleday Books.

Stack, J. and Burlingham, B. 2013. *The Great Game of Business – The Only Sensible Way to Run a Company.* New York: Currency.

Starr, J. 2003. *The Coaching Manual*. London: Pearson Education.

Stewart, Neil. 9 September 2010. *An Audience with the GRI's King*. Inside Investor Relations. [Archived from the original on 13 January 2011]

T

Tama-Rutigliano, K. 2019. *How To Draw The Line On Unethical Marketing***.** Forbes. https://www.forbes.com/sites/forbescommunicationscouncil/2019/06/24/how-to-draw-the-line-on-unethical-marketing/?sh=450a51875736.

Taplin, D.H. and Clark, H. 2012. *Theory of Change Basics: A primer on Theory of Change*. New York: Act Knowledge.

The Canadian CED Network. https://www.slideserve.com/vila/introduction-to-community-economic-development-powerpoint-ppt-presentation

The King IV Report on Corporate Governance for South Africa 2016, Copyright and trademarks are owned by the Institute of Directors in Southern Africa and the IoDSA website link is: http://www.iodsa.co.za/?page=AboutKingIV

The Laureus Monitoring & Evaluation Toolkit. 2009. https://www.yumpu.com/en/document/read/37514505/laureus-monitoring-evaluation-training-streetgames

The Startup. 2020. *Design Thinking vs. Systems Thinking*. https://medium.com/swlh/design-thinking-vs-systems-thinking-ca13caa17557

U

US Crisis Monitor. 2020. *Demonstrations and Political Violence in America – New Data for Summer 2020.* https://acleddata.com/2020/09/03/demonstrations

-political-violence-in-america-new-data-for-summer-2020/

V

VanderSpek, T., Schreven, A-M & VanderVelden, F. 2013. *Leadership in Social Business.* https://www.thebrokeronline.eu/the-three-roles-of-social-business-leadership-d68/

W

Weiss, C. 1995. *New Approaches to Evaluating Community Initiatives.* Washington DC: The Aspen Institute.

Williams, C. 2019. *Management – Principles of Management* 11th ed. Boston: Cengage.

Willoughby, R. 2021. Email to Harold Tessendorf. April 22, 2021.

Wiseman, L. 2010. *Multipliers: How the Best Leaders Make Everyone Smarter.* New York: HarperCollins.

World Fair Trade Organization. https://wfto.com/our-fair-trade-system#10-principles-of-fair-trade.

BIOGRAPHY

Megan-Lee Meredith has over 25 years of experience in community social development, policy and strategy formulation and implementation, as well as executive and life coaching, counselling and mediation. She has consulted to some of the top companies in South Africa and to networks on both grassroots and government level. Megan-Lee holds a BA in Social Work, a Postgraduate Diploma in HIV Management in the World of Work from the University of Stellenbosch, and a Certificate in Coaching Practice from the University of Stellenbosch Business School. She is a qualified mediator (South African Association of Mediators). The author of *Advanced Counselling for HIV/AIDS*, published by Juta (2009), Megan-Lee has also won awards for her social impact development work. In her private practice, she provides consultancy services in HIV/AIDS workplace management, workplace wellness, corporate social responsibility, conflict mediation and wellness therapy.

As a scholar-practitioner, Harold Tessendorf has spent the past three decades working in social enterprise and conflict management spaces in the United States of America, South Africa, Haiti, Sierra Leone, and Mozambique. Harold holds a Master of Arts in Political Studies (Conflict Resolution) from Nelson Mandela University in Port Elizabeth, South Africa, and a Master of Science in International Community Economic Development from Southern New Hampshire University in the United States. He has published several peer-reviewed articles on conflict and conflict management techniques. He is an accomplished trainer, presenter, mediator, and executive coach and has served as a senior executive for social enterprises which provide opportunities for affordable homeownership. Harold teaches social business and management classes in the Stetson-Hatcher School of Business at Mercer University in Macon, GA. As the Founder of Tessendorf Consulting, he advises, trains, and coaches businesses, non-profits, and coalitions about housing development, social enterprise, conflict management, and governance.

INDEX

Made in the USA
Columbia, SC
29 August 2022

66269677R00133